Contents

Introduction to the course

Syllabus overview

This unit introduces students to the double entry bookkeeping system and the associated documents and processes. This unit provides students with the skills necessary to operate a manual double entry bookkeeping system and provides a strong foundation for progression to more advanced manual and computerised activities.

This unit is the first of two mandatory bookkeeping units at Level 2. The second of these units, *Bookkeeping Controls*, builds on the knowledge and skills acquired from studying *Bookkeeping Transactions*. Studying *Bookkeeping Transactions* will also provide an important foundation for the financial accounting units at Level 3 – *Advanced Bookkeeping* and *Final Accounts Preparation*.

Assessment type	Marking type	Duration of exam
Computer based unit assessment	Computer marked	2 hours

Learning outcomes		Weighting
1	Understand financial transactions within a bookkeeping system	10%
2	Process customer transactions	10%
3	Process supplier transactions	15%
4	Process receipts and payments	25%
5	Process transactions through the ledgers to the trial balance	40%
Total		**100%**

AAT

Bookkeeping Transactions
Level 2
Foundation Certificate in
Accounting
Course Book

Fourth edition June 2018

ISBN 9781 5097 1819 1
ISBN (for internal use only) 9781 5097 1815 3

British Library Cataloguing-in-Publication Data
A catalogue record for this book is available from the British Library

Published by

BPP Learning Media Ltd
BPP House, Aldine Place
142-144 Uxbridge Road
London W12 8AA

www.bpp.com/learningmedia

Printed in the United Kingdom

BPP
LEARNING MEDIA

Assessment structure

2 hours duration

Competency is 70%

*Note that this is only a guideline as to what might come up in your assessment. The format and content of each task may vary from what we have listed below.

The table below shows the content of the AAT Sample Assessment 1 for *Bookkeeping Transactions*.

Your assessment will consist of 10 tasks.

Task	AAT Sample Assessment 1 content	Max marks	Chapter ref	Study complete
Task 1	**Recording credit sales** **The question involved:** • Calculating amounts to be included on an invoice • Recording the invoice in the day books • Checking a payment from a credit customer • Calculating an amount due from a customer, including a prompt payment discount	12	Business documentation; The books of prime entry; VAT and discounts; Recording credit sales	
Task 2	**Recording credit purchases** **The question involved:** • Identifying discrepancies on a supplier invoice • Recording a supplier invoice in the day books	9	The books of prime entry; Recording credit purchases	
Task 3	**Recording credit purchases** **The question involved:** • Checking a supplier statement to the purchases ledger • Calculating the amounts to be paid to suppliers, including prompt payment discounts	9	The books of prime entry; VAT and discounts; Recording credit purchases	

Task	AAT Sample Assessment 1 content	Max marks	Chapter ref	Study complete
Task 4	**Cash book** **The question involved:** • Recording transactions in the cash book • Calculating the cash and bank balances	15	Maintaining the cash book	
Task 5	**Petty cash** **The question involved:** • Entering transactions in to the petty cash book and calculating the balance carried down • Calculating the amount required to restore the imprest amount	15	Accounting for petty cash	
Task 6	**Posting day books to the general ledger** **The question involved:** • Posting the totals of the discounts allowed day book to the general ledger • Posting to the sales ledger	12	VAT and discounts; Double entry for sales and trade receivables	
Task 7	**Posting day books to the general ledger** **The question involved:** • Posting the debit and credit side of the cash book to the general ledger	12	Maintaining the cash book; Double entry for sales and trade receivables; Double entry for purchases and trade payables	
Task 8	**Balancing T-accounts** **The question involved:** • Calculating the balance b/d on two general ledger accounts • Completing an account in the sales ledger by calculating the balance b/d and c/d	12	Double entry bookkeeping (Part 2)	

Task	AAT Sample Assessment 1 content	Max marks	Chapter ref	Study complete
Task 9	**Trial balance** **The question involved:** • Transferring the balances on T-accounts to the debit or credit side of the trial balance • Creating a trial balance from a list of account balances	12	Initial trial balance	
Task 10	**Coding; prompt payment discounts; double entry bookkeeping principles** **The question involved:** • Creating a supplier code • Determining the actions required when a customer takes a discount • Calculating capital using the accounting equation • Distinguishing between capital and revenue expenditure	12	Business documentation; VAT and discounts; Double entry bookkeeping (Part 2)	

Skills bank

Our experience of preparing students for this type of assessment suggests that to obtain competency, you will need to develop a number of key skills.

What do I need to know to do well in the assessment?

Bookkeeping Transactions is the first of the two financial accounting assessments at level two. It is designed to introduce students to the double entry bookkeeping system and associated documents and processes, to the point of extracting an initial trial balance, before any adjustments are made.

To be successful in the assessment you need to:

- Be able to prepare and check the accuracy of invoices, credit notes, remittance advices, statements of account and petty cash vouchers.

- Use business documentation to make entries in the day books.

- Be able to transfer the totals of the day books to the ledgers, using double entry bookkeeping.

- Know how to make entries in the cash book and petty cash book, and transfer the totals of those books to the ledgers.

- Be able to perform appropriate checks on supplier invoices and credit notes and reconcile supplier statements with the supplier's purchases ledger account.

- Prepare payments to suppliers and check receipts from customers.

- Demonstrate an understanding of double entry bookkeeping principles, such as the use of the accounting equation.

- Prepare a trial balance from T-accounts and from a list of T-account balances, distinguishing between debit and credit balances.

Assessment style

In the assessment you will complete tasks by:

1. Entering narrative by selecting from drop down menus of narrative options known as **picklists**

2. Using **drag and drop** menus to enter narrative

3. Typing in numbers, known as **gapfill** entry

4. Entering **ticks**

5. Entering **dates** by selecting from a calendar

You must familiarise yourself with the style of the online questions and the AAT software before taking the assessment. As part of your revision, login to the **AAT website** and attempt their **online practice assessments**.

Introduction to the assessment

The question practice you do will prepare you for the format of tasks you will see in the *Bookkeeping Transactions* assessment. It is also useful to familiarise yourself with the introductory information you **may** be given at the start of the assessment. For example:

Each task is independent. You will not need to refer to your answers to previous tasks.

Read every task carefully to make sure you understand what is required.

Where the date is relevant, it is given in the task data.

Both minus signs and brackets can be used to indicate negative numbers UNLESS task instructions say otherwise.

You must use a full stop to indicate a decimal point. For example, write 100.57 NOT 100,57 OR 100 57.

You may use a comma to indicate a number in the thousands, but you don't have to. For example, 10000 and 10,000 are both OK.

Other indicators are not compatible with the computer-marked system.

Complete all 10 tasks

The tasks are set in a business situation where the following apply:

- You are employed by the business, Gold, as a bookkeeper.

- Gold uses a manual accounting system.

- Double entry takes place in the general ledger. Individual accounts of trade receivables and trade payables are kept in the sales and purchases ledgers as memorandum accounts.

- The cash book and petty cash book should be treated as part of the double entry system unless the task instructions say otherwise.

- The VAT rate is 20%.

1   As you revise, use the **BPP Passcards** to consolidate your knowledge. They are a pocket-sized revision tool, perfect for packing in that last-minute revision.

2   Attempt as many tasks as possible in the **Question Bank**. There are plenty of assessment-style tasks which are excellent preparation for the real assessment.

3   Always **check** through your own answers as you will in the real assessment, before looking at the solutions in the back of the Question Bank.

Key to icons

	Key term	A key definition which is important to be aware of for the assessment
	Formula to learn	A formula you will need to learn as it will not be provided in the assessment
	Formula provided	A formula which is provided within the assessment and generally available as a pop-up on screen
	Activity	An example which allows you to apply your knowledge to the technique covered in the Course Book. The solution is provided at the end of the chapter
	Illustration	A worked example which can be used to review and see how an assessment question could be answered
	Assessment focus point	A high priority point for the assessment
	Open book reference	Where use of an open book will be allowed for the assessment
	Real life examples	A practical real life scenario

AAT qualifications

The material in this book may support the following AAT qualifications:

AAT Foundation Certificate in Accounting Level 2, AAT Foundation Certificate in Accounting at SCQF Level 5 and AAT Foundation Diploma in Accounting and Business Level 2.

Supplements

From time to time we may need to publish supplementary materials to one of our titles. This can be for a variety of reasons, from a small change in the AAT unit guidance to new legislation coming into effect between editions.

You should check our supplements page regularly for anything that may affect your learning materials. All supplements are available free of charge on our supplements page on our website at:

www.bpp.com/learning-media/about/students

Improving material and removing errors

There is a constant need to update and enhance our study materials in line with both regulatory changes and new insights into the assessments.

From our team of authors BPP appoints a subject expert to update and improve these materials for each new edition.

Their updated draft is subsequently technically checked by another author and from time to time non-technically checked by a proof reader.

We are very keen to remove as many numerical errors and narrative typos as we can but given the volume of detailed information being changed in a short space of time we know that a few errors will sometimes get through our net.

We apologise in advance for any inconvenience that an error might cause. We continue to look for new ways to improve these study materials and would welcome your suggestions. Please feel free to contact our AAT Head of Programme at nisarahmed@bpp.com if you have any suggestions for us.

Business documentation

Learning outcomes

1.1	**Indicate the purpose of business documents**
	• Petty cash voucher
	• Invoice
	• Credit note (including for prompt payment discounts)
	• Remittance advice
1.3	**Demonstrate an understanding of a coding system**
	• The different types of code: customer account, supplier account, product
	• Where to use codes: sales, sales returns and discounts allowed daybooks, and purchases, purchases returns and discounts received daybooks, sales and purchases ledgers
	• How to create codes: alphabetical, numerical, alphanumerical

Assessment context

Business documentation is one of the key areas of the syllabus and therefore very examinable. The main documents you could be tested on are introduced in this chapter in the context of the sales process. You could be asked to complete these documents in the assessment, as you will see in the two assessment-standard activities in this chapter.

Qualification context

This chapter includes source documents and terminology which will be used frequently during your AAT studies. *Bookkeeping Controls* builds on the knowledge gained in *Bookkeeping Transactions*. The use of codes links with the *Elements of Costing* unit. *Bookkeeping Transactions* provides the underlying knowledge required in the *Using Accounting Software* unit.

Business context

Businesses have many transactions taking place throughout the financial year which must be controlled, monitored and recorded. Documentation is an essential part of this process.

Chapter overview

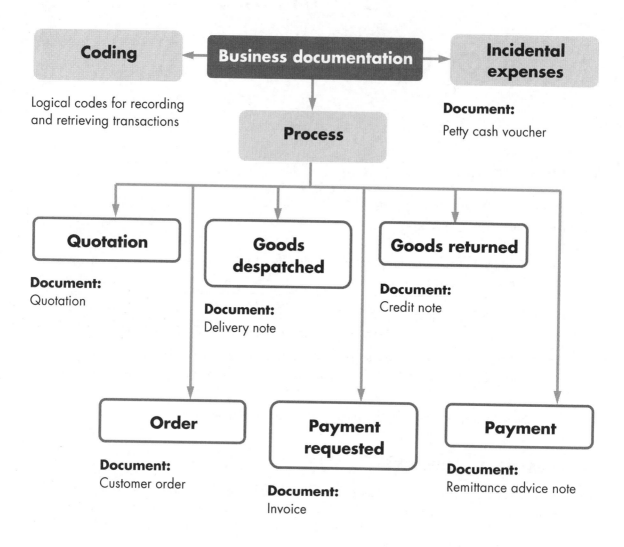

Coding

Logical codes for recording and retrieving transactions

Business documentation

Incidental expenses

Document:
Petty cash voucher

Process

Quotation

Document:
Quotation

Goods despatched

Document:
Delivery note

Goods returned

Document:
Credit note

Order

Document:
Customer order

Payment requested

Document:
Invoice

Payment

Document:
Remittance advice note

Introduction

Every business carries out typical **business transactions**, including:

- Selling goods or services
- Buying goods to resell
- Withdrawing **cash** from the bank
- Paying expenses from the bank account or from small amounts of cash
- Paying taxes such as VAT

The basic purpose of **accounting** is to record and classify accurately the business's transactions.

It is the business's **documentation** that contains details of its transactions, so the information on this documentation must be complete, accurate and valid.

In this chapter we will look at the documents that are issued and received by a business, using illustrations from the **sales process**. Similar documentation is used in the purchases process, as we will see in Chapter 5.

1 Types of business entities

A business can be set up in a number of ways depending upon the size and the nature of the organisation. There tend to be three main types:

(a) **Sole trader**

This is the simplest form of business. A sole trader business is owned and managed by one person. This person may employ one or two assistants, and control their work. The **owner** of a sole trader business contributes the **capital** to start the business and receives all the benefits (eg profits). They are also liable for all the debts of the business.

(b) **Partnership**

Partnerships are owned and managed by two or more people. Profits are shared between the partners in accordance with a profit-sharing agreement. The partners are also jointly responsible for the debts of the business.

(c) **Limited liability company**

In a limited liability company, the owners (the 'shareholders') and the **managers** of the business are separate. Limited liability status means that the business's debts and the personal debts of the shareholders are legally separate. The shareholders cannot be sued for the debts of the business unless they have given a personal guarantee.

2 Financial records

Most businesses exist to make a **profit**, by selling goods or providing services. In order to measure performance and year-end position (cash, inventory, loans etc) businesses prepare **financial statements** for the end of each accounting year. **Financial statements** are based on the business's financial records.

Consequently, **financial records**:

(a) Need to be maintained for all commercial transactions undertaken by a business

(b) Must contain **complete, accurate** and **valid** financial information

To ensure that the financial records are complete, accurate and include valid information, all business transactions are supported by **financial documentation**. A financial document is a document that is recorded in a **book of prime entry**, which we will cover in detail later in the course.

3 Introduction to sales income

Providing goods and services to customers generates **sales income**. The terms 'revenue' and 'sales revenue' are also used to describe sales income.

Sales could be sales of **goods** (eg dishwashers, cars, biscuits) or of **services** (eg using broadband, staying in a hotel).

It is important to distinguish between **cash sales** and **credit sales**.

	Cash sales	Credit sales
Action	The sale and the payment happen **at the same time**.	The seller provides the buyer with the goods or services but no payment is made at that time.
Payment	Payment can be made by **cash, cheque, debit or credit card**, all of which are regarded as cash.	The seller **invoices** the buyer and payment is made 30 or 60 days later depending on the seller's credit terms. Payment could then take the form of cash, cheque, card or automated payment (eg BACS or direct debit).
Usage	Cash sales tend to be the **minority** of a business's sales, except in the case of a retailer, such as a supermarket.	The **majority** of goods or services are sold on credit, except in the case of a retailer, such as a supermarket.
Business documentation	The primary documentation created is a **till receipt**.	The seller issues an **invoice** to the customer.

Activity 1: Cash or credit sale

Tara sells goods to Cathy for £100 and they agree Cathy will pay Tara in cash in two weeks' time.

Is this a cash transaction or a credit transaction?

	✓
A cash transaction	
A credit transaction	

3.1 Credit sales: risks

When a business sells on credit, it supplies the goods or services **before** payment is requested. So there is always a risk that the customer does not:

- Pay at the appropriate time; and/or
- Pay at all.

Credit may not be extended to all customers. Whether a particular customer is offered credit is decided by a business's **credit control function**.

We will now look at the process involved where a business offers credit to a customer.

4 Business documentation (sales)

There are six stages of the sales process and at each stage a document is generated:

Stage	Process	Document
1	Quotation is requested for goods/services	Quotation/price list
2	Order is placed	Customer order (or sales order)
3	Goods are despatched	Delivery note
4	Payment requested	Invoice
5	Goods may be returned to vendor*	Credit note
6	Payment	Remittance advice note

* This (of course!) does not happen with every sale – credit notes are issued if goods are returned to the business or a service is found to be unsatisfactory.

The style and format of business documents varies from business to business. However, the essential features are the same.

As mentioned, it is important that these documents contain **complete, accurate** and **valid** information. Errors and omissions can:

- Delay the sale of goods or provision of services
- Hinder payment for goods or services
- Lead to errors in the accounting records

Errors in financial documentation are explored later in the course. Issues to consider while working through the various types of documentation in this chapter are:

Item	Consideration
Name of the customer/supplier	Are these correct?
Goods or services provided	Are the correct names given?
Product codes	Are these correct?
Price per unit	For example, does the price shown on the invoice agree with the price on the quotation or order?
Quantities	Does the quantity of goods invoiced agree to the quantity delivered?
Arithmetic	Does the financial document add up, both in terms of the individual product lines and in total?
Discounts and VAT	Are they correctly calculated?

Assessment focus point

In your assessment you could be asked to check that the details on the documents match. You can use the three-way matching technique: check the details on the sales order match those on the delivery note which match those on the invoice.

4.1 Stage 1: price list and quotation

The first stage in the sales process is that a potential customer will enquire about the price of goods or provision of a service. They will be sent a **price list** and/or a **quotation** by the prospective seller.

This quotation should clearly state:

- The goods or services to be supplied
- The price
- The terms and conditions that will govern the contract, including any discounts

Illustration 1: Quotation and price list

Toby Parts Ltd

31 Cannon Way, Amersham

Bucks HP8 3LD

QUOTATION

To:

Paving Co Ltd

24 George Street, Amersham

Bucks HP3 5BJ

Date: 23 October 20XX

Thank you for your enquiry. The prices you requested are as follows:

Dishwashers (product code 1842)   £300 per unit plus VAT

Discount: less 10% trade discount

Toby Parts Ltd
PRICE LIST (extract)

Product code	Product description	Unit price (excl VAT) £
1842	Dishwasher	300.00

The potential customer (in this illustration, Paving Co Ltd) will have to decide whether to accept this quotation or not.

4.2 Stage 2: customer order

If the potential buyer finds the price and terms acceptable they will produce an order. Following on from the quotation in Illustration 1, Paving Co Ltd will produce an order which, as far as Toby Parts Ltd is concerned, is a **customer order**.

Illustration 2: Customer order

Paving Co Ltd

24 George Street, Amersham

Bucks HP3 5BJ

ORDER PP4252

To: Delivery address: as per address above

Toby Parts Ltd
31 Cannon Way
Amersham
Bucks HP8 3LD

Date: 1 November 20XX

Please supply 40 dishwashers (product code 1842)

Purchase price per unit: £300 plus VAT

Discount: less 10% trade discount, as agreed.

Authorised by: ....   Date: ....

Let's consider the details of this order:

- Using a coding system it has its own unique, sequential document number (PP4252) which will be quoted on subsequent documentation such as the **delivery note** and **invoice**.

- The address to which the goods are to be delivered is given, as this may be different from the address of the purchasing department if there is, for example, a separate warehouse.

- The product is described in words but is also given a **product code** – coding is useful in all areas of the accounting process to identify goods and transactions. If a code is used as well as words it helps to reduce the chances of an error being made in the sale, but it is very important that the code is used accurately.

- The price has been confirmed in order to avoid any misunderstanding at a later date.

- The order must be signed by an appropriate person within Paving Co Ltd.

4.3 Stage 3: delivery note

Once the order is received, it will be checked against the quotation to ensure that this was the quantity and price that had been quoted. The seller will now deliver the goods to the customer.

Illustration 3: Delivery note

Toby Parts Ltd

31 Cannon Way, Amersham

Bucks HP8 3LD

DELIVERY NOTE

Delivery note no: 33562

Order no: PP4252

04 November 20XX

Paving Co Ltd   Customer account code: PAV001
24 George Street
Amersham
Bucks HP3 5BJ

40 dishwashers (product code 1842)

Received by: (signature) .... (print name) ....

Date: ....

On the delivery note:

- The address of the delivery is included so that the carrier knows where to take the goods.

- The delivery note has its own unique, sequential number which can be used on other documentation and in any dispute.

- A precise description of the goods is given by including both the description in words and the product code. Again, this is important as the goods despatched must be exactly what the customer has ordered.

- When the delivery note leaves Toby Parts Ltd it is unsigned. The signature that is required is that of the person receiving the dishwashers at Paving Co Ltd. The stores department at Paving Co Ltd must check that the goods that have been delivered were the ones ordered and stated on the delivery note. If there is any discrepancy then this must be recorded on the delivery note.

- There will normally be more than one copy of the delivery note. Once it has been signed to confirm that the correct goods have been delivered, the carrier and the customer will keep one copy each as proof of delivery and a further copy will be returned to Toby Parts Ltd as proof of delivery and acceptance by Paving Co Ltd.

- No price information is included on the delivery note as this is not relevant at this stage.

Assessment focus point

You won't be asked to put together a quotation, a customer order or a delivery note in your assessment, but you may be asked to check them against other documentation, such as the invoice.

4.4 Stage 4: invoice

Once the goods/services have been supplied (and therefore the delivery note has been sent to the customer), the accounts department will raise an **invoice** to the customer.

Receipt of the invoice is the customer's prompt to pay for the goods or services received.

Illustration 4: Invoice

Toby Parts Ltd

31 Cannon Way, Amersham

Bucks HP8 3LD

VAT Registration No. 424 5242 42

INVOICE

Paving Co Ltd

24 George Street

Amersham

Bucks HP3 5BJ

Customer account code: PAV001

Delivery note number: 33562

Invoice no: 298   Date: 5 November 20XX

Quantity	Product code	Total list price £	Net amount after discount £	VAT £	Gross £
40	1842	12,000.00	10,800.00	2,160.00	12,960.00

Terms 30 days net

Note the following key points:

- It shows the supplier's name, address and VAT registration number.

- It has its own unique, sequential document number or code (298), which allows it to be identified easily (it is much more accurate to refer to 'Invoice 298' rather than 'the invoice we sent the other day').

- The date of the invoice (also known as the tax point) is important information for the customer. It allows the customer to see when the invoice is due for payment – in this case 30 days after the invoice date.

- The customer account code is example of **coding** in accounting. Eventually Toby Parts Ltd will have to enter this invoice into its accounting records and this shows exactly which account relates to Paving Co Ltd.

- The total price is the quantity (40) multiplied by the unit price (£300) to arrive at the total list price.

- The customer was offered a 10% trade discount, so this is then deducted from the total list price to give the net amount after discount.

- To this net amount must be added VAT charged at 20%. The resulting invoice total (also known as the 'gross' total since it includes VAT) is the amount that Paving Co Ltd must pay.

- The term '30 days net' shows that payment of the invoice total is due 30 days after the invoice date.

4.4.1 VAT

You can see that the invoice includes **VAT** of £2,160. The VAT is added to the net amount after discount to get the gross amount owed by the customer. VAT is covered in detail in Chapter 3, but for now the main points you need to know are:

- A business that is registered for VAT must charge VAT on its sales

- The current rate of VAT is 20%

- The amount before VAT is added is known as the **net** amount

- Gross amount = net amount + VAT

- To calculate VAT:

  VAT = Net amount × rate of VAT as a percentage
  So, using the invoice above and a VAT rate of 20%
  VAT = 10,800.00 × 20% = £2,160.00

The following illustration walks step by step through the process of preparing an invoice using the information given in other business documents.

Illustration 5: The process of preparing an invoice

You work for Southfield Electrical and are responsible for preparing sales invoices. Today is 8 October 20XX and you have on your desk the following customer order from Whitehill Superstores for which an invoice must be prepared.

ORDER

WHITEHILL SUPERSTORES
28 Whitehill Park
Benham DR6 5LM
Tel 0303446 Fax 0303447

To: Southfield Electrical
Industrial Estate
Benham
DR6 2FF

Number: 32174

Date: 2 Oct 20XX

Delivery address: Whitehill Superstores
28, Whitehill Park
Benham DR6 5LM

Product code	Quantity	Description	Unit list price £
6160	4	Hosch Washing Machine	300.00
3172	10	Temax Mixer	40.00

Authorised by: *P. Winterbottom*   **Date:** *2 Oct 20XX*

Step 1   You must first check that the goods were in fact sent to Whitehill, so you find the delivery note that relates to order 32174.

DELIVERY NOTE

Southfield Electrical
Industrial Estate
Benham DR6 2FF
Tel 0303379 Fax 0303152

Delivery address:

Whitehill Superstores
28, Whitehill Park
Benham DR6 5LM

Number: 34772

Date: 5 Oct 20XX

Order number: 32174

Product code	Quantity	Description
6160	4	Hosch Washing Machine
3172	9	Temax Mixer

Received by: [Signature] *J. Jones*   **Print name:** *J. JONES*

Date: *5 Oct 20XX*

Step 2 You should note that only nine mixers were delivered and accepted (the delivery note is signed by J Jones at Whitehill) and therefore only nine mixers must be invoiced, not the ten that were ordered. You might also make a note to follow up why only nine and not ten were delivered, or to inform the appropriate person in your organisation.

Step 3 The prices quoted on the order are the unit list prices. You must now check that these list prices are correct. An extract from Southfield's price list is given below.

SOUTHFIELD ELECTRICAL
PRICE LIST (extract)

Product code	Product description	Unit price (excl VAT) £
HOSCH		
6150	Washing machine	260.00
6160	Washing machine	300.00
TEMAX		
3172	Mixer	40.00
3174	Mixer	46.00

The prices included on the order agree with the list prices and therefore can be used on the invoice.

Step 4 You must now find the customer file for Whitehill Superstores, which will show details of addresses and the customer code. The customer file for Whitehill Superstores shows the customer code is SL 44.

Step 5 You now have all the information required to start preparing the invoice. The final invoice is now shown and we will then work through the remaining steps in completing it.

INVOICE	Invoice number 56483
Southfield Electrical **Industrial Estate** **Benham DR6 2FF** **Tel: 01239 345639**	
VAT registration:	0264 2274 49
Date/tax point:	8 October 20XX
Order number:	32174
Customer:	Whitehill Superstores 28 Whitehill Park Benham DR6 5LM
Account number (customer code)	SL 44

Description/product code	Quantity	Unit amount £	Total £
Hosch washing machine / 6160	4	300.00	1,200.00
Temax Mixer / 3172	9	40.00	360.00
List price			1,560.00
Net total			1,560.00
VAT at 20%			312.00
Gross total			1,872.00

Step 6   Enter the customer's name and address and customer code from the customer file. The invoice number is the next number in sequence after the previous invoice. Enter today's date.

Step 7   Enter the quantities, codes and descriptions from the delivery note – remember that only nine mixers were delivered.

Step 8 Enter the unit prices from the price list. Calculate the total list price by multiplying the quantity by the list price:

4 × £300 = £1,200.00
9 × £40 = £360.00

Step 9 Calculate the total list price by adding together the totals for each product:

£1,200.00 + £360.00 = £1,560.00

Step 10 Calculate the VAT at 20%:

£1,560.00 × 20% = £312.00

Step 11 Add the VAT calculated to the net total to arrive at the gross total for the invoice:

£1,560.00 + £312.00 = £1,872.00

Assessment focus point

Activity 2 below provides assessment-standard practice at completing an invoice. Ahead of this it is useful to consider some of the features of the assessment.

Feature	Data entry method
Dates	If dates require entry a calendar menu is attached to the relevant cell. You click on the date to enter it in the solution box.
Numbers	Numbers can be typed in. This is known as a 'gapfill' answer.
Narrative	The general rule is that narrative answers are entered by selecting from picklists or drag-and-drop options. In other words, narrative **cannot** be typed in.
	The **exception** is when just one or two letters need to be entered, such as a customer account code or a product code. Here, the computer will accept narrative (as well as numbers) in that cell.
VAT rate	This is given at the start of the assessment, in the introductory screen.

Activity 2: Preparing an invoice

On 1 August 20XX Garden Greats delivered the following goods to a credit customer, Super Stores.

Garden Greats

16 Vash Lane, Elstree, KH3 9GH

Delivery note no: 39483

Order no: 36952

01 August 20XX

Customer account code: SS454

Super Stores
42 The Pitch
Old Crabtree
Wellington GK34 9HL

200 cases of bottled vinegar, product code F250.

The list price of the goods was £10 per case plus VAT at 20%.

Complete the invoice.

Garden Greats

16 Vash Lane, Elstree, KH3 9GH

VAT Registration No. 284 4924 93

INVOICE

Super Stores
42 The Pitch
Old Crabtree
Wellington GK34 9HL

Invoice no: 571

Customer account code:

Delivery note number:

Date: | 1 August 20XX

Quantity	Product code	Total list price £	VAT £	Gross £

4.5 Stage 5: credit note

If a customer receives goods that are faulty or the incorrect item was sent, the goods will be returned to the seller.

If an invoice has already been issued then it will be necessary to raise a **credit note** to reduce the amount owed by the customer. The credit note provides written confirmation that the customer either owes nothing to the seller in respect of that invoice, or owes **less** than the amount shown on the original invoice.

Illustration 6: Credit note

Toby Parts Ltd
31 Cannon Way, Amersham
Bucks HP8 3LD

VAT Registration No. 424 5242 42

CREDIT NOTE

Paving Co Ltd   Customer account code: PAV001
24 George Street
Amersham
Bucks HP3 5BJ   Invoice no: 298

Credit note no: 104   Date: 10 November 20XX

Quantity	Product code	Total list price £	Net amount after discount £	VAT £	Gross £
1	1842	300.00	270.00	54.00	324.00

Reason: faulty item returned

The credit note is almost identical to an invoice. The only differences are:

- It is described as a credit note
- It has a unique, sequential credit note number rather than an invoice number
- A reason for the credit is often noted at the bottom of the credit note

To make sure that buyers do not get invoices and credit notes mixed up, credit notes are often printed in red.

Assessment focus point

Students often forget to include the discount when preparing a credit note, so remember to check whether a discount was applicable and needs to be included on the credit note. Discounts are covered in Chapter 3.

4.6 Stage 6: remittance advice note

A customer may place several orders with a preferred seller in any month. Consequently, they will receive various invoices from that seller. The credit customer may pay each seller just once a month and so will often settle several invoices (less any credit notes) in one payment.

When the customer pays the supplier in a credit transaction, a variety of payment methods may be used, such as a cheque, debit card or an automated payment from the customer's bank account to the seller's.

To let the supplier know which invoices are being paid, and which credit notes are being deducted (or netted off), the buyer usually sends the supplier a **remittance advice note** which contains that information.

Illustration 7: Remittance advice note

REMITTANCE ADVICE NOTE

Paving Co Ltd

24 George Street, Amersham

Bucks HP3 5BJ

Remittance advice note number 0937498

To: Toby Parts Ltd   Date: 31 December 20XX

Supplier number: PL 23

Please find attached our cheque in payment of the following amounts.

Invoice number	Credit note number	Amount £
298		12,960.00
	104	(324.00)
Total amount paid		12,636.00

Note that this remittance advice note:

- Is described as a remittance advice note
- Has a unique, sequential remittance advice note number
- Is going from the buyer to the supplier, so instead of a customer code it contains a supplier code
- Deducts the amount of the credit note from the amount of the invoice to arrive at the amount of the payment made – though it could contain other invoices or credit notes, and other reductions in the amount owed (especially discounts, which we shall see in Chapter 3)

5 Incidental expenses

Most businesses hold **petty cash** in a **petty cash box** on their premises to pay for small incidental expenses, such as stationery, milk and taxi fares. This is discussed in more detail later in the course. In this section we will look at the documentation used to record **petty cash transactions**.

Illustration 8 shows a typical **petty cash voucher**. It is an **internal document**, which must be completed and authorised before any cash can be paid out of the petty cash box. Receipts are attached to the voucher to prove the expenditure.

Illustration 8: Petty cash voucher

Petty cash voucher	
Date: 4.12.XX	Number: PC436

Stationery

Net £ 18.00
VAT £ 3.60
Gross £ 21.60

We shall see much more about petty cash vouchers in Chapter 11.

6 Coding

We saw above that sales invoices generally have a **customer code** on them to denote the particular customer, and similarly communications from buyers have a **supplier code** on them. Invoices and credit notes also routinely include product codes for the items sold. In general, all documents will also have a **document number**.

The use of **coding systems** in an organisation is designed to ensure that:

(a) Information can be recorded accurately and in a timely manner

(b) Documents can be filed and retrieved efficiently

6.1 Types of coding system

Each organisation will have its own coding system, designed to help it run its processes in the most efficient manner. The system may be:

System	Explanation
Numeric	All documents are given a sequential code number or **document number**, with the most recent document being given the document number that immediately follows the one before.
	Different types of document (for example, sales invoices and purchase orders) are part of different numbering systems.
	For example, the last sales invoice sent to a customer on 29 August 20XX is 1204; the first sales invoice sent to a customer on 30 August 20XX is 1205.
Alphabetical	Documents are filed in alphabetical order. For example, customer files are filed alphabetically by name.
Alpha-numeric	There is an initial run of letters that tells us something about the items being coded. For example, the letters may be the first few letters of a supplier name or a customer name.
	The alpha run is followed by a sequential numeric system as well (as described above).
	For example, a business has suppliers called Wellington Ltd and Wells Co. The supplier codes may be:
	• Wellington Ltd – WEL001
	• Wells & Co – WEL002

Illustration 9: Coding systems

In the case of Southfield Electrical in Illustration 5, we saw that the customer code on its invoice was 'SL 44'. An alpha-numeric coding system has been used to create a customer code for its sales invoices:

- The 'alpha' part is SL, which stands for 'Sales Ledger', part of the accounting system for credit customers which we shall come back to in later chapters. All customer codes for credit customers of Southfield Electrical will have this prefix.

- The 'numeric' part is 44, which is the unique part of the code. This will have been allocated because, at the time when Whitehill Superstores became a customer, Southfield had allocated 43 customer codes and so Whitehill was given the 44th.

The invoice document number, however, was 56483, a simple numeric code (the next invoice issued will be 56484).

Activity 3: Coding an invoice

Paving Co Ltd codes all purchase invoices with a supplier code and a general ledger code. A selection of the codes used is given below.

Supplier	Supplier account code
Angus Ltd	ANG42
Doris Day	DOR32
Harold & Co	HAR04
Tobias & Sons	TOB49
Toby Parts Ltd	TOB51

Item	General ledger code
Office chair	GL103
Office desk	GL108
Office lamp	GL114
Office shelf	GL117
Office telephone	GL119

This is an invoice received from a supplier.

Toby Parts Ltd
31 Cannon Way, Amersham
Bucks HP8 3LD
VAT Registration No. 424 5242 42

INVOICE

Paving Co Ltd
24 George Street
Amersham
Bucks HP3 5BJ

Customer account code: PAV001

Date: 5 November 20XX

Invoice number: 694

Delivery note number: 43456

10 telephones @ £50	£500.00
VAT @ 20%	£100.00
Total	£600.00

Supplier code: [   ]   General ledger code: [   ]

Code the supplier's invoice by selecting the appropriate codes from the items below.

Items	ANG42	DOR32	HAR04	TOB49	TOB51
	GL103	GL108	GL114	GL117	GL119

Activity 4: Creating a code

Toby Parts Ltd allocates a customer code to each of its customers as shown below. The code is made up of the first three letters of the customer's name, followed by a number, which is allocated sequentially to the next customer in that alphabetical group.

Customer name	Customer code
Aga Ltd	Aga01
Arundel Ltd	Aru02
Carlisle Ltd	Car01
Hill Products	Hil01
Jamji Ltd	Jam01
Juno Designs	Jun02
Paving Co Ltd	Pav01
Zoom Ltd	Zoo01

Toby Parts Ltd has two new credit customers which need to be allocated a customer code.

Insert the relevant customer codes for each customer.

Customer	Customer code
Docoa Ltd	
Jury Ltd	

Chapter summary

- There are three types of business entities: sole trader, partnership and limited liability company.

- Every business carries out typical business transactions such as buying and selling goods. For each transaction, business documentation is produced.

- A business's sales transactions can be categorised as either cash or credit sales.

- It is important that the documentation contains complete, accurate and valid information.

- A quotation is sent to a potential customer. It details the goods or services to be supplied, the price and the terms and conditions of the sale.

- If the potential customer wishes to make an order, a customer order document is produced.

- When goods are delivered to a customer, they are usually accompanied by a delivery note.

- An invoice is used in credit transactions to show how much is owed by the customer and when it should be paid.

- A credit note is used in credit transactions to show that less is owed than was originally invoiced.

- A remittance advice note is used in credit transactions to help the business receiving the advice note to identify which invoices and credit notes are being paid.

- A petty cash voucher is used to record payments of petty cash.

- Coding systems are used to ensure accuracy of recording and filing.

- **Capital:** The amount of money invested by the owner in the business

- **Cash:** Amounts of cash held physically by the business as notes and coin, usually as a result of making cash sales, pending banking

- **Cash sales:** Sales that are made for immediate payment by cash, cheque, credit or debit card

- **Coding systems:** Used to ensure accuracy of filing and recording

- **Credit note:** A document issued to a customer who returns goods, showing the details of the goods returned and their value

- **Credit sales:** Sales that are made now but payment is not required for a specified period of time

- **Customer code:** A unique code given to a customer by a supplier when recording transactions that relate to that customer

- **Customer order:** Sent from the customer to the supplier confirming the required purchase

- **Delivery note:** Document sent to the customer with the items being despatched, which must be signed by the customer confirming receipt of the items

- **Document number:** The unique number allocated from a sequence to a particular document as part of the business's coding system

- **Invoice:** A document issued by the seller to the purchaser of goods on credit showing the details of the goods sold, the amount due and the due date of payment

- **Limited liability company:** A business that is owned by shareholders and managed by directors, who are not necessarily the same people. The debts of the business and the personal debts of the owners (shareholders) are legally separate

- **Owner:** The person who has invested money in the business

- **Partnership:** A business that is jointly owned and managed by two or more individuals

- **Petty cash:** Small amounts of cash held physically within the business and used to make small payments

- **Petty cash voucher:** A document that records payments out of petty cash

- **Price list:** Written confirmation from a supplier as to the price of goods

- **Product code:** A unique code given to a product by a supplier or customer to help in recording transactions involving that product

- **Profit:** The excess of income over expenses made by a business

- **Quotation:** A written statement sent from supplier to customer advising them of the price of a specific good or service (or combination of the two)

- **Remittance advice note:** A document sent with a payment setting out which amounts are being paid and whether any credit notes are being applied

- **Sales income:** What the business earns when it makes sales of goods or services to other parties; can also be called 'revenue' or 'sales revenue'

- **Sole trader:** A business that is owned and managed by an individual

- **Supplier code:** A unique code given to a supplier by a customer when recording transactions that relate to that supplier

- **Till receipt:** The primary documentation for a sale or purchase in cash

1 For each of the following transactions determine whether it should be classified as a cash or credit transaction.

	Cash ✓	Credit ✓
Purchase of a van with an agreed payment date in one month's time		
Sale of goods by credit card in a shop		
Purchase of computer disks by cheque		
Purchase of computer disks which are accompanied by an invoice		
Sale of goods which are paid for by cheque		

2 Tara agrees to sell goods to Cathy for £100 and they agree Cathy will pay Tara in 2 weeks' time. The business document that Tara should send to Cathy to record this agreement is (tick **one**):

	✓
An invoice	
A receipt	
A remittance advice	
A credit note	

3 Cathy is not happy with her goods when she receives them and Tara agrees that they are not quite of the required standard, so she will only expect payment of £80 rather than £100 at the due time. The business document that Tara should send to Cathy to record this is (tick **one**):

	✓
An invoice	
A delivery note	
A remittance advice	
A credit note	

4 Cathy sends a cheque to Tara for £80 and wishes to make it clear that both the invoice and the credit note are being settled by means of this payment. To clarify this matter for Tara, Cathy should send her (tick **one**):

	✓
An invoice	
A delivery note	
A remittance advice	
A credit note	

5 For each of the following transactions, indicate the primary business document that will be created, by drawing an arrow from each of the four boxes on the left to one of the boxes on the right.

Sale of goods for cash		Credit note
Return of goods purchased on credit		Remittance advice note
Reimbursement of employee for expense by cash		Till receipt
Indication of which amounts that are owed are being paid		Cheque
		Petty cash voucher
		Invoice

6 An organisation codes all invoices received from suppliers with a supplier code. A selection of the codes used is given below:

Supplier	Supplier code
Benson Ltd	BEN41
Immer plc	IMM56
Presley Co	PRE62

The organisation has received an invoice from Presley Co. What supplier code should it use for the invoice?

✓	Supplier code
	BEN41
	IMM56
	PRE62

The books of prime entry

2

Learning outcomes

1.4	Demonstrate an understanding of the process of recording financial transactions
	• The role of the books of prime entry: sales and sales returns daybooks, purchases and purchases returns daybooks, discounts allowed and discounts received daybooks.
2.2	Enter sales invoices and credit notes into books of prime entry
	• The books of prime entry: sales, sales returns and discounts allowed daybooks
	• The columns within books of prime entry: customer name, customer account code, total, VAT, net, analysis (including product codes).
3.2	Enter supplier invoices and credit notes into books of prime entry
	• The books of prime entry: purchases, purchases returns and discounts received daybooks
	• The columns within books of prime entry: supplier name, supplier account code, total, VAT, net, analysis (including product codes).

Assessment context

Entering invoices and credit notes in the books of prime entry is an important part of the syllabus. It is likely that you will have to complete a partially completed day book and total the day book in your assessment.

Qualification context

In the Level 3 *Advanced Bookkeeping* paper, you need to understand the importance of maintaining financial records and the types of records that should be maintained, including the books of prime entry and ledger accounts.

Business context

Transactions must be recorded accurately in the books of prime entry as these books are the source of information which is ultimately included in the financial statements.

Chapter overview

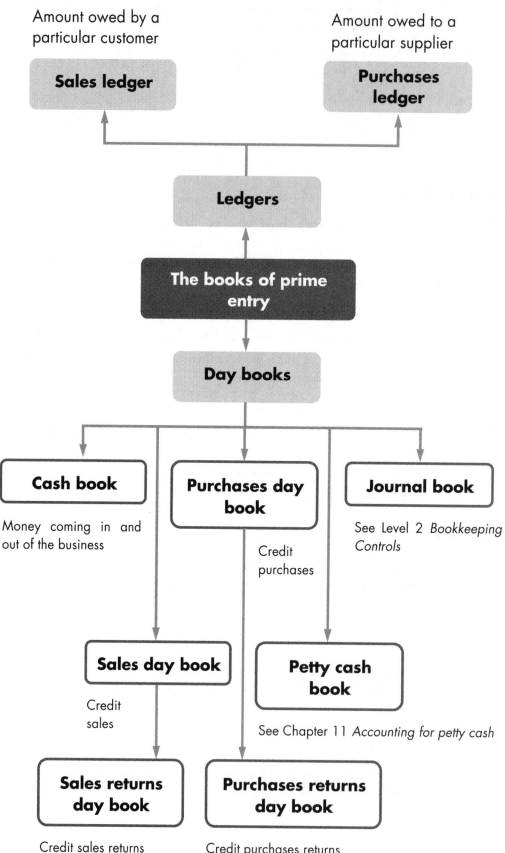

Amount owed by a particular customer

Sales ledger

Amount owed to a particular supplier

Purchases ledger

Ledgers

The books of prime entry

Day books

Cash book

Money coming in and out of the business

Purchases day book

Credit purchases

Journal book

See Level 2 *Bookkeeping Controls*

Sales day book

Credit sales

Petty cash book

See Chapter 11 *Accounting for petty cash*

Sales returns day book

Credit sales returns

Purchases returns day book

Credit purchases returns

Introduction

In the previous chapter we looked at some of the basic transactions of a business. We are now ready to start recording some of these transactions in the business's accounting system, beginning with the books of prime entry.

1 The accounting process

A business exists so that its activities make a profit for its owner. In order to know whether it is profit or loss making, the business must keep a record of its income and expenses in a process known as **accounting**.

Chapter 1 introduced business documents, including invoices, credit notes and remittance advice notes. At this stage they are just a pile of documents and from them it is not easy to see:

- The amount of income the business has generated in the year
- The expenditure incurred
- How much cash has been received and paid
- Which customers still owe money to the business
- Which suppliers are awaiting payment from the business

To obtain this information we need to find a way of categorising like information together and then summarising it so that we can understand its meaning.

This is achieved by entering details from key business documents into the appropriate **book of prime entry**. These books of prime entry are often known as **day books** as, in theory at least, they would be written up every day.

On a regular basis (eg weekly, monthly or quarterly) these books of prime entry are **totalled** and the totals entered into the **general ledger** (which we will cover later in the course).

Categorising the documents in the day books is an important step in the process of building the accounting records which ultimately feed into the financial statements. This is illustrated in the following diagram:

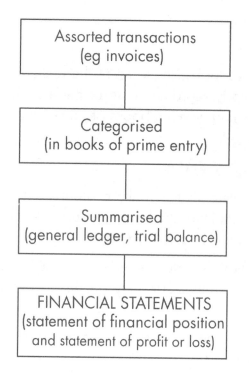

In your assessment you may be asked to complete the following books of prime entry:

- Sales day book
- Sales returns day book
- Purchases day book
- Purchases returns day book
- Cash book
- Petty cash book
- Discounts allowed day book
- Discounts received day book

The discounts allowed and discounts received day books are covered in Chapter 3. The journal book is also a book of prime entry. You will not be asked to complete the journal book in your assessment. The journal book is covered in *Bookkeeping Controls*.

2 Sales day book

As we saw in Chapter 1, when a business makes a sale on **credit**, payment is not received at the point of sale. Therefore, the business must generate an invoice to send to the customer.

The **sales day book** lists all the business's invoices sent to credit customers.

Illustration 1: Sales day book

Date 20XX	Details	Invoice number	Customer code	Total	VAT	Net	Sales type 1	Sales type 2
31 Aug	J Beadle	2041	SL21	9,600	1,600	8,000	8,000	
31 Aug	M Ralph	2042	SL05	3,600	600	3,000		3,000
31 Aug	Tom Ltd	2043	SL17	720	120	600	600	
	Totals			13,920	2,320	11,600	8,600	3,000

To enter information into the sales day book:

Step 1 Gather the invoices that have been sent out to the customers since the sales day book was last written up and check that there are no invoices missing (the invoice numbers should be in sequence).

Step 2 Enter the dates of the invoices, the names of the customers and the invoice numbers in the appropriate columns of the sales day book.

Step 3 The customer code column is also sometimes headed up 'reference' or 'folio'. This is the column where the account numbers for the customers are entered from the invoices. The customer code is the account number given to the customers in the **sales ledger** (which we will come back to shortly) and therefore is often given the prefix 'SL'.

Step 4 Only three figures are entered from the invoices:

- The total column contains the gross total including VAT shown on the invoice.

- VAT is the VAT amount shown on the invoice.

- The net column is the net total (before VAT) on the invoice.

Step 5 Finally, analyse the net amounts into the different types of sales. For example, sales to J Beadle and Tom Ltd were of sales type 1, sales to M Ralph were of sales type 2.

Most businesses include a more detailed analysis of the net amount of sales by using analytical columns in an **analysed sales day book**. For example, a business may wish to analyse its sales by **type of product**. So a computer manufacturer may wish to analyse net sales between computers, printers and scanners. In this case there would be a column for each in the sales day book. The amounts included in the analysis columns are **net amounts**.

Alternatively, a business that makes sales of its products around the country may wish to analyse its sales by geographical area. **Shading** is often used to denote the analysis columns.

On a regular basis (eg daily, weekly or monthly) the sales day book columns are **totalled** and entered into the **general ledger** (we will come back to this later in the course).

Activity 1: Sales day book

Sales invoices have been prepared and partially entered in the sales day book, as shown below. The rate of VAT is 20%.

Required

(a) **Complete the entries in the sales day book by inserting the appropriate figures for each invoice.**

(b) **Total the last five columns of the sales day book.**

Sales day book

Date 20XX	Details	Invoice number	Customer code	Total £	VAT £	Net £	Sales type 1 £	Sales type 2 £
31 Aug	K Lead	2041	SL15				2,500	
31 Aug	O Ball	2042	SL02					300
31 Aug	P Reed	2043	SL10				665	
	Totals							

3 Sales returns day book

Goods may be returned to the seller if the items were faulty or are no longer required, and a credit note raised to reimburse the customer. Credit notes also need to be recorded in the day books.

They can be recorded in one of two ways:

- Either as a **negative entry** in the sales day book; or
- In a separate book of prime entry known as the **sales returns day book**.

Assessment focus point

In your assessment a separate sales returns day book will be used.

The sales returns day book is a list of all the credit notes raised against sales which have been made on credit. It works in a similar way to the sales day book.

Illustration 2: Sales returns day book

Date 20XX	Details	Credit note number	Customer code	Total £	VAT £	Net £	Sales returns £
31 Aug	M James	831	SL98	360	60	300	300
31 Aug	F Rally	832	SL01	240	40	200	200
31 Aug	G Walter	833	SL15	480	80	400	400
	Totals			1,080	180	900	900

The sales returns day book is also totalled periodically (usually with the same frequency as the sales day book).

Combining the information in the sales day book and the sales returns day book will give the business an idea of the **net income** it has earned in a given period.

Activity 2: Sales returns day book

Sales credit notes have been prepared and partially entered in the sales returns day book, as shown below. The rate of VAT is 20%.

(a) **Complete the entries in the sales returns day book by inserting the appropriate figures for each credit note.**

(b) **Total the last four columns of the sales returns day book.**

Sales returns day book

Date 20XX	Details	Credit note number	Customer code	Total £	VAT £	Net £	Sales returns £
31 May	K Farm	751	SL08				350
31 May	S Fred	752	SL11	270			
31 May	J Irons	753	SL07		200		
	Totals						

4 Cash book – introduction

The **cash book** is a book of prime entry used to record money received and paid out by the business.

The cash book is a large book and therefore often split into two books:

Terms used	Explanation
Cash book – debit side	This records money **received** by the business, together with the appropriate analysis.
Cash book – credit side	This records money **paid out** by the business, together with the appropriate analysis.

'Debits' and 'credits' are explained later in this Course Book. For now, just think of a **debit** as being something the business owns, such as money in the bank account. In contrast, a **credit** is something the business owes, such as a bank loan.

In *Bookkeeping Transactions* we study the **two-column cash book**. This means that on each side of the cash book there are two main columns:

- Cash – this column is used to record amounts received or paid in **cash only**

- Bank – this column is used to record all other amounts paid or received through the bank, including cheques, direct debits and **BACS**

The other columns (such as VAT, cash sales and cash purchases) are analysis columns.

4.1 Cash book – debit side

All money received by a business is recorded in the **cash book – debit side**, whether it is a receipt of cash, cheque, credit card or debit card or passed directly through the banking system by automated payment.

Generally a business receives cash for the following reasons:

(a) Cash sales
(b) Cash received from credit customers (receivables)
(c) Other miscellaneous receipts (bank interest, contributions from the owner)

Illustration 3: Cash book – debit side

Date 20XX	Details	Cash £	Bank £	VAT £	Trade receivables £	Cash sales £	Sundry £
9 May	Balance b/f	400	1,000				
10 May	J Jones	600		100		500	
10 May	B Kindly		800		800		
10 May	Bank interest		100				100
10 May	F Feather		1,200		1,200		
10 May	I Glue	300		50		250	
	Totals	1,300	3,100	150	2,000	750	100

The **date** recorded will be the date the payment was received or written up in the cash book, depending on the business's policy.

The figure in the Cash column is the total amount of the receipt of notes and coin only.

The figure in the Bank column is the total amount of the receipts into the business's bank account, including **cheques** paid in.

When money is received from a **credit customer**, **no entry is made to the VAT** column as the VAT was recorded when the original sales invoice was entered into the sales day book. However, when **cash sales which include VAT** are made, the **VAT element** must be entered in the **VAT column**, and the net amount must be entered into the Cash sales column, so that the total of the Cash sales and VAT amounts is the figure in the Cash or Bank column.

5 Purchases day book

A business that makes sales will, of course, also make **purchases** of goods and services. When purchases are made on credit the business will **receive an invoice** from the credit supplier.

Purchases invoices are recorded in the book of prime entry known as the **purchases day book**.

Illustration 4: Purchases day book

Date 20XX	Details	Invoice number	Supplier code	Total £	VAT £	Net £	Purchases £	Expenses £
28 Feb	Callum	3252	PL23	6,000	1,000	5,000		5,000
28 Feb	Mavis	PO521	PL14	5,112	852	4,260	4,260	
28 Feb	Henry	JK411	PL06	10,104	1,684	8,420	8,420	
	Totals			21,216	3,536	17,680	12,680	5,000

To enter invoices into the purchases day book:

Step 1 Gather the invoices that have been received from suppliers since the purchases day book was last written up.

Step 2 Enter the date of the invoice, the name of the supplier and the supplier's invoice number in the appropriate columns – note that as all suppliers are likely to have different ways of numbering their invoices, the invoice numbers in the purchases day book will not be sequential.

Step 3 The supplier code column is entered with the account number for the supplier. The supplier code is the account number given to the supplier in the purchases ledger (which we will come back to shortly) and therefore is often given the prefix 'PL'. This code is important as it helps with the eventual entry of these figures into the accounts.

Step 4 Enter the figures from the invoice.

- The total column contains the gross total including VAT shown on the face of the invoice.

- VAT is the VAT amount shown on the invoice.

- The net total on the invoice (ie the gross amount less the VAT) is then entered into the net column and into appropriate analysis columns, which are often shaded in practice to denote their separation from the net amount.

Like the other day books, the purchases day book is totalled periodically (eg every week, fortnight or month).

The purchases day book is nearly always **analysed** into different types of purchases or expenses. The **purchases analysis** column contains items bought for use in the business's primary products (eg flour for a baker) whereas the **expenses analysis** column contains overhead expenditure, such as stationery and utility bills. The analysis columns show the **net amount**.

Activity 3: Purchases day book

Purchases invoices have been checked and partially entered in the purchases day book, as shown below. The VAT rate is 20%.

Required

(a) **Complete the entries in the purchases day book by inserting the appropriate figures for each invoice.**

(b) **Total the last five columns of the purchases day book.**

Purchases day book

Date 20XX	Details	Invoice number	Supplier code	Total £	VAT £	Net £	Purchases £	Expenses £
28 Feb	Dill Ltd	5215	PL05					9,520
28 Feb	Neil Co	PO8214	PL17				130	
28 Feb	Elkin	SS852	PL33				5,240	
	Totals							

6 Purchases returns day book

If the business finds it has been invoiced for goods that were faulty or not ordered then it will request and receive a credit note against the invoice. These credit notes also need to be recorded.

They can be recorded in one of two ways:

- Either as a **negative entry** in the purchases day book; or

- In a separate book of prime entry known as the **purchases returns day book**.

> **Assessment focus point**
>
> In your assessment a separate purchases returns day book will be used.

The purchases returns day book is simply a **list of all the credit notes received** against purchases which have been made on credit.

Illustration 5: Purchases returns day book

Date 20XX	Details	Credit note number	Supplier code	Total £	VAT £	Net £
31 Mar	Eliza Ltd	82	PL13	624	104	520
31 Mar	Florence	KJ42	PL04	456	76	380
	Totals			1,080	180	900

The credit note numbers are unlikely to be sequential as each supplier will have their own way of numbering credit notes.

Activity 4: Purchases returns day book

Purchases credit notes have been checked and partially entered in the purchases returns day book, as shown below. The rate of VAT is 20%.

(a) Complete the entries in the purchases returns day book by inserting the appropriate figures for each credit note.

(b) Total the last three columns of the purchases returns day book.

Purchases returns day book

Date 20XX	Details	Credit note number	Supplier code	Total £	VAT £	Net £
31 Mar	Horace	NH94	PL01			120
31 Mar	Jameson	313	PL23	1,050		
	Totals					

7 Cash book – credit side

When **payments** are made by a business they are recorded in the **cash book – credit side**. This book of prime entry is the mirror image of the cash book – debit side.

Generally a business makes a payment for the following reasons:

(a) Purchases (goods for resale) made for cash
(b) Payments made to credit suppliers
(c) Regular payments made for other expenses (for example wages and salaries)
(d) Drawings (money taken out of the business by the proprietor for personal use)
(e) Other miscellaneous payments, such as bank charges

Illustration 6: Cash book – credit side

Date 20XX	Details	Cash £	Bank £	VAT £	Trade payables £	Cash purchases £	Expenses £
11 May	Mole Co		200				200
11 May	Adams	360		60		300	
11 May	Polly & Sons		3,000		3,000		
11 May	Oscar Ltd		4,000		4,000		
11 May	Fishers	90		15		75	
	Totals	450	7,200	75	7,000	375	200

There are many similarities between the cash book – credit side and the cash book – debit side.

The **date** recorded will be the date on which the transaction was authorised (such as when the cheque was written or the BACS payment was notified to the bank) or the date on which the cash book is written up, depending on the business's policy.

The figure in the Cash column is the total amount of the payment of notes and coin.

The figure in the Bank column is the total value of the payment leaving the bank account by cheque, debit card or automated payment.

When a payment is made to a **credit supplier, no entry is made to the VAT column**, as the VAT was recorded when the original purchases invoice was entered into the purchases day book. However, when **cash purchases** are made on which VAT is charged the **VAT element** is recorded in the **VAT column**, and the net amount is recorded in the Cash purchases column, so that the total of the Cash purchases and VAT amounts is the figure in the Cash or Bank column.

8 Sales and purchases ledgers

8.1 Purpose of the ledgers

As we have seen, the purpose of the books of prime entry is to categorise like business documentation together (for example, invoices and credit notes) so that we can see the level of sales and expenditure for a particular period.

While this is very useful information, businesses are faced with another challenge. They need to know **how much is owed from each credit customer** and the **amount due to each supplier** at any point in time.

This way, if there are queries or disagreements with a customer or supplier the business can locate the information it needs easily and without trawling back through the detailed information in each of the books of prime entry.

To achieve this, a **sales ledger** (for customers) and a **purchases ledger** (for suppliers) are maintained. These ledgers are known as **subsidiary ledgers**, which we will come back to later in the course.

Ledger	Purpose
Sales ledger	A record that contains **ledger accounts** for every credit customer.
	The customer's ledger account shows the amount owed by that individual customer.
	It helps with customer queries over invoices, credit notes and receipts.
Purchases ledger	A record that contains ledger accounts for every credit supplier.
	The supplier's ledger account shows the amount owed to that individual supplier.
	It helps the business identify how much to pay each supplier and the date the payment should be made.

8.2 Sales ledger

Each credit customer's **ledger account** contains two sides:

- On the **left-hand side** we record invoices, which **increase** the amount owed by the customer.

- On the **right-hand side** we record credit notes, prompt payment discounts taken and payments received from the customer, all of which **decrease** the amount owed by the customer.

Illustration 7: Sales ledger

Gregory & Sons has two customers, Harvey Ltd and Fred & Co. The following transactions take place with Harvey Ltd:

Type	Detail required for sales ledger	Total £
Sales invoice	Invoice 88	3,000
Sales invoice	Invoice 94	5,000
Payment	Bank	3,000
Credit note	Credit note 13	1,000

Sales ledger

Harvey Ltd

Details	Amount £	Details	Amount £
Invoice 88	3,000	Bank	3,000
Invoice 94	5,000	Credit note 13	1,000

Remember, entries on the left-hand side **increase** the amount owed by the customer, and entries on the right-hand side **decrease** the amount owed by the customer.

To calculate how much is owed by Harvey Ltd to Gregory & Sons, you **should total the left-hand side** of the account, and **total the right-hand side** of the account, then **subtract** the right-hand side total from the left-hand side total.

	£
How much does Harvey Ltd owe Gregory & Sons? (3,000 + 5,000) – (3,000 + 1,000) = 4,000	4,000

Activity 5: Sales ledger

Following on from Illustration 7, these transactions take place with Fred & Co:

Type	Detail required for sales ledger	Total £
Sales invoice	Invoice 121	3,425
Sales invoice	Invoice 125	4,561
Payment	Bank	1,952
Credit note	Credit note 31	553

Required

(a) Complete the sales ledger for Fred & Co, in the books of Gregory & Sons.

Sales ledger

Fred & Co

Details	Amount £	Details	Amount £

(b) Answer the following question.

	£
How much does Fred & Co owe Gregory & Sons?	

8.3 Purchases ledger

Each credit supplier's ledger account contains two sides:

(a) On the **right-hand side** we record invoices, which **increase** the amount owed to the supplier.

(b) On the **left-hand side** we record credit notes, prompt payment discounts taken and payments to the supplier, all of which **decrease** the amount owed to the supplier.

Illustration 8: Purchases ledger

Gregory & Sons has two suppliers, Tiger Ltd and Cyril & Co. The following transactions take place with Tiger Ltd:

Type	Detail required for purchases ledger	Total £
Purchases invoice	Invoice 56	8,550
Purchases invoice	Invoice 78	510
Payment	Bank	7,425
Credit note	Credit note 21	325

Purchases ledger

Tiger Ltd

Details	Amount £	Details	Amount £
Bank	7,425	Invoice 56	8,550
Credit note 21	325	Invoice 78	510

Remember, entries on the left-hand side **decrease** the amount the business owes the supplier, and entries on the right-hand side **increase** the amount the business owes the supplier.

To calculate how much Gregory & Sons owes Tiger Ltd, you should **total the left-hand side** of the account, and **total the right-hand side** of the account, then **subtract** the left-hand side total from the right-hand side total.

	£
How much does Gregory & Sons owe Tiger Ltd? (8,550 + 510) – (7,425 + 325) = 1,310	1,310

Activity 6: Purchases ledger

Following on from Illustration 8, the following transactions take place with Cyril & Co:

Type	Detail required for purchases ledger	Total £
Purchases invoice	Invoice 101	4,250
Purchases invoice	Invoice 107	9,682
Payment	Bank	4,250
Credit note	Credit note 87	1,032

Required

(a) **Complete the purchases ledger for Cyril & Co, in the books of Gregory & Sons.**

Purchases ledger

Cyril & Co

Details	Amount £	Details	Amount £

(b) **Answer the following question.**

	£
How much does Gregory & Sons owe Cyril & Co?	

Chapter summary

- Documents of the same type are recorded in the books of prime entry.

- Sales invoices are all recorded initially in the sales day book, which shows the net amount, VAT and gross totals from each invoice. The net amount may also be analysed to show the different types of sale.

- Sales credit notes are initially recorded in the sales returns day book. It shows the net amount, VAT and gross total from each credit note, and may be analysed.

- Purchases invoices are all recorded initially in the purchases day book. It shows the net amount, VAT and gross totals from each supplier invoice, and the net amount is nearly always analysed to show the different types of purchase or expense.

- Purchase credit notes from suppliers are initially recorded in the purchases returns day book. It shows the net amount, VAT and gross total from each credit note, and may be analysed.

- Receipts of money into the business are recorded in the cash book – debit side.

- Payments of money by the business are recorded in the cash book – credit side.

- The sales ledger shows the amount owed by each individual credit customer.

- The purchases ledger shows the amount owed to each individual credit supplier.

- **Analysed sales day book:** A sales day book where the net amount is analysed into the different types of sale for each invoice

- **BACS:** Bankers' Automated Clearing Service – automated payment method

- **Books of prime entry:** The books in which the details of the organisation's transactions are initially recorded, using details from business documents

- **Cash book:** The book of prime entry in which all receipts and payments by the business are recorded

- **Cash book – credit side:** The part of the cash book in which payments are recorded

- **Cash book – debit side:** The part of the cash book in which receipts are recorded

- **Day books:** Another name for books of prime entry

- **Purchases day book:** The book of prime entry where all the supplier invoices received by the business are listed

- **Purchases ledger:** Record that contains ledger accounts for every credit supplier

- **Purchases returns day book:** The book of prime entry where all the credit notes received by the business are listed

- **Sales day book:** The book of prime entry where all the business's invoices sent to credit customers are listed

- **Sales ledger:** Record that contains ledger accounts for every credit customer

- **Sales returns day book:** The book of prime entry where all the credit notes issued by the business are listed

Test your learning

1   An invoice shows the following amounts. Which columns in the sales day book would each amount appear in? Tick **one** box for each amount.

	£	Total	VAT	Net
Goods total	1,236.00			
VAT	247.20			
Total	1,483.20			

2   (a)   Complete the following sentences:

An invoice is entered on the	left right	side of the customer's ledger account
A credit note is entered on the	left right	side of the customer's ledger account

   (b)   The ledger account for Harris & Sons is shown here:

   Harris & Sons   SL 17

Details	£	Details	£
Invoice 1898	120	Credit note 55	96

   How much does Harris & Sons owe the business?

   £ [   ]

3   An extract from an invoice for a computer manufacturer that analyses its sales into those for computers, printers and scanners is given below:

Quantity	Description	£
1	GH3 Computer	800.00
1	Z3 Colour printer	300.00
1	S4 Scanner	200.00
		1,300.00
VAT		260.00
		1,560.00

Show how this invoice would be entered into the analysed sales day book.

Total £	VAT £	Net £	Computers £	Printers £	Scanners £

4   An extract from an invoice from a supplier of dishwashers is given below:

Quantity	Description	£
1	RDX dishwasher	650.00
1	KJG dishwasher	480.00
1	XXX dishwasher	520.00
		1,650.00
VAT		330.00
		1,980.00

Show how this invoice would be entered into the analysed purchases day book for a business that sells dishwashers and other electrical goods to consumers.

Total £	VAT £	Net £	Purchases £	Expenses £

5   Write up the sales day book and the sales returns day book from the invoices and credit notes given below.

Invoice no. 44263	1 June	J Jepson	SL34	£118.00 + VAT
Invoice no. 44264	2 June	S Beck & Sons	SL01	£320.00 + VAT
Credit note 3813	2 June	Scroll Ltd	SL16	£18.00 + VAT
Invoice no. 44265	3 June	Penfold Ltd	SL23	£164.00 + VAT
Invoice no. 44266	4 June	S Beck & Sons	SL01	£256.00 + VAT
Invoice no. 44267	4 June	J Jepson	SL34	£144.00 + VAT
Credit note 3814	5 June	Penfold Ltd	SL23	£16.80 + VAT

Sales day book

Date	Customer	Invoice number	Customer code	Total £	VAT £	Net £
Total						

Sales returns day book

Date	Customer	Credit note number	Customer code	Total £	VAT £	Net £
Total						

6   Today's date is 6 June and you are required to write up the purchases day book and the purchases returns day book from the invoices and credit notes given below. It is organisational policy to use the date column to record the date of entry rather than the date of invoice.

1 June	Invoice 224363 from Y H Hill (PL16)	£158.40 + VAT
1 June	Credit note CN92 from Letra Ltd (PL24)	£100.00 + VAT
2 June	Invoice PT445 from Letra Ltd (PL24)	£228.00 + VAT
2 June	Invoice 77352 from Coldstores Ltd (PL03)	£158.00 + VAT
5 June	Credit note C7325 from Y H Hill (PL16)	£26.00 + VAT

Purchases day book

Date	Supplier	Invoice number	Supplier code	Total £	VAT £	Net £
Total						

Purchases returns day book

Date	Supplier	Credit note number	Supplier code	Total £	VAT £	Net £
Total						

7   Given below are two invoices received from suppliers by Whitehill Superstores.
    An extract from the supplier code listing is given:

Bass Engineers   PL 13

Herne Industries   PL 15

Today's date is 20 October. You are required to record the invoice details in the
purchases day book and then total the purchases day book.

Purchases day book

Date	Supplier	Invoice number	Supplier code	Total £	VAT £	Net £
		Total				

INVOICE

Herne Industries
Fuller House
Bean Park
Benham DR6 3PQ
Tel 0303226 Fax 0303582
VAT Reg 0624 3361 29

To: Whitehill Superstores
     28, Whitehill Park
     Benham DR6 5LM

Invoice number: 46121

Date/tax point: 16 Oct 20XX

Order number: 32216

Account number: SL 23

Quantity	Description	Product code	Unit amount £	Total £
3	Komax Camcorder	KC410	240.00	720.00
		Net total		720.00
		VAT		144.00
		Invoice total		864.00

Terms
Net 30 days
E & OE

INVOICE

Bass Engineers
Bass House
Parrish DR3 2FL
Tel 0462333 Fax 0462334
VAT Reg 2016 2131 87

To: Whitehill Superstores
28, Whitehill Park
Benham DR6 5LM

Invoice number: 663211

Date/tax point: 15 Oct 20XX

Order number: 32213

Account number: W15

Quantity	Description	Product code	Unit amount £	Total £
16	Standard lamps	33116	24.00	384.00
			Net total	384.00
			VAT	76.80
			Invoice total	460.80

Terms
Net 30 days
E & OE

8   Today's date is 20 October. Given below are two credit notes received by Whitehill Superstores. Enter the details of these credit notes into the purchases returns day book and then total the day book.

An extract from the supplier code listing is given:

Southfield Electrical   PL 20

Herne Industries   PL 15

Purchases returns day book

Date	Supplier	Credit note number	Supplier code	Total £	VAT £	Net £
		Total				

CREDIT NOTE

SOUTHFIELD ELECTRICAL
INDUSTRIAL ESTATE
Benham DR6 2FF
Tel 0303379 Fax 0303152
VAT Reg 0264 2274 49

Invoice to:

Whitehill Superstores
28 Whitehill Park
Benham DR6 5LM

Credit note number: 08702
Date/tax point: 16 Oct 20XX
Order number 32217
Account number: SL 44

Quantity	Description	Product code	Unit amount £	Total £
2	Temax Coffee maker	9130	50.00	100.00

Net total	100.00
VAT	20.00
Gross total	120.00

Reason for credit note:

Not ordered by customer

CREDIT NOTE

HERNE INDUSTRIES
Fuller House
Bean Park
Benham DR6 3PQ
Tel 0303226 Fax 0303582
VAT Reg 0624 3361 29

Invoice to:

Whitehill Superstores
28 Whitehill Park
Benham DR6 5LM

Credit note number: CN 4502
Date/tax point: 17 Oct 20XX
Order number 32221
Account number: SL 23

Quantity	Description	Product code	Unit amount	Total
			£	£
1	Kemax Camera	KC450	110.00	110.00
			Net total	110.00
			VAT	22.00
			Gross total	132.00

Reason for credit note:

Wrong items

BPP
LEARNING MEDIA

VAT and discounts

3

Learning outcomes

1.2	Distinguish between prompt payment, trade and bulk discounts
	• The difference between discounts offered: prompt payment, trade and bulk
	• How discounts are shown on invoices: prompt payment, trade and bulk
	• How prompt payment discounts are recorded: credit note, discounts allowed or discounts received daybook, sales or purchases ledger
1.4	Demonstrate an understanding of the process of recording financial transactions
	• The role of the books of prime entry: discounts allowed and discounts received daybooks

Assessment context

An assessment question may give you an invoice with the net sales amount and details of discount(s). You could be asked to calculate the discount(s) and VAT on the sale or purchase. You could also be asked to identify when errors have been made in the discount and VAT calculations on invoices/credit notes sent by customers or suppliers.

Qualification context

This chapter includes VAT and discount calculations that will be used in the Level 3 *Advanced Bookkeeping* and *Final Accounts Preparation* courses. VAT is also studied in *Indirect Tax*.

Business context

Most companies offer discounts to win business. It is important to understand their effect on the financial statements.

Chapter overview

- A registered business charges output tax on its sales
- This is paid over to the tax authority once any recoverable input tax is deducted

A registered business will recover input tax on its purchases

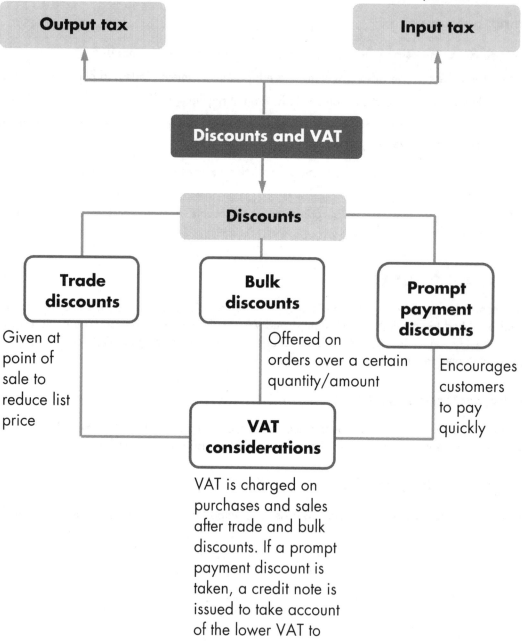

Output tax

Input tax

Discounts and VAT

Discounts

Trade discounts

Given at point of sale to reduce list price

Bulk discounts

Offered on orders over a certain quantity/amount

Prompt payment discounts

Encourages customers to pay quickly

VAT considerations

VAT is charged on purchases and sales after trade and bulk discounts. If a prompt payment discount is taken, a credit note is issued to take account of the lower VAT to be paid

Introduction

We saw on the invoice, credit note and petty cash voucher in Chapter 1 that **value added tax (VAT)** is an issue for businesses that buy and sell. But what is VAT? VAT may also be referred to as **sales tax** or an **indirect tax**. In this chapter, we will look at how VAT is charged and how to calculate it.

We will then move on to look at the different types of discounts offered by suppliers to their customers – trade, bulk and prompt payment discounts – before considering how discounts and VAT interact and how discounts are recorded in the books of prime entry.

1 Value added tax (VAT)

1.1 Principles of VAT

If the sales of a business exceed a certain amount for a year then a business **must** register for VAT with HM Revenue & Customs (HMRC).

As a registered business it must:

- Charge VAT on sales (also known as **output tax**)
- Suffer VAT on purchases (also known as **input tax**)

This means that goods/services are sold to customers at a higher price as VAT is added on. However, registered businesses can **recover** VAT on purchases from HMRC.

This means that VAT is a tax that is **paid by the final consumer** but is collected along the way by each seller in the supply chain.

Usually every three months, the business must complete a **VAT return** showing output and input tax. The excess of output tax over input tax must be paid to HMRC. However, if the input tax exceeds the output tax then a refund is due from HMRC.

1.2 Rates of VAT

The standard rate of VAT in the UK is 20%.

> **Assessment focus point**
>
> The rate of VAT applicable in your assessment will be given in the instruction screen at the start of your assessment. Read this carefully as from time to time it may change. AAT are currently using 20% as the standard rate of VAT in all assessments. Therefore, 20% is the rate used in this Course Book.

1.3 Calculating VAT

The two main calculations that you might be required to make are:

- Calculating VAT on the **net total**
- Calculating VAT from the **gross total** (note that sometimes this may be referred to as the invoice total, or just 'total', or just 'gross')

The **net total** is the total of the invoice **before** VAT is applied.

The **gross total** is the total of the **net amount plus VAT**.

The total VAT shown on an invoice should be **rounded down to the nearest 1p**. In other words, if the VAT calculation gives a figure of more than two decimal places you should always round VAT down to the nearest penny.

> **Assessment focus point**
>
> Where it is relevant, AAT will provide advice on rounding in the task instructions. If advice is given, you should follow it.
>
> If no advice is given in the task instructions:
>
> - you should round down the VAT on **invoices** to the nearest penny.
>
> - you can choose whether to round up or down the VAT on **credit notes** and you will be given credit for either.

1.3.1 Calculating VAT on the net amount

To calculate VAT on the **net** sales or purchases amount, the method is:

> **Formula to learn**
>
> VAT = Net amount × rate of VAT as a %

With a rate of VAT of 20% this is: VAT = Net amount × 20%

> **Assessment focus point**
>
> To calculate 20%, you can multiply by 0.2 or by the fraction 20/100. The fraction 20/100 can also be expressed as 1/5, so you could instead divide by 5 to calculate the VAT.

> **Illustration 1: Calculating VAT on the net amount**
>
> The net amount is £50.00 and the rate of VAT is 20%. Calculate the gross amount.
>
> $$VAT = 50.00 \times 0.2 = \textbf{£10.00}$$
>
> $$Or, VAT = \frac{50.00}{5} = \textbf{£10.00}$$
>
> The gross amount is then the net amount plus the VAT
>
> $$50.00 + 10.00 = \textbf{£60.00}$$

Activity 1: Calculating VAT on the net amount

The rate of VAT is 20%.

Complete the table below. Show all answers to two decimal places.

Net £	VAT £	Gross £
100.00		
350.00		
3,898.34		
6,500.00		

1.3.2 Calculating VAT from the gross amount

To calculate VAT from the **gross** sales or purchases amount, the method is:

Formula to learn

$$\text{VAT} = \text{Gross amount} \times \frac{\text{VAT rate}}{\text{VAT rate plus } 100}$$

With a rate of VAT of 20% this is:

$$\text{VAT} = \text{Gross amount} \times \frac{20}{120}$$

Assessment focus point

The fraction 20/120 can also be expressed as 1/6, so you could instead divide by 6 to calculate the VAT.

Illustration 2: Calculating VAT from the gross amount

The gross amount is £900.00 and the rate of VAT is 20%. Calculate the net amount.

$$\text{VAT} = 900.00 \times \frac{20}{120} = \textbf{£150.00}$$

$$\text{Or, VAT} = \frac{900.00}{6} = \textbf{£150.00}$$

The net amount is then the gross **minus** the VAT

£900.00 – £150.00 = £750.00

Activity 2: Calculating VAT from the gross amount

The rate of VAT is 20%.

Complete the table below. Show all answers to two decimal places.

Net £	VAT £	Gross £
		240.00
		660.00
		594.00
		1,260.00

2 Discounts

Many businesses offer discounts to their customers. There are three types of discount: trade discounts, bulk discounts and prompt payment discounts.

2.1 Trade discount

A **trade discount** is a **percentage reduction** from the **list price** of goods or services. The list price is the seller's standard price before any discounts have been deducted.

This reduced price may be offered:

- Because the customer is regular and valued;

- As an incentive to a new customer to buy; or

- Because the customer is in the same trade as the supplier and the supplier wants to develop good relations.

The amount of the trade discount will be **shown on the invoice** as a **deduction** from the list price before arriving at the net total.

2.2 Bulk discount

A **bulk discount** is also a **percentage reduction** from the list price of goods or services, offered because the customer's order is large. The business will offer this to encourage customers to place large orders, so costs of administration and delivery are reduced.

Like the trade discount, the amount of the bulk discount will be **shown on the invoice** as a **deduction** from the list price before arriving at the net total. It may be offered as well as, or instead of, a trade discount.

If a bulk discount is offered in addition to a trade discount, it is normal practice to calculate the bulk discount on the amount **after** the trade discount has been deducted.

Illustration 3: Trade and bulk discounts

Southfield Electrical sells six dishwashers to Whitehill Superstores. The dishwashers have a list price of £200 per dishwasher. Southfield Electrical's discount policy in relation to Whitehill is:

- 10% trade discount is allowed on all sales

- 5% bulk discount on orders where list price net of trade discount exceeds £1,000

The net amount after discounts have been deducted is calculated as follows.

Amount	Calculation	£
List price	6 × 200	1,200
Less trade discount	1,200 × 0.1	120
Net amount after trade discount	1,200 – 120	1,080
Less bulk discount	1,080 × 0.05	54
Net amount after trade and bulk discounts	1,080 – 54	1,026

2.3 Prompt payment discount

A **prompt payment discount** is a **percentage discount** of the gross total that is offered to a customer to encourage that customer to pay the invoice earlier.

For example, if it is normal policy to request that payment is made by customers 30 days after the invoice date, a prompt payment discount of 4% might be offered for payment within 10 days of the invoice date.

A prompt payment discount differs from a trade or bulk discount in that although the seller offers the discount to the customer it is up to the **customer** to **decide whether or not** to accept the offer of the discount. Therefore the discount is not shown as a deduction from the invoice total. Instead it is noted at the bottom of the invoice in the 'Terms' section.

2.4 Trade/Bulk discounts and VAT

The VAT shown on the invoice is the VAT calculated on the net amount **after trade and bulk discounts** have been deducted.

The steps for calculating VAT are:

Step 1   Identify the total amount **before** any discounts.

Step 2   Deduct any trade or bulk discounts to find the net amount **after** trade/bulk discounts.

Step 3   Multiply the net amount after trade/bulk discounts by the **VAT rate**.

Illustration 4: VAT and discounts

A customer buys goods costing £200 before VAT and discounts. A trade discount of 10% is offered.

Calculate the VAT to be shown on the invoice.

Step	Method	Calculation	£
1	Identify total before any discounts.	Per question	200.00
2	Deduct trade/bulk discounts to find the net amount after these discounts.	200 × 10% = 20.00 200.00 – 20.00 = 180.00	180.00
3	Multiply net amount after trade/bulk discounts by VAT rate.	180.00 × 20% = 36.00	36.00

2.5 Prompt payment discounts and VAT

As we have seen, customers may be offered a prompt payment discount (PPD). If a customer chooses to take a PPD, the total amount of cash received by the business for that sale will be **less** than the invoice total, and so the amount of **VAT charged should also be less**.

To account for this reduction in VAT charged, HMRC requires the business to issue a **credit note** (sometimes called a **VAT credit note**) to the customer, showing the discount taken and the relevant VAT.

Assessment focus point

HMRC has allowed two different methods for accounting for the reduction in VAT due to a PPD. However, the *Bookkeeping Transactions* syllabus only includes the method shown in this Course Book.

2.5.1 Preparing a credit note for a PPD

Where a PPD has been taken, the steps for calculating the amounts to include on the credit note are:

Step 1   **Identify** or **calculate** the PPD taken by the customer (calculated as invoice gross amount × prompt payment discount percentage). This is the gross amount for the credit note.

Step 2   Calculate the **VAT** on the PPD taken (VAT = PPD × 20/120).

Step 3   Calculate the **net amount of the discount** (gross amount less VAT)

Illustration 5: VAT and prompt payment discount

A customer buys goods with a list price of £200. The following information is given on the invoice:

- Net amount £200.00
- Gross amount £240.00
- Prompt payment discount of 2% if payment made in 20 days
- VAT rate 20%

The customer pays within 20 days and takes the prompt payment discount.

Calculate the net, VAT and total amounts to be shown on the VAT credit note.

Step	Method	Calculation	£
1	Calculate the discount taken.	240.00 × 2% = 4.80	4.80
2	Calculate the VAT on the prompt payment discount taken.	4.80 × 20/120 = 0.80	0.80
3	Calculate the net amount.	4.80 – 0.80 = 4.00	4.00

Credit note

Amount	£
Net amount	4.00
VAT	0.80
Gross amount	4.80

Now try the following three activities.

Activity 3: VAT and discounts

Car Parts R Us sells a car engine with a list price of £15,000 to Marcus Cars on 9 August 20XX. A trade discount of £4,000 is available and a 10% prompt payment discount is offered if the invoice is paid within 14 days.

The company is registered for VAT and the VAT rate is 20%.

Required

Complete the table to show the amounts to be included on the invoice.

Amount	£
List price	
Trade discount	
Sales price net of trade discount	
VAT	
Gross	

Activity 4: VAT, discounts and business documentation

The bookkeeper at Car Parts R Us is preparing an invoice to send to Marcus Cars in respect of the car engine sold in Activity 3. The following details are also available:

- Invoice date 9 August 20XX
- Invoice number 5353
- Customer account code for Marcus Cars MC001
- Product code 9315
- VAT rate 20%

Required

Complete the invoice.

<table>
<tr><td colspan="5" align="center">Car Parts R Us
14 Maze Road
Essex, UG1 7SG
VAT Registration No: 472 3591 71
INVOICE</td></tr>
<tr><td rowspan="3">Marcus Cars
3 Viewpoint Way
Birmingham
BH12 3LK</td><td colspan="3">Customer account code:</td><td></td></tr>
<tr><td colspan="3">Invoice no:</td><td></td></tr>
<tr><td colspan="3">Date:</td><td></td></tr>
<tr><td>Quantity</td><td>Product code</td><td>Total list price £</td><td>Net amount after discount £</td><td>VAT £</td></tr>
</table>

Quantity	Product code	Total list price £	Net amount after discount £	VAT £	Gross £

Payment terms: 10% discount if paid within 14 days
Otherwise, pay within 30 days.

Activity 5: Discounts and credit notes

Marcus Cars pays the invoice from Car Parts R Us within 14 days and takes the prompt payment discount.

Required

Complete the table below to show the amounts to be included on the credit note for Marcus Cars.

Credit note

Amount	£
Net amount	
VAT	
Gross amount	

3 Recording discounts in the books of prime entry

Trade discounts and bulk discounts are deducted from the list price to give the net amount on the invoice. As we saw in Chapter 2, the net, VAT and gross amounts on an invoice are recorded in the sales day book for sales and the purchases day book for purchases. So trade and bulk discounts are automatically recorded in a business's accounting records.

Prompt payment discounts are an optional discount which the customer can choose whether or not to take. If a customer chooses to take a prompt payment discount, the business must issue the customer with a credit note to show the discount taken and the related VAT. These credit notes are then recorded in the **discounts allowed day book**.

3.1 Discounts allowed day book

The **discounts allowed day book** is a book of prime entry used to record prompt payment discounts taken by credit customers. It is a discount **allowed** as the business has allowed the customer to take the discount.

Illustration 6: Discounts allowed day book

Date 20XX	Details	Credit note number	Customer code	Total £	VAT £	Net £
31 May	K Sweeney	23	SL09	60.00	10.00	50.00
31 May	S Grass	24	SL11	12.00	2.00	10.00
31 May	J Flower	25	SL22	30.00	5.00	25.00
	Totals			102.00	17.00	85.00

3.2 Discounts received day book

When a business chooses to take a prompt payment discount offered by a credit supplier, that supplier must then send a credit note to the business, showing the discount and the related VAT. These credit notes are recorded in **the discounts received day book**. It is a discount **received** as the business has received the discount from the supplier.

Illustration 7: Discounts received day book

Date 20XX	Details	Credit note number	Supplier code	Total £	VAT £	Net £
31 Jan	K Hill	CR35	PL05	6.00	1.00	5.00
31 Jan	S Fretwell	231	PL13	30.00	5.00	25.00
31 Jan	J Brookes	CN52	PL22	3.60	0.60	3.00
	Totals			39.60	6.60	33.00

Activity 6: Discounts and day books

The credit note below has been sent to a customer in respect of a prompt payment discount.

Toby Parts Ltd
31 Cannon Way, Amersham
Bucks HP8 3LD

VAT Registration No. 424 5242 42

PROMPT PAYMENT DISCOUNT CREDIT NOTE

Paving Co Ltd
24 George Street
Amersham
Bucks HP3 5BJ

Customer account code: PAV001

Invoice no: 298

Credit note no: 105

Date: 10 November 20XX

Net £	VAT £	Gross £
10.00	2.00	12.00

Required

Record the credit note in the appropriate day book by:

- **Selecting the correct day book title**
- **Making the necessary entries.**

Day book:	▼				
Date 20XX	Details	Credit note number	Total £	VAT £	Net £
10 Nov	▼	105			

Picklist:

Discounts allowed day book
Discounts received day book
Paving Co Ltd
Purchases returns day book
Sales returns day book
Toby Parts Ltd

Chapter summary

- If the sales of a business exceed a certain amount in a year, then the business must register for VAT.

- Businesses that are registered for VAT must add VAT to the list price of the goods or services charged to the customer on the invoice.

- The current rate of VAT used in your assessment is 20%.

- From a net total, calculate VAT at 20/100 or 1/5 of the net amount.

- From a gross total, calculate VAT at 20/120 or 1/6 of the gross amount.

- The seller may offer the customer a trade discount, a bulk discount and/or a prompt payment discount.

- Trade and bulk discounts are reductions of list price and are shown on the invoice as deductions before arriving at the net total.

- A prompt payment discount may be offered to the customer who may or may not take up the offer, and is shown at the bottom of the invoice as part of the terms.

- VAT on the invoice is calculated after deducting trade and bulk discounts.

- If the customer takes the prompt payment discount, a credit note should be issued showing the decrease in net, VAT and gross amounts from the original invoice due to the prompt payment discount.

- These credit notes are recorded in the discounts allowed day book.

- Prompt payments offered by credit suppliers and taken by a business are documented on a credit note received by the business and those credit notes are recorded in the discounts received day book.

- **Bulk discount:** A percentage discount from the list price of goods and services. Calculated after any trade discount has been deducted. Designed to encourage large orders

- **Discounts allowed day book:** The book of prime entry where all the credit notes for prompt payment discounts taken by credit customers are listed

- **Discounts received day book:** The book of prime entry where all the credit notes for prompt payment discounts received by the business are listed

- **Gross total:** The total of the invoice after VAT is added to the net total

- **Input tax:** VAT on purchases and expenses. Input VAT can be recovered from HMRC

- **List price:** The seller's standard price before any discounts have been deducted

- **Net total:** The total of the invoice before VAT is added

- **Output tax:** VAT on sales. Output VAT is paid to HMRC

- **Prompt payment discount:** A percentage discount from the net total offered in order to provide an incentive to pay the invoice amount early. Appears only in a terms note on the invoice, not as a deduction from the net or gross total

- **Trade discount:** A percentage discount deducted from the list price of goods and services. Offered to some long-standing customers or participants in the same trade, or as an incentive to new customers

- **Value added tax (VAT):** A government tax which must be added to the selling price of goods and services. The difference between input tax and output tax is paid to HMRC, or refunded from HMRC, every three months

- **VAT credit note:** A credit note issued to a customer if the customer chooses to take a prompt payment discount, showing the decrease in the invoice net, VAT and gross total due to the prompt payment discount

- **VAT return:** A statement sent every three months to HMRC showing the total input tax suffered, the total output tax charged and the balance due for payment/refund

Test your learning

1   A business sells 400 items to its customer for £30 per item. Trade discount of 5% is offered, plus a bulk discount of 10% for orders after trade discount of £1,000 or more. No prompt payment discount is offered.

   What is the net total on the invoice?

   £ _____

2   (a)   A sale is made for £378.00 plus VAT. How much VAT should be charged?

      £ _____

   (b)   A sale is made for £378.00 including VAT. How much VAT has been charged and what is the net amount of the sale?

VAT	£
Net amount	£

3   For each of the following gross amounts, calculate the VAT and the net amount.

Gross amount	VAT	Net amount
(a) £3,154.80	£	£
(b) £446.40	£	£
(c) £169.20	£	£

4   (a)   A customer is purchasing 23 items each with a list price of £56.00. A trade discount of 15% is given to this customer. The VAT rate is 20%.

   Calculate:

(i)	Total cost before discount	£
(ii)	Trade discount	£
(iii)	Net total	£
(iv)	VAT	£
(v)	Gross total	£

(b) A prompt payment discount of 10% is also offered and is taken by the customer. Calculate the amounts to be included on the credit note sent to the customer in respect of this discount. Round down all VAT amounts to the nearest penny.

(i)	Net total	£	
(ii)	VAT	£	
(iii)	Gross total	£	

5   Goods with a list price of £2,400.00 are to be sent to a customer. The customer is allowed a trade discount of 15% and VAT is to be charged at 20%. What is the gross total?

£

6   Goods with a list price of £2,400.00 are to be sent to a customer. The customer is allowed a trade discount of 10% and a bulk discount of 12% for orders of £2,000 and over after trade discount has been deducted. VAT is to be charged at 20%. What is the gross total?

£

7   Goods with a net total of £368.00 are to be sold to a customer and the customer is offered a 3% prompt payment discount for payment received within 14 days of the invoice date. Payment is received within 14 days. What amount of VAT should be included on the credit note for this customer in respect of this discount?

£

Recording credit sales

Learning outcomes

2.1	Calculate invoice and credit note amounts
	• The documents to be used: quotations, discount policy, customer order, delivery note, price list.
	• Calculate invoice amounts: item price, net, value added tax (VAT) and total amounts, trade and bulk discounts
	• Calculate credit note amounts: item price, net, value added tax (VAT) and total amounts, trade, bulk and prompt payment discounts
2.3	Check the accuracy of receipts from customers
	• The records and documents to use: sales ledger account, sales invoice, sales credit note, remittance advice, discount policy.
	• Identify discrepancies: under- or over-payment, incorrect discount taken, incorrect amounts
	• Calculate amounts due from customers, including prompt payment discount.

Assessment context

You could be asked to complete invoices, credit notes and remittance advice notes. You will be given an outline document and required to enter data into certain boxes. You may also be asked to identify errors in business documentation, and calculate the correct entries.

Qualification context

In the optional Level 4 *Credit Management* unit one of the key themes is managing credit customers.

Business context

It is essential for a business to be able to record sales completely, accurately and efficiently, as income and receivables are key figures in the financial statements.

Chapter overview

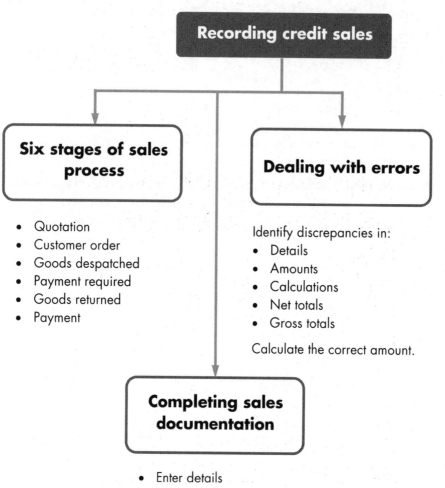

Recording credit sales

Six stages of sales process

- Quotation
- Customer order
- Goods despatched
- Payment required
- Goods returned
- Payment

Dealing with errors

Identify discrepancies in:
- Details
- Amounts
- Calculations
- Net totals
- Gross totals

Calculate the correct amount.

Completing sales documentation

- Enter details
- Enter amounts
- Perform calculations
- Calculate totals

Introduction

In this chapter we will first take a closer look at the **financial statements** of a business – the statement of profit or loss and the statement of financial position. This will give you a greater understanding of the bigger picture in the accounting process. We will then move on to consider in more detail the documents involved in making credit sales, and the checks that must be made on those documents.

1 Introduction to the financial statements

In Chapter 2 we discussed the importance of categorising like information together and summarising it so that we can understand its meaning. This is achieved by having accounting records to record each stage of the process:

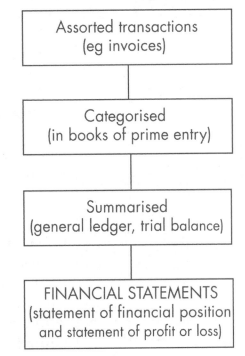

The financial statements of a business are the **statement of financial position** and the **statement of profit or loss**. The information contained in the financial statements comes from the accounting records, mainly from the balances of the ledger accounts, which also form the basis of the **trial balance**.

You need to be able to categorise account names in the financial statements as **assets, liabilities, income** or **expenses**. The best way to understand these terms is to look at financial statements, which we will do next.

Assessment focus point

You will **not** be required to prepare a statement of financial position or a statement of profit or loss in your assessment. However, you should familiarise yourself with these statements as it will help you to make sense of the bigger picture.

1.1 Statement of financial position

The statement of financial position is a **snapshot** of the business at **one** point in time.

It shows what a business owns (**assets**) and what it owes (**liabilities**).

Illustration 1: Statement of financial position

Fred Designs
Statement of financial position as at 31 December 20X8

	£
ASSETS	
Non-current assets	
Property, plant and equipment	160,000
Current assets	
Inventories	55,000
Trade and other receivables	28,000
Cash and cash equivalents	7,000
	90,000
LIABILITIES	
Current liabilities	
Bank overdraft	16,000
Trade and other payables	44,000
	60,000
Net current assets	30,000
Net assets	190,000
CAPITAL	
Capital	170,000
Profit	45,000
Less drawings	(25,000)
	190,000

The **assets** section of the statement of financial position contains '**non-current assets**' which are assets that the business will hold for more than one year and '**current assets**' which are assets which the business will hold for less than one year.

The **liabilities** section is made up of **current liabilities** which are amounts the business owes which must be paid within one year. It is also possible to have **non-current liabilities**, which are amounts the business owes which are due to be paid in more than one year, eg bank loans.

The **capital** section is made up of the **cash injected** by the owner, plus the **profit** the business has made, less any **drawings** the owner has taken.

You can see from the statement of financial position that:

Assets	-	Liabilities	=	Capital
£250,000	-	£60,000	=	£190,000

This equation is known as the **accounting equation** which we will consider in more detail in Chapter 7.

Assessment focus point

You will **not** be required to produce a statement of financial position in the assessment, but you could be asked to categorise items as **assets** or **liabilities**.

1.2 Statement of profit or loss

The statement of profit or loss gives a summary of trading activities over a period of time (usually 12 months).

It shows earnings that a business has received **(income)** and costs that a business has incurred **(expenses)**. Income less expenses gives the **profit** the business has generated.

The following are examples of income:

(a)   Revenue (or sales) – this is all the income generated from selling the business's primary product

(b)   Interest received – eg interest received from bank savings accounts

(c)   Rental income

The following are examples of expenses:

(a)   Cost of goods sold – this is the cost of the products that the business sells
(b)   Interest paid – eg interest paid on bank loans
(c)   Gas, electricity, stationery and rent and rates costs

Illustration 2: Statement of profit or loss

Fred Designs
Statement of profit or loss for the year ended 31 December 20X8

	£
Revenue	200,000
Less cost of goods sold	
Opening inventory	40,000
Purchases	130,000
Closing inventory	(50,000)
	(120,000)
Gross profit	80,000
Sundry income	5,000
Discounts received	3,000
	88,000
Expenses	
Rent and rates	21,000
Telephone	3,000
Electricity	4,000
Wages and salaries	9,000
Motor expenses	5,000
Discounts allowed	1,000
	(43,000)
Profit	45,000

Cost of goods sold is calculated as the **opening inventory** (all the goods the business purchased in the last period but didn't sell) plus **purchases** (all the goods the business has bought to sell in this period) less **closing inventory** (all the goods the business has bought in this period but not yet sold).

Gross profit is the profit from the business's **trading activity**.

Discounts received are prompt payment discounts the business has received from suppliers.

The expenses listed here in this section are the business's **overheads**.

The **profit** is then transferred to the capital section of the statement of financial position.

Assessment focus point

As with the statement of financial position, you will **not** be required to produce a statement of profit or loss in the assessment but you could be asked to categorise items as **income** or **expenses**.

BPP
LEARNING MEDIA

1.2.1 Terminology

The financial statements here use terminology that you might not be familiar with. That's because they use **international terminology**, based on International Financial Reporting Standards (IFRS), whereas you may be familiar with **UK terminology** which is often used in the workplace.

The AAT standards and assessments use international terminology, so you need to be familiar with it. Below is a short list of the most important terms you are likely to use or come across in this course, together with their UK equivalents.

UK term	International term
Profit and loss account	Statement of profit or loss
Balance sheet	Statement of financial position
Fixed assets	Non-current assets
Stocks	Inventories
Trade debtors or Debtors	Trade receivables
Trade creditors or Creditors	Trade payables

2 Recap – business documentation

In Chapter 1 we looked at the six stages of the sales process, and the documents associated with each stage. Complete the following activity to refresh your memory.

Activity 1: Business documentation

Required

Complete the table.

Stage	Process	Document
1		
2		
3		
4		
5		
6		

3 Preparing sales documentation

In Chapter 1 we looked at completing an invoice where there were no discounts on offer. The next illustration continues the process of preparing an invoice (shown in Illustration 5 in Chapter 1), but here the customer is offered trade, bulk and prompt payment discounts.

Illustration 3: The process of preparing an invoice including discounts

You work for Southfield Electrical and are responsible for preparing sales invoices. Today is 8 October 20XX and you have on your desk a customer order number 32174 from Whitehill Superstores for which an invoice must be prepared.

Step 1 You first check that the goods were in fact sent to Whitehill, so you find the delivery note that relates to order 32174.

Step 2 You identify from the delivery note that only nine mixers were delivered and accepted and therefore only nine mixers must be invoiced, not the ten that were ordered.

Step 3 The prices quoted on the order are the unit list prices. You check the prices against Southfield's price list and confirm they are correct and therefore can be used on the invoice.

The documentation relating to the first three steps was shown in Illustration 5 in Chapter 1. Go back to Chapter 1 to refresh your memory.

Step 4 You must now find the customer file for Whitehill Superstores. The customer file shows details of addresses, the customer code and **discount policy** in respect of the customer (ie what trade, bulk and prompt payment discounts should be applied to sales to the customer).

The customer file for Whitehill Superstores shows the following:

- Customer code – SL 44
- Discount policy effective 1 Oct 20XX:

    – 10% trade discount is allowed on all sales

    – 5% bulk discount on orders where list price net of trade discount exceeds £1,000

    – 4% prompt payment discount for payment within 10 days, otherwise net 30 days

You now have all the information required to start preparing the invoice. The final invoice is now shown and we will then work through the remaining steps in completing it.

INVOICE	Invoice number 56483		
Southfield Electrical **Industrial Estate** **Benham DR6 2FF** **Tel: 01239 345639**			
VAT registration:	0264 2274 49		
Date/tax point:	8 October 20XX		
Order number:	32174		
Customer:	Whitehill Superstores 28 Whitehill Park Benham DR6 5LM		
Account number (customer code)	SL 44		
Description/product code	**Quantity**	**Unit amount** **£**	**Total** **£**
Hosch washing machine / 6160 Temax mixer / 3172 List price Less trade discount 10% List price net of trade discount Less bulk discount 5%	4 9	300.00 40.00	1,200.00 360.00 1,560.00 (156.00) 1,404.00 (70.20)
Net total			1,333.80
VAT at 20%			266.76
Gross total			1,600.56
Terms 4% discount for payment within 10 days of invoice date, otherwise 30 days net			

Step 5   Enter the customer's name and address and customer code from the customer file. The invoice number is the next number in sequence after the previous invoice. Enter today's date.

Step 6   Enter the quantities, codes and descriptions from the delivery note – remember that only nine mixers were delivered.

Step 7   Enter the unit prices from the price list. Calculate the total list price by multiplying the quantity by the list price:

$4 \times £300 = £1,200.00$
$9 \times £40 = £360.00$

Step 8   Calculate the total list price by adding together the totals for each product:

$£1,200.00 + £360.00 = £1,560.00$

Step 9   Calculate the trade discount as 10% of the total list price:

$£1,560.00 \times 10\% (10/100) = £156.00$

Deduct the trade discount from the total list price:

$£1,560.00 - £156.00 = £1,404.00$

Step 10   As the list price net of trade discount is more than £1,000, calculate the bulk discount as 5% of the list price net of trade discount:

$£1,404.00 \times 5\% (5/100) = £70.20$

Deduct the bulk discount from the list price net of trade discount to arrive at the net total:

$£1,404.00 - £70.20 = £1,333.80$

Step 11   Calculate the VAT at 20% based on the net amount after the trade and bulk discounts have been deducted:

$£1,333.80 \times 0.2 = £266.76$

Step 12   Add the VAT calculated to the net total to arrive at the gross total for the invoice:

$£1,333.80 + £266.76 = £1,600.56$

Step 13   Enter the prompt payment discount terms at the bottom of the invoice.

The next activities require you to complete invoices and credit notes, **including trade** and **bulk discounts**.

Activity 2: Sales invoice

On 24 March 20XX Hugh Houghton delivered the following goods to a credit customer, Elizabeth Elstree.

Hugh Houghton

24 Bottrels Lane

Crewe CA3 DF

DELIVERY NOTE

Delivery note no: 84251

24 March 20XX

Elizabeth Elstree   Customer account code: ELI053

89 Somerset Way

Moreton MK8 4JD

2,500 tins of tomato soup, product code 8321

The list price of the goods was £0.30 per tin plus VAT at 20%. Elizabeth Elstree's customer file shows the following:

Discount policy

- 15% trade discount
- 5% bulk discount for orders over 2,000 tins

Required

Complete the invoice.

Hugh Houghton

24 Bottrels Lane

Crewe CA3 DF

VAT Registration No. 482 4995 24

INVOICE

Elizabeth Elstree   Customer account code:

89 Somerset Way

Moreton MK8 4JD

Delivery note number:

Invoice no: 1031   Date: 24 March 20XX

Quantity	Product code	Total list price £	Net amount after discount £	VAT £	Gross £

Activity 3: Credit note

On 21 July 20XX Jasper & Co returned 5 faulty DVD players to Darren Dunn. The VAT rate is 20%. A credit note needs to be raised, including details as follows:

- Product code 5295
- Price per unit prior to trade discount £55
- Trade discount offered on original sale 5%
- Customer account number JAS003

Required

Complete the credit note.

Darren Dunn
482 The Lagger
Liverpool LI4 9MG

VAT Registration No. 424 5242 42

CREDIT NOTE

Jasper & Co
52 The Hilltop
Liverpool
LN8 8DW

Customer account code:

Date: 21 July 20XX

Credit note no: 454
Invoice no: 3567

Quantity	Product code	Total list price £	Net amount after discount £	VAT £	Gross £

4 Checking the accuracy of business documentation

Business documents are used to provide documentary evidence of transactions between customers and suppliers. They must be accurate as otherwise:

- Disagreements will arise between companies
- Incorrect, invalid transactions may be recorded in the accounting records

The following questions can help you identify any errors and discrepancies in business documentation.

Possible questions
Is the correct product name included on the invoice?
Are the correct quantities shown on the invoice?
Has the correct product code been shown on the invoice?
Is the customer code correct?
Does the invoice show the correct sales price?
Have the correct discounts been applied?
Has the VAT been correctly calculated?
Has the invoice been correctly cast*?
If errors have been made, what is the correct entry?

* **'Cast'** is used in accounting to mean 'check the addition' of a column or row of numbers. So if a question asks if an invoice has been correctly cast, it means has the invoice been correctly added up, eg does the net total plus VAT equal the gross total.

Assessment focus point

In the assessment you may be given two business documents, such as an order and an invoice, and you may be asked to identify errors and discrepancies between them.

You may also be asked to calculate the correct entries, such as the VAT charge or the gross total which **should** be shown on the invoice.

Activity 4: Checking business documentation

A supply of wheelbarrows have been delivered to Judy Hutchins by Garden Fittings Ltd. The order sent from Judy Hutchins and the invoice from Garden Fittings Ltd are shown below.

Order

Judy Hutchins
49 Aston Way
Wormley
LI9 3JN
Order no. GT4295
To: Garden Fittings Ltd

Date: 2 March 20XX

Please supply 35 wheelbarrows product code 841951

Purchase price: £60 plus VAT at 20%

Discount: less 10% trade discount and 5% prompt payment discount, as agreed.

Invoice

Garden Fittings Ltd
Cheston Garden Centre
Wormley
LI8 4MD
VAT Registration no. 482 4991 32
Invoice no. 3278

Judy Hutchins
49 Aston Way
Wormley
LI9 3JN
5 March 20XX

	£
35 wheelbarrows product code 814951 @ £60.00 each	
Total list price	2,100.00
Less trade discount (5%)	(105.00)
Net amount after discount	1,995.00
VAT @ 20%	399.00
Total	2,394.00

Terms: 30 days net, 10% prompt payment discount

Required

(a) Check the invoice against the customer order and answer the following questions.

	Yes ✓	No ✓
Is the product code on the invoice correct?		
Has the correct unit price per wheelbarrow been charged?		
Has the correct trade discount been applied?		

(b) Answer the following questions.

	£
What would be the VAT charge if the invoice was correct?	
What would be the total amount charged if the invoice was correct?	

4.1 Checking the accuracy of customer receipts

When money is received from customers, the business must check to make sure that the amount received is accurately calculated and valid (ie ties in with supporting documentation).

The following checks should be completed.

Check	Details
Is it the correct amount?	Check the payment received against the **remittance advice note** (seen in Chapter 1)
	If there is no remittance advice note, you need to work out which invoices have been paid by looking at the customer's account in the **sales ledger**
Has any **prompt payment discount** been correctly taken and correctly calculated?	Check the terms of the **prompt payment discount** against the **invoice**
	Check the customer has paid within the required timescale
	Check the discount has been correctly calculated

Common reasons for **discrepancies** in amounts received from customers are:

- The customer **underpaying** an invoice by mistake, for instance by making a payment of £210.36 when the invoice was for £210.63, so the customer still owes 27p

- The customer **overpaying** the invoice by mistake, for instance by making a payment of £54.00 when the invoice was for £45.00, so the business owes the customer £9.00

- The customer deducting the **wrong amount** of prompt payment discount

- The customer deducting prompt payment discount even though the **deadline** for taking advantage of this **has passed**

If any discrepancies arise with a payment from a customer, the payment should still be recorded, but the discrepancy should be reported to the appropriate person within the business, such as your supervisor.

Activity 5: Checking the accuracy of customer receipts

The account shown below is in the sales ledger of Silver. A cheque for £750 has now been received from this customer.

Heidi Ltd

Date 20XX	Details	Amount £	Date 20XX	Details	Amount £
1 July	Balance b/f	6,000	5 August	Bank	6,000
25 July	Invoice 501	1,200	29 August	Credit note 130	450
30 August	Invoice 505	1,310			

Required

(a) **Which item has not been included in the payment?**

▼

Picklist:

Balance b/f £6,000
Bank £6,000
Credit note 130
Invoice 501
Invoice 505

An invoice is being prepared to be sent to Heidi Ltd for £3,200 plus VAT of £640.00. A prompt payment discount of 2% will be offered for payment within 15 days. The invoice is dated 4 September 20XX.

(b) What is the amount Silver should receive if payment is made within 15 days?

£

(c) What amounts should be included on the credit note to Heidi Ltd if the prompt payment discount is taken?

Net	£	
VAT	£	
Gross	£	

(d) What amount should Silver receive if payment is NOT made within 15 days?

£

Chapter summary

- The financial statements of a business are the statement of profit or loss and the statement of financial position.

- The financial statements contain assets, liabilities, income and expenses.

- The sales process contains six steps: quotation, order, goods despatched, payment requested, goods returned (not always) and payment received. Each step has related documentation.

- Many checks are necessary when preparing an invoice to ensure that it is for the correct goods, to the correct customer and for the correct amount.

- Similar checks are also required for credit notes, in particular details of the goods that have been returned.

- Receipts from customers must be checked – is it for the correct amount? Is any prompt payment discount deducted valid and correctly calculated?

- If no remittance advice is received with the payment then the customer's sales ledger account must be examined to determine which invoices (less credit notes) are being paid.

- If any discrepancies arise with a payment from a customer the payment should still be recorded, but the discrepancy should be reported to the appropriate person within the organisation.

BPP
LEARNING MEDIA

Keywords

- **Assets:** Something that a business owns

- **Capital:** The amount of money invested by the owner in the business

- **Discount policy:** A business's system for giving the different types of discount to customers in order to encourage certain buying behaviours

- **Expenses:** What the business spends to purchase goods or services for the company

- **Financial statements:** The statement of profit or loss and the statement of financial position of a business

- **Income:** What the business earns when it makes sales of goods or services to other parties

- **Liabilities:** Something that a business owes

Test your learning

1   Identify which type of document would be used for the following purposes.

To inform the customer of the amount due for a sale	▼
To inform the supplier of the quantities required	▼
To inform the customer of the quantity delivered	▼
To inform the customer that the invoiced amount was overstated	▼

Picklist:

Credit note
Customer order
Delivery note
Invoice
Quotation
Returns note

2   A customer, Sally, is purchasing 23 items each with a list price of £56.00. A trade discount of 15% is given to Sally.

(a) Calculate the total price before the discount, the discount, the net of discount price, the VAT and the gross amount.

	£
Price before discount	
Trade discount	
Net	
VAT	
Gross	

A prompt payment discount of 3% is also offered and taken by Sally.

(b) Calculate the figures to be included on the credit note to Sally in relation to the prompt payment discount.

	£
Net	
VAT	
Gross	

3   Given below is a sales invoice. Check it carefully, state what is wrong with it and calculate the correct figures.

INVOICE

Southfield Electrical
Industrial Estate
Benham DR6 2FF
Tel 0303379 Fax 0303152
VAT Reg 0264 2274 49

To:
G. Bender & Sons
14, High St.
Wentford
DR10 6LT

Invoice number: 56503

Date/tax point:

Order number: 32216

Account number:

Quantity	Description	Stock code	Unit amount £	Total £
21	Zanpoint Tumble Dryer	4610	180.00	3,870.00
10	Temax Mixer	3172	40.00	400.00
				4,270.00
Less:	15% discount			683.20

Net total	3,586.80
VAT	717.36
Invoice total	4,304.16

Terms
5% cash discount for payment within 10 days, otherwise 30 days net
E & OE

Errors:

	Description of error or omission
1	
2	
3	
4	

Corrected figures:

	£
Tumble dryers	
Mixers	
Goods total	
Trade discount	
Net total	
VAT	
Invoice total	

4 Here are two cheques received by Southfield Electrical in the post this morning and the accompanying remittance advices. Today's date is 22 October 20XX. Check each receipt carefully, state what is wrong with it and calculate the correct figures.

first national

20 - 26 - 33
004621 3266892

26 Pinehurst Place, London EC1 2AA

Date 20 October 20XX

Pay *Southfield Electrical*

Seven hundred and seventy pounds

and 80 pence

£ **770.80**

J. D. Feltz

140600
Cheque No.   Sort Code   Account No.

004621   20—26—33   3266892

Quinn Ltd

REMITTANCE ADVICE

To: Southfield Electrical
Industrial Estate
Benham
DR6 2FF
Tel 0303379 Fax 0303152

From: Quinn Ltd

Date: 20 October 20XX

Reference	Amount	Paid (✓)
30128	325.61	✓
CN2269	18.80	✓
30201	463.27	✓

CHEQUE ENCLOSED	£770.08

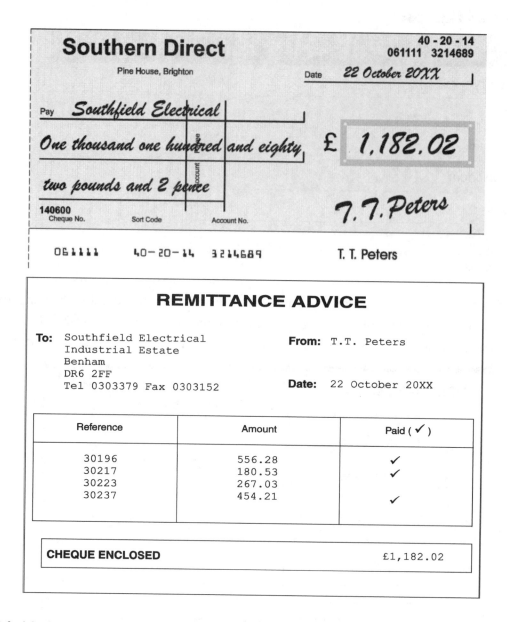

REMITTANCE ADVICE

To: Southfield Electrical
Industrial Estate
Benham
DR6 2FF
Tel 0303379 Fax 0303152

From: T.T. Peters

Date: 22 October 20XX

Reference	Amount	Paid (✓)
30196	556.28	✓
30217	180.53	✓
30223	267.03	
30237	454.21	✓

CHEQUE ENCLOSED	£1,182.02

5 Southfield Electrical has received a cheque from a customer, Long Bros, for £226.79 with no accompanying documentation. The sales ledger account for this customer is given below. **Determine which invoices/credit notes are being paid by this cheque.**

Long Bros

SL 42

Details	£	Details	£
Invoice 30219	88.37	Credit note CN2381	15.80
Invoice 30234	157.35		
Invoice 30239	85.24		
Invoice 30250	265.49		

Invoice/credit note number	£
Total	

6 On 1 December Wendlehurst Trading delivered the following goods to a credit customer, Stroll In Stores.

Wendlehurst Trading

Delivery note No. 8973
01 Dec 20XX

Stroll In Stores

Customer account code: ST725

600 1 litre bottles Tiger pop, product code TIG300.

The list price of the goods was £10 per case of 12 bottles plus VAT. Stroll In Stores is to be given a 15% trade discount and a 4% prompt payment discount.

Complete the invoice below.

Wendlehurst Trading

VAT Registration No. 876983479

Stroll In Stores

Customer account code:
Delivery note number:
Date: 1 Dec 20XX

Invoice No: 624

Quantity of cases	Product code	Total list price £	Net amount after discount £	VAT £	Gross £

Recording credit purchases

Learning outcomes

3.1	Check the accuracy of supplier invoices and credit notes
	• The documents to use: quotations including discounts, purchase orders, goods received notes, delivery notes, goods returned notes.
	• Identify discrepancies that may be found: non-delivery of goods, incorrect type or quantity of goods, incorrect calculations, incorrect discounts (trade, bulk and prompt payment), date and terms of payment.
3.3	Prepare payments to suppliers
	• The records and documents to use: purchases ledger account, invoices and credit notes (including discounts and VAT), statement of account
	• The information to take into account: agreed payment terms.
	• Identify discrepancies between the supplier's statement of account and the purchases ledger account: timing differences, wrong amounts, missing transactions, duplicated transactions
	• Calculate payments due to suppliers, including prompt payment discount

Assessment context

Accounting for purchases is very examinable and a topic which is developed in later chapters. You could be asked to complete purchases invoices, identify discrepancies and complete a remittance advice note.

Qualification context

The themes in this chapter are explored in the optional Level 4 *Credit Management* unit.

Business context

It is essential for a business to be able to record purchases completely, accurately and efficiently, as purchases and payables are key balances in the financial statements.

Chapter overview

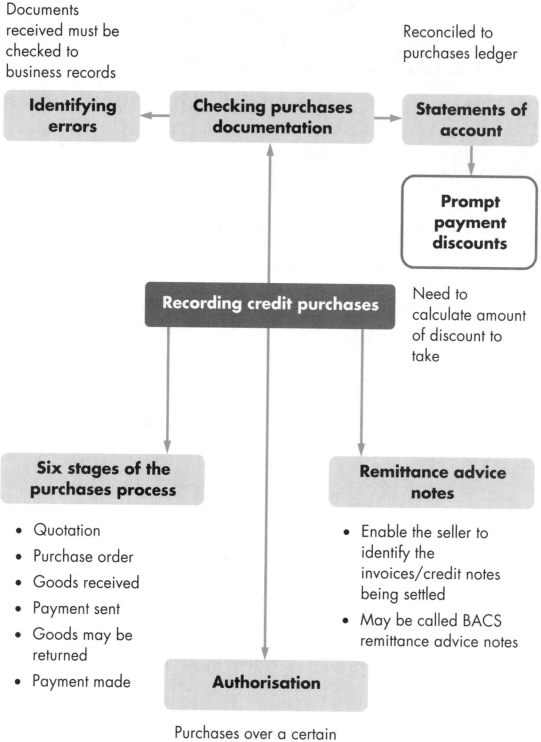

Documents received must be checked to business records

Reconciled to purchases ledger

Identifying errors

Checking purchases documentation

Statements of account

Prompt payment discounts

Need to calculate amount of discount to take

Recording credit purchases

Six stages of the purchases process

- Quotation
- Purchase order
- Goods received
- Payment sent
- Goods may be returned
- Payment made

Remittance advice notes

- Enable the seller to identify the invoices/credit notes being settled
- May be called BACS remittance advice notes

Authorisation

Purchases over a certain amount must be authorised

Introduction

In the previous chapter, we looked at the documents and processes involved when a business **sells** goods. In this chapter, we will consider what happens when a business **purchases** goods from a supplier. We will consider the documents involved and the checks carried out before paying a supplier.

1 Introduction to purchases

In Chapter 1 and Chapter 4 we looked at the business documents needed at each stage of the **sales process**. The documents needed for the **purchases process** are very similar, only prepared from the point of the business being the 'buyer' and having to pay for goods or services they have received from a supplier.

Businesses buy goods or engage employees/other companies to provide services so that they in turn can **generate sales income**. The ultimate goal is to make a **profit**.

Try the following activity to identify some goods or services a business may purchase.

Activity 1: Expenses: goods or services

Required

Give three examples as to what business expenses might be classified as:

(a) Goods

- –

- –

- –

(b) Services

- –

- –

- –

Earlier in the course we distinguished between cash and credit sales. Here, the same principles apply to **cash purchases** and **purchases made on credit**.

	Cash purchases	Credit purchases
Action	The purchase and the payment happen **at the same time**.	The supplier (seller) provides the buyer with the goods (or services) but **no payment** is made at that time.
Payment	Payment can be made by **cash, cheque, debit or credit card**, all of which are regarded as cash.	The supplier **invoices** the buyer and payment is made 30 or 60 days later, depending on the seller's credit terms. Payment could be made in the form of cheque, card or automated payment.
Usage	Cash purchases tend to be the **minority** of a business's purchases.	Most businesses will buy the **majority** of their goods/services on credit.
Document	The primary documentation created is a **till receipt**.	The seller issues an **invoice** to the customer.

2 Stages in a typical purchases process

There are **six stages** of the **purchases process**. At each stage a document is generated:

Stage	Process	Document
1	Quotation is requested for goods/services	Quotation
2	Order is placed	Purchase order
3	Goods are received	Delivery note/Goods received note
4	Payment requested	Invoice
5	Goods are returned to vendor*	Credit note
6	Payment made	Remittance advice note

* This (of course!) does not happen with every purchase – credit notes are issued if goods are returned to the vendor, or a service is found to be unsatisfactory.

You will notice that these are the same six steps as in the sales process – this is not surprising, as a **purchase** made by one business is a **sale** for the other business.

2.1 Stages 1 to 3: quotation to delivery

The first stage in the purchases process is to identify a number of **potential suppliers** and request a **quotation** from each of them. This is called **tendering** and ensures the business gets the best value for money.

As was discussed with the sales process, a **quotation** will detail the price, terms and conditions and the specification of the goods or service.

Once the business has secured an acceptable quotation it raises a **purchase order** and sends this to the seller.

Upon receipt of the purchase order, the supplier will arrange to deliver the goods.

The goods will be sent with a **delivery note** drawn up by the supplier. This will be signed by the purchasing business as proof of receipt. The goods are usually delivered to the purchasing business's stores, so it will be the stores manager who will sign the delivery note.

The stores manager may also complete a **goods received note** (GRN). A GRN contains similar information to the delivery note but the delivery note is produced by the seller and the goods received note by the purchaser.

Illustration 1: Goods received note

Henry Hotsphur
84 The Green
Colchester CE0 8MD

GOODS RECEIVED NOTE

Goods received note no: 47241
09 August 20XX
Jill Thurston
51 Hill Lane
Chalfonts NE3 4MD

Delivery note no: 49241
Order no: 31455

Quantity	Description	Product code
40	White lampshades	5324

Received by: M Matthews
Checked by: S Horne
Comments: All items satisfactory

Note the main points of the GRN:

- It has its own sequential number.

- It is referenced to the order number and delivery note number, both taken from the copy of the supplier's delivery note.

- The quantity and precise detail of the goods received are noted.

- In order to ensure the security of the goods being received, the GRN is signed by not only the person who received delivery of the goods but also a second person who checked them.

- Once there has been a chance to examine the goods in detail, any comments on their condition can then be added to the GRN.

Once the goods have been received and checked, all the documentation is then passed over to the accounts department. At this stage the accounts department will have a price list and quotation from the supplier, its own purchase order, a delivery note from the supplier and its own GRN.

The accounts department must check that the delivery note agrees with the purchase order to ensure that what was **ordered** has **actually arrived**. The details should then be compared with the GRN to ensure that the goods that were actually delivered were of the **correct quality** and **condition**.

Activity 2: Accuracy of business documentation

Ashtons Ltd placed an order with a new supplier Whales Way and has now received a delivery from them.

Order

Ashtons Ltd
The Studio
Marston ME0 3JD
PURCHASE ORDER PP8471

To:

Whales Way
The Port
Brighton BE3 9MJ

Date: 3 October 20XX
Please supply:

Product	Product code	Quantity
Aluminium sheets	5366	50
Red plastic squares	4529	45
Discount: less 10% trade discount, as agreed		

Goods received note

Ashtons Ltd
The Studio
Marston ME0 3JD
GOODS RECEIVED NOTE

Goods received note no: 56731
10 October 20XX
Whales Way

Delivery note no: 84293

The Port
Brighton BE3 9MJ

Purchase order no: PP8471

Quantity	Description	Product code
45	Aluminium sheets	5366
50	Red plastic squares	4529

Received by: B Bob
Checked by:
Comments: 3 plastic squares damaged on arrival

Required

Check the purchase order against the goods received note and answer the following questions.

	Yes ✓	No ✓
Is the purchase order number correctly included on the goods received note?		
Has the correct quantity of aluminium sheets been delivered?		
Has the correct quantity of red plastic squares been delivered?		
Are the product codes correctly included on the goods received note?		
Has the goods received note been signed to confirm the goods were checked on arrival?		

2.2 Stage 4: request for payment

Once the goods have been received, the supplier will then send an **invoice** requesting payment for the goods.

The invoice **must** be checked **before** it is paid to identify any discrepancies. In particular, the buyer must confirm that:

Step 1   The **details** on the invoice are correct.

Check the details against the **purchase order**, the **delivery note** and the **goods received note**. Check:

(a)   Quantity – were the right number of goods delivered? Were any goods not delivered at all?

(b)   Quality – were the correct type of goods delivered? Were the goods of an acceptable standard?

(c)   Price – is the price as agreed on the quotation?

(d)   Date and terms of payment – correct?

(e)   Codes – are they correct (product codes, purchase order number)?

Step 2   The **calculations** on the invoice are correct. Check:

(a)   The price before discounts
(b)   Any discounts applied
(c)   The VAT
(d)   The total of the invoice

If any of the details on the invoice are incorrect, this should be queried with the supplier.

Illustration 2: Checking the invoice

Given below is an invoice that Whitehill Superstores received from Southfield Electrical (which we saw in Chapter 4):

INVOICE	Invoice number 56483
Southfield Electrical **Industrial Estate** **Benham DR6 2FF** **Tel: 01239 345639**	
VAT registration:	0264 2274 49
Date/tax point:	8 October 20XX
Order number:	32174
Customer:	Whitehill Superstores 28 Whitehill Park Benham DR6 5LM
Account number (customer code)	SL 44

Description/product code	Quantity	Unit amount £	Total £
Hosch washing machine / 6160	4	300.00	1,200.00
Temax mixer / 3172	9	40.00	360.00
List price			1,560.00
Less trade discount 10%			(156.00)
List price net of trade discount			1,404.00
Less bulk discount 5%			(70.20)

Net total	1,333.80
VAT at 20%	266.76
Gross total	1,600.56

Terms

4% discount for payment within 10 days of invoice date, otherwise 30 days net

The checks that the customer, Whitehill Superstores, should make on this invoice before paying it are as follows.

- Compare the purchase order, delivery note and GRN to the invoice to ensure that the correct quantity has been invoiced. The purchase order and delivery note are shown in Illustration 5 in Chapter 1. The GRN is shown below. Ten mixers were ordered, but only nine were received into the warehouse. The invoice reflects this, only nine mixers have been included. Note that the purchase order number, 32174, is shown on both the GRN and the invoice.

Whitehill Superstores

GOODS RECEIVED NOTE

Goods received note no: G765
5 October 20XX
Southfield Electrical   Delivery note no: 34772
Industrial Estate
Benham DR6 2FF   Purchase order no: 32174

Quantity	Description	Product code
5	Hosch Washing Machine	6160
9	Temax Mixer	3172

Received by: J Jones
Checked by: S Smith
Comments: Only 9 Temax Mixers received with order

- Check the percentage discounts agree to the **discount policy** agreed with this supplier: 10% trade discount, 5% bulk discount for orders over £1,000, 4% prompt payment discount for payment within 10 days.

- Check that the unit prices are correct – this may be noted from the supplier's quotation or price list.

- Check that the total price for each item has been correctly calculated by multiplying the unit price by the quantity, eg 4 × £300 = £1,200.

- Check that the total list price has been correctly added up, eg £1,200 + £360.00 = £1,560.00.

- Check that the trade discount has been correctly calculated, eg £1,560 × 10% = £156, and that it has been deducted correctly, eg £1,560.00 – £156.00 = £1,404.00.

- Check that the bulk discount has been deducted as due (since the total after trade discount exceeds £1,000) and that it has been calculated correctly, eg £1,404.00 × 5% = £70.20; net total is therefore £1,404.00 – £70.20 = £1,333.80.

- Check that the VAT is correct, eg £1,333.80 × 20% = £266.76.

- Check that the VAT has been correctly added to the net total, eg £1,333.80 + £266.76 = £1,600.56.

2.3 Stage 5: returning goods

If the business receives goods that are faulty or incorrect, the goods will be returned to the supplier. Often the return of the goods will be accompanied by a **goods returned note** detailing the goods returned and the reason for their return. The contents of a goods returned note are very similar to a goods received note.

Illustration 3: Goods returned note

Ashtons Ltd
The Studio
Marston ME0 3JD

GOODS RETURNS NOTE

Goods returned note no: 8909
Goods received note no: 56731

11 October 20XX

Whales Way   Delivery note no: 84293
The Port
Brighton BE3 9MJ   Purchase order no: PP8471

Quantity	Description	Product code
3	Red plastic squares	4529

Returned by: B Bob
Comments: 3 plastic squares damaged

The business should request a **credit note** from the supplier for the returned goods.

As we saw in Chapter 1, a credit note provides written confirmation that the business either owes nothing to the supplier in respect of that invoice, or owes **less** than the amount shown on the original invoice.

When the credit note arrives, it should be **checked** to make sure that it is correct and that it fully resolves the discrepancy. As with the invoice, the buyer should:

Step 1   Check the details on the credit note against the **invoice**, **purchase order**, **delivery note**, **goods received note** and **goods returned note**.

Step 2   Check the calculations on the credit note.

2.4 Services

One of the initial checks on goods is that they are **actually received**, evidenced by a delivery note or GRN. With **services** there will not be any physical goods. It is still important to check that the services that have been invoiced have **been received**.

Typical invoices for services might include utilities such as electricity, gas and phone bills. Such bills can usually be checked to meter readings and for **reasonableness**; for example, each business should have an idea of the normal value of the phone bill and therefore if a very different amount is billed then this should be investigated.

3 Communication with credit suppliers

3.1 The objectives of managing credit suppliers

Most businesses enjoy credit from their suppliers. However, while it is important that a business **maximises the credit period taken**, it must be careful not to leave payments so overdue as to jeopardise its relationship with the supplier.

There are practical steps a business can take to manage its relationships with suppliers:

(a)   Negotiate credit terms with suppliers. The business may be able to negotiate longer credit terms with non-critical suppliers.

(b)   Hold regular meetings with suppliers.

(c)   Share information on suppliers with others.

(d)   If cash flow is tight, pay key suppliers before others.

(e)   Choose the payment method carefully. BACS is easier but paying by cheque can give the business a few extra days' cash flow advantage.

3.2 Statements of account

A business may have many transactions with a supplier. On a monthly basis, the supplier will send a **statement of account** which will show all the invoices and credit notes sent to the business and payments received from the business during the month.

Illustration 4: Statement of account

Barry Bannister
85 Dalton Road
Highbury
BK4 9MG

STATEMENT OF ACCOUNT

To: Anthony Ltd   Date: 31 October 20XX

Date 20XX	Details	Transaction amount £	Outstanding amount £
11 October	Invoice 2535	5,241	5,241
15 October	Invoice 2645	4,675	9,916
18 October	Credit note 150	572	9,344
21 October	Invoice 2690	2,545	11,889
25 October	Cheque	6,421	5,468

A supplier's statement of account is a very important **double check** on the accuracy of the purchasing business's accounting records. In theory, the statement of account should **agree** to the balance in the **individual supplier's account** in the business's purchases ledger. However, there may be differences and so it is important that the business checks the statement of account against the purchases ledger to identify any differences.

Assessment focus point

In your assessment you may be given a statement of account and a purchases ledger account and asked to identify any differences. The best way to start such a question is to compare the statement of account with the purchases ledger and tick off the items that appear in both.

Activity 3: Checking a statement of account

Shown below is a statement of account received from a credit supplier, and the supplier's account as shown in the purchases ledger of Peter Ltd.

Samuel Ltd
Unit 5, Watford Estates
Watford
HS2 2MT

STATEMENT OF ACCOUNT

To: Peter Ltd

Date 20XX	Invoice number	Details	Invoice amount £	Cheque amount £	Balance £
11 May	405	Goods	5,500		5,500
15 May	406	Goods	4,200		9,700
18 May	407	Goods	500		10,200
21 May	408	Goods	2,200		12,400
28 May		Cheque		5,500	6,900

Purchases ledger

Samuel Ltd

Date 20XX	Detail	Amount £	Date 20XX	Detail	Amount £
28 May	Bank	5,500	11 May	Invoice 405	5,500
1 June	Bank	4,200	15 May	Invoice 406	4,200
			18 May	Invoice 407	500

Required

(a) Answer the following questions.

Which item is missing from the statement of account from Samuel Ltd?	▼
Which item is missing from the supplier account in Peter Ltd's purchases ledger?	▼

Picklist:

Cheque for £4,200
Cheque for £5,500
Invoice 405
Invoice 406
Invoice 407
Invoice 408

(b) Answer the following question.

	£
Assuming any differences between the statement of account from Samuel Ltd and the supplier account in Peter Ltd's purchases ledger are simply due to omission errors, what is the amount owing to Samuel Ltd?	

3.3 Reconciliation of purchases ledger to supplier statement of account

It is important that the information recorded in a business's purchases ledger is complete, accurate and valid. To help a business identify any errors or missing information, it can perform a **reconciliation** between the supplier's **statement of account** and the supplier's **individual account** in the purchases ledger, to show and explain any differences.

Differences between the two balances can occur due to:

(1) **Errors** or **omissions** in the purchases ledger or the supplier statement; these could include wrong amounts recorded, missing transactions or duplicated transactions

(2) **Timing differences**; for example, the business sent a payment to the supplier but the supplier hadn't received the payment on the date the statement of account was prepared

Illustration 5: Reconciliation of purchases ledger to supplier statement of account

At the end of February 20XX Whitehill Superstores has the following transactions recorded in its purchases ledger account for Southfield Electrical:

Purchases ledger

Southfield Electrical

Detail	Amount £	Detail	Amount £
Credit note 09543	734.25	Invoice 58256	2,089.76
Bank payment	1,355.51	Invoice 58311	1,240.00
		Invoice 58325	3,287.09

Whitehill Superstores knows that the history of the account in February is as follows:

- Three invoices from Southfield were recorded towards the end of the month.

- In respect of the first invoice (total £2,089.76) a credit note for £734.25 was received.

- Whitehill wished to settle the remaining amount of the first invoice (£2,089.76 – £734.25 = £1,355.51), so it sent an automated payment of £1,355.51.

- Whitehill decided to leave paying the second and third invoices until March, so at the end of February it owed Southfield £1,240.00 + £3,287.09 = **£4,527.09**.

At the beginning of March Whitehill received the following statement of account from Southfield:

STATEMENT OF ACCOUNT	
Southfield Electrical **Industrial Estate** **Benham DR6 2FF** **Tel: 01239 345639**	
VAT registration:	0264 2274 49
Date:	28 February 20XX
Customer:	Whitehill Superstores 28 Whitehill Park Benham DR6 5LM
Account number (customer code)	SL 44

Date	Details	Amount £	Balance £
23 Feb	Invoice 58256	2,089.76	2,089.76
27 Feb	Credit note 09543	(734.25)	1,355.51
27 Feb	Invoice 58311	1,240.00	2,595.51
28 Feb	Invoice 58325	3,287.09	5,882.60
Amount now due			5,882.60
Terms 30 days net			

The customer and the supplier do not agree on how much is outstanding. The difference between them is:

	£
Amount per supplier statement	5,882.60
Amount per purchases ledger	4,527.09
Difference	1,355.51

The supplier, Southfield Electrical, is saying that the customer, Whitehill Superstores, owes £1,355.51 more than Whitehill thinks it does.

By looking at the amount of the difference it is clear that Southfield Electrical thinks that Whitehill still owes the net amount of the first invoice and the credit note, while Whitehill shows in the purchases ledger account that it has settled this amount. This is confirmed when we note that the supplier's statement does not contain details of the automated payment made. The automated payment had not yet reached Southfield Electrical by the time it prepared the statement.

We can therefore explain the difference between the parties as a **timing difference**, and produce a **reconciliation** which shows how the difference is made up:

Reconciliation statement

As at 28 February 20XX	£
Balance on Southfield's supplier statement	5,882.60
Balance on Southfield's account in Whitehill purchases ledger	4,527.09
Difference	1,355.51

Explained by: timing differences

Automated payment made, not received as at 28 Feb	1,355.51

Assessment focus point

To perform a reconciliation, you should start by comparing the supplier's statement of account to the supplier's account in the purchases ledger and tick off all items that agree. The remaining unticked items will usually represent the difference.

Activity 4: Reconciliation of a purchases ledger account and a supplier statement

Shown below is a statement of account received from a credit supplier, and the supplier's account as shown in Silver's purchases ledger.

Jen Jackson

The Cause
Elstree EL1 3MD

To: Silver
25 Lancaster Road
Percival
P3 4NF

Statement of account

Date 20XX	Invoice or credit note number	Details	Invoice amount £	Credit note amount £	Cheque amount £	Balance £
01 May		Opening balance				900
02 May		Cheque			750	150
10 May	Inv – 841	Goods	2,342			2,492
17 May	CN – 76	Goods returned		150		2,342
22 May	Inv – 878	Goods	725			3,067
29 May	Inv – 891	Goods	1,250			4,317

Jen Jackson

Date 20XX	Details	Amount £	Date 20XX	Details	Amount £
02 May	Cheque	750	01 May	Balance b/f	900
17 May	Credit note 76	150	10 May	Invoice 841	2,342
			22 May	Invoice 878	725

(a) **Calculate the balance on the supplier's account in Silver's purchases ledger and reconcile this with the balance showing on the supplier's statement of account.**

	£
Balance on supplier's statement of account	4,317
Balance on supplier's account in purchases ledger	
Difference	

(b) **Which item on the supplier's statement of account has not yet been entered in the supplier's account in Silver's purchases ledger?**

Items	✓
Cheque for £750	
Invoice number 841	
Credit note number 76	
Invoice number 878	
Invoice number 891	

4 Stage 6: paying the supplier

The final stage of the purchases process is to pay the supplier. There are several issues to consider before the business can pay the supplier:

(a) **Prompt payment discount** – has any prompt payment discount been offered, and will it be taken? What is the amount to be paid after deducting the discount?

(b) **Authorisation** – has the invoice been properly authorised by the appropriate person?

(c) **Remittance advice note** – a remittance advice note will need to be prepared to show the supplier which invoices are being paid.

4.1 Prompt payment discount

As we saw in Chapter 3, a **prompt payment discount** (PPD) is a **percentage discount** of the **gross total** that is offered to a customer to encourage that customer to pay or settle the invoice earlier.

If a PPD is offered on an invoice from a supplier, then the business needs to decide **whether or not to take that discount**. If the PPD is taken then a smaller amount is paid to the supplier, but it is paid earlier, meaning that money leaves the business's bank account earlier. This reduces any interest receivable on the account or increases any overdraft interest. The business will usually have a **policy** to determine whether a PPD should be taken.

If the business decides to take the PPD, it must pay the invoice within the required time frame. The total amount to be paid will be **the total invoice amount less the PPD**.

Illustration 6: Taking a prompt payment discount

Given below is an extract from one of Whitehill Superstores' invoices:

Invoice date: 8 December 20XX

	£
Net total	3,000
VAT	600
Gross total	3,600
Terms 2% prompt payment discount for payment received within 14 days of the invoice date	

Whitehill Superstores wishes to take the prompt payment discount. How much should Whitehill Superstores pay and when should that payment reach the supplier?

The payment that will be made if the discount is taken is calculated as follows:

Step 1 Calculate the discount to be deducted:

£3,600 × 2% = £72

Step 2 Deduct the discount from the gross total to find the amount to be paid:

£3,600 – £72 = **£3,528**

The total amount to be paid is **£3,528**.

The invoice is dated 8 December, so to take advantage of the prompt payment discount, the payment must reach the supplier within 14 days of this date: 8 December plus 14 days = 22 December.

After payment has been received by the supplier, the supplier will then send a **credit note**, detailing the discount and related VAT. These credit notes are then recorded in the discounts received day book. Now try this activity.

Activity 5: Prompt payment discount

Ashtons Ltd has received an invoice from supplier Whales Way. The invoice has been checked and agreed as correct and can now be paid. It is Ashtons' policy to take all prompt payment discounts offered by Whales Way.

Whales Way
The Port
Brighton BE3 9MJ
VAT Registration No. 482 4995 24

INVOICE

Ashtons Ltd
The Studio
Marston ME0 3JD

Customer account code: | ASH053

Delivery note number: | 84295

Invoice no: 1031 | Date: | 01 December 20XX

Quantity	Product code	Total list price £	Net amount after discount £	VAT £	Gross £
50	4529	750.00	637.50	127.50	765.00

Terms: 2% prompt payment discount for payment received within 14 days of invoice date

---

Required

(a) What is the latest date payment can be received by Whales Way if Ashtons Ltd is to take advantage of the prompt payment discount?

	✓
31 December 20XX	
15 December 20XX	
01 December 20XX	

(b) What is the total amount that should be paid to Whales Way after deducting the prompt payment discount?

£ _____

Ashtons Ltd took the prompt payment discount and so paid a reduced amount to Whales Way. Whales Way must now prepare a credit note for Ashtons Ltd detailing the prompt payment discount taken and the related VAT.

(c) **What amounts will be shown on the credit note from Whales Way to Ashtons Ltd?**

Amount	£
Net amount	
VAT	
Gross amount	

4.2 Authorisation of invoices

It is essential that a business only pays for goods and services which:

(a) Are genuine expenses for the business
(b) Have been ordered by the business
(c) Have been received in the correct quantity
(d) Are of satisfactory quality

In order to achieve this, businesses will have measures in place to ensure that expenditure is **authorised** by **appropriate personnel**.

For example, all purchases invoices should be checked against the purchase order and delivery note before being authorised for payment by an appropriate supervisor. Usually a business has different levels of authorisation depending on the amount of the expenditure.

All businesses should have a list of authorised persons which includes a specimen signature.

Activity 6: Authorisation

At Timothy Toys Ltd, the authorisation procedures are as follows.

Expenditure £	Authorisation required
< 1,000	Line manager
1,000 to 5,000	Line manager plus manager from another department
> 5,000	Line manager plus finance director

Required

Answer the following questions by dragging the relevant item into the table. Not all items will be used; however, items can be used more than once.

The purchase of raw materials costing £300 should be authorised by	
The purchase of an item of machinery costing £49,999 should be authorised by	
The purchase of goods costing £3,500 should be authorised by	

Drag items

line manager	line manager plus finance director	line manager plus manager from another department
line manager plus two managers from other departments	warehouse staff	

4.3 Remittance advice note

It is normal for a business to pay several invoices together, typically at the end of the month. Payments to suppliers will usually be accompanied by a **remittance advice note**, which details the invoices and credit notes covered by the payment.

Chapter 1 showed an example of a remittance advice note which would accompany a cheque payment. Payments may also be made by **BACS transfer**, as is shown in the next activity.

Activity 7: BACS remittance advice note

Justin Jukes sends BACS remittance advice notes to suppliers on the last day of the month following the month of invoice. Credit notes are taken immediately. Justin Jukes banks with HNB3 Bank plc and Rose Reed banks with Cardleys Bank plc. Below is an uncompleted BACS remittance advice and an extract from Justin Jukes's purchases ledger.

Justin Jukes

45 High Street

Nottingham NH4 9MD

BACS REMITTANCE ADVICE

To: Date:

The following payment will reach your bank account within 3 working days.

Invoice number	Credit note number	Amount £
	Total amount paid	

Rose Reed

Date 20XX	Details	Amount £	Date 20XX	Details	Amount £
16 Feb	Credit note 56	332	14 Feb	Invoice 4560	8,472
27 Feb	Credit note 67	875	19 Mar	Invoice 4591	3,295
31 Mar	Bank	7,265	14 Mar	Invoice 5003	2,031
			12 Apr	Invoice 5115	4,067

Required

(a) To whom will the BACS remittance advice be addressed? (Select one)

	✓
Cardleys Bank plc	
HNB3 Bank plc	
Justin Jukes	
Rose Reed	

(b) What will be the date shown on the BACS remittance advice? (Select one)

	✓
31 January	
28 February	
31 March	
30 April	

(c) What will be the TWO items shown on the BACS remittance advice?

	✓
Invoice 4560	
Invoice 4591	
Invoice 5003	
Invoice 5115	
Credit note 56	
Credit note 67	

(d) What will be the total amount paid?

	£
Total amount paid	

Chapter summary

- The first stage in the purchases process is to identify a number of potential suppliers and request a quotation from each of them.

- Once a supplier has been selected, the business will place an order using a purchase order.

- When the ordered goods are received they will normally be accompanied by a delivery note which must be checked and signed as evidence that the stated quantity of goods was delivered.

- On receipt of goods many businesses also complete an internal document, the goods received note (GRN), detailing the quantity and condition of the goods received.

- If goods have to be returned to the supplier a goods returns note may be issued and the business will request a credit note from the supplier for the returned goods.

- When the invoice is received it should be carefully checked to make sure the details are correct (check against order and delivery documents) and that it is correctly calculated.

- When any related credit note is received it should be checked to make sure it resolves the discrepancy and to make sure the details and calculations are correct.

- When invoices for services are received there will be no delivery note or GRN but evidence must be sought that the service has been provided and that the amount charged is reasonable or the agreed amount.

- At regular intervals it is likely that the business may receive a statement of account from suppliers showing the amount currently owed.

- A reconciliation can be carried out between the statement of account and the business's purchases ledger. This will identify any differences between the two.

- When all the checks have been carried out and it has been determined that the invoice is correct then it must be passed for payment.

- At this point it may be the business's policy for the amount of any prompt payment discount offered to be calculated – this is the given percentage of the net total of the invoice.

- All invoices must be authorised before they are paid.

- A remittance advice note will be sent with any payment to the supplier, detailing the invoices and credit notes being paid.

Keywords

- **BACS transfer:** Bankers Automated Clearing Service – an automated payment method

- **Delivery note:** The document sent by the supplier with the goods detailing which goods, and in what quantities, are being sent

- **Goods received note (GRN):** An internal document completed by the buyer on receipt of the goods showing the quantity and condition of the goods received

- **Goods returned note:** The document sent by the customer to the supplier detailing the goods returned and the reason for their return

- **Purchase order:** The written document sent from the buyer to the supplier detailing the goods that are being ordered and the agreed price

- **Reconciliation:** A check of a supplier's statement of account against the business's purchases ledger, and finding reasons for any discrepancies

- **Remittance advice note:** A document setting out exactly how a payment is made up (ie the invoices/credit notes that it is paying/netting off)

- **Tendering:** The process of requesting and receiving quotations from several suppliers

- **Timing difference:** A reason for a variance in a reconciliation – for example, a payment has been made but has not yet reached the supplier's account when the statement is prepared

Test your learning

1   Identify which type of document would be used for the following purposes.

To accompany goods being returned to a supplier	▼
To record for internal purposes the quantity of goods received	▼
To request payment from a purchaser of goods	▼
To order goods from a supplier	▼
To accompany payment to a supplier	▼

Picklist:

Credit note
Delivery note
Goods received note
Invoice
Purchase order
Quotation
Remittance advice note
Returns note

BPP
LEARNING MEDIA

2   Given below are an invoice and credit note received by A J Hammond and the related purchase order, delivery note and goods received note. Check the invoice and credit note thoroughly and note any problems that there might be.

INVOICE

P T Cards
Foram Road
Winnesh DR3 4TP
Tel 0611223 Fax 0611458
VAT Reg 0661 3247 98

To:

A.J. Hammond
Brockham Park Estate
Winnesh DR3 2XJ

Invoice number: 46298

Date/tax point: 5 Oct 20XX

Order number: 304051

Account number: H03

Quantity	Description	Product code	Unit amount £	Total £
200	Birthday Cards	TN451	0.89	178.00
600	Christmas Cards	SJ106	0.45	270.00
100	Get Well Cards	GW444	0.33	33.00

Net total	481.00
VAT	96.20
Invoice total	577.20

Terms
E & OE

CREDIT NOTE

P T Cards
Foram Road
Winnesh DR3 4TP
Tel 0611223 Fax 0611458
VAT Reg 0661 3247 98

Credit note to:

A.J. Hammond
Brockham Park Estate
Winnesh DR3 2XJ

Credit note number: 31313
Date/tax point: 10 Oct 20XX
Order number: 304051
Account number: H03

Quantity	Description	Product code	Unit amount	Total
			£	£
30	Get Well Cards	GW444	0.25	7.50
			Net total	7.50
			VAT	1.50
			Gross total	9.00

Reason for credit note:

Not ordered

PURCHASE ORDER

A J HAMMOND
Brockham Park Estate
Winnesh DR3 2XJ

To: P.T.Cards
Foram Road
Winnesh DR3 4TP

Number: 304051

Date: 13 Sept 20XX

Delivery address: As above

Product code	Quantity	Description	Price (£)
SJ106	600	Christmas Cards	0.45
GW444	70	Get well Cards	0.33
TN451	200	Birthday Cards	0.89

Authorised by: *P T Thomas*   **Date:** *13 Sept 20XX*

DELIVERY NOTE

P T Cards
Foram Road
Winnesh DR3 4TP
Tel 0611223 Fax 0611458

Delivery address:

A.J.Hammond
Brockham Park Estate
Winnesh DR3 2XJ

Number: 21690
Date: 20 Sept 20XX
Order number: 304051

Product code	Quantity	Description
SJ106	600	Christmas Cards
GW444	100	Get Well Cards
TN451	200	Birthday Cards

Received by: [Signature]   *J T Turner*   **Print name:**   *J T TURNER*

Date: *20 Sept 20XX*

GOODS RECEIVED NOTE

A J Hammond
Brockham Park Estate
Winnesh DR3 2XJ

Supplier:

GRN number: 27420

Date: 21 Sept 20XX

Order number: 304051

Delivery Note No: 21690

Quantity	Description	Product code
200	Birthday Cards	TN 451
100	Get Well Cards	GW 444
600	Christmas Cards	SJ 106

Received by: *P Darren*

Checked by: *D Gough*

Comments: *All in good condition*

3   A supply of printer paper has been delivered to Wendlehurst Trading by Patel Stationery. The purchase order sent from Wendlehurst Trading, and the invoice from Patel Stationery, are shown below.

Wendlehurst Trading
Purchase Order No. PO89346

To: Patel Stationery

Date: 7 Dec 20XX

Please supply 100 reams printer paper product code PAP6735

Purchase price: £80 per box of 20 reams, plus VAT

Discount: less 12.5% trade discount, as agreed.

BPP
LEARNING MEDIA

```
                    Patel Stationery
                    Invoice No. 109273
Wendlehurst Trading

10 Dec 20XX

100 reams printer paper product code PAP6735 @ £4 each      £400.00
Trade discount                                              (£40.00)
Net amount                                                  £360.00
VAT @ 20%                                                    £ 72.00
Total                                                       £432.00
                    Terms: 30 days net
```

Check the invoice against the purchase order and answer the following questions.

	Yes ✓	No ✓
Has the correct purchase price of the printer paper been charged?		
Has the correct trade discount been applied?		

	£
What should the corrected VAT amount be?	
What should be the total amount charged?	

4   An invoice for goods shows the net total of the goods as £800.00 and the VAT as £160.00, giving a gross total of £960.00. A prompt payment discount of 3% is offered. The business decides to take the prompt payment discount. How much should be paid to the supplier?

£ _____

5   An invoice dated 23 November is received on 25 November. The prompt payment discount of 4% for payment within 10 days of the invoice date is to be taken and the payment will be received by the supplier 2 days after the cheque is written.

What is the latest date that the cheque should be written?

Date	

Double entry bookkeeping (Part 1)

Learning outcomes

5.1	Transfer data from the books of prime entry to the ledgers
	• The books of prime entry: sales and sales returns daybooks, purchases and purchases returns daybooks, discounts allowed and discounts received daybooks, cash book, petty cash book
	• The ledgers: sales, purchases, general
	• Know that the sales and purchases ledger control accounts are part of the double entry system
	• Transfer data from books of prime entry to the relevant accounts in the ledgers

Assessment context

Your understanding of double entry is a key skill which is needed to pass *Bookkeeping Transactions*. It is introduced in this chapter, and then studied further in Chapters 7 to 10.

The assessment will directly test double entry in two different ways. You could be asked to complete T-accounts by selecting an account name from a picklist (choice of account names) and entering the correct amount in the debit or credit column. You will then have to balance the T-account and show the closing amount.

Alternatively, you could be asked to enter the information in tabular format by selecting account names from a picklist and entering the relevant amount and ticks to indicate debit or credit entries.

Qualification context

Double entry bookkeeping is introduced in *Bookkeeping Transactions* and then developed in the Level 2 *Bookkeeping Controls* and Level 3 *Advanced Bookkeeping* and *Final Accounts Preparation* courses. It is applied at Level 4 *Financial Statements of Limited Companies*.

Business context

Double entry is used to prepare financial statements which show the company's financial performance over the year and closing assets and liabilities. It is therefore essential in helping users of the financial statements to make business decisions.

Chapter overview

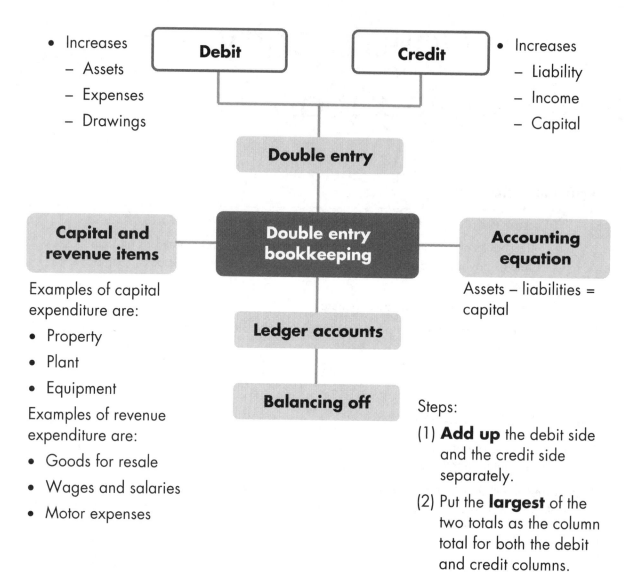

- Increases
  - Assets
  - Expenses
  - Drawings

Debit **Credit**

- Increases
  - Liability
  - Income
  - Capital

Double entry

Capital and revenue items

Double entry bookkeeping

Accounting equation

Examples of capital expenditure are:

- Property
- Plant
- Equipment

Assets – liabilities = capital

Ledger accounts

Examples of revenue expenditure are:

- Goods for resale
- Wages and salaries
- Motor expenses

Balancing off

Steps:

(1) **Add up** the debit side and the credit side separately.

(2) Put the **largest** of the two totals as the column total for both the debit and credit columns.

(3) Calculate the **balancing figure** on the side with the lower total and describe this as the **balance carried down** (balance c/d).

(4) Show this balancing figure on the **opposite side**, below the totals line, and describe this figure as the **balance brought down** (balance b/d).

Introduction

In the chapters we have covered so far we have seen that all businesses need to keep records in order to know how they are performing, and that this is done by a system of accounting.

A business should maintain accounting records to record each stage of the process:

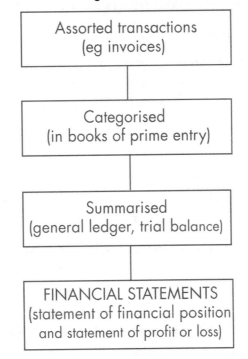

In Chapter 2 we saw how transactions were categorised in **books of prime entry**. The next step is to include that information in the **general ledger**, and we use **double entry bookkeeping** to do that.

1 The principles of double entry bookkeeping

The three main principles that underlie the practice of recording transactions in a double entry bookkeeping system are:

(a)   The **separate entity concept** – the owner of a business is a completely separate entity to the business itself

(b)   There is an **accounting equation** which always holds true:

ASSETS – LIABILITIES = CAPITAL

(c)   The **dual effect** of transactions – each and every transaction that a business undertakes has two effects on the business

1.1 The accounting equation

To understand the accounting equation a little better you need to know more about its different **elements.**

- **Assets** are items that the business owns, such as cash and machinery and amounts owed to the business by credit customers.

- **Liabilities** are amounts that are owed to other parties, such as loans, overdrafts and amounts owed to credit suppliers.

- **Capital** is the amount of **cash injected** by the owner, plus the **profit** the business has made, less any **drawings** the owner had taken.

Profit is the business's income less its expenses:

- The main sources of **income** for a business will be from sales of goods and services, but may also include **sundry income**, such as interest paid to the business by its bank, rent received from tenants, and commission received from acting as an agent.

- The main **expenses** of the business will be the goods that it purchases for resale as well as the other ongoing costs of running the business such as wages to employees (but **not** the owner, as these are actually drawings), rent paid for its premises, utilities and stationery.

Assets, **liabilities**, **capital, income** and **expenses** are known as the **elements** of the financial statements, which we saw in Chapter 4.

1.2 The dual effect

Double entry bookkeeping is based on the fundamental principle that every transaction has **two effects** on the business; this is called the **dual effect**.

For example:

(a) A business makes a cash sale for £200:

Cash increases by £200

Sales increase by £200

(b) A business makes a sale on credit for £500:

Trade receivables increase by £500

Sales increase by £500

1.3 Ledger accounts

The two effects of each transaction need to be recorded in the organisation's accounting records.

The traditional method of recording these transactions is in a **ledger account** in the organisation's **general ledger**.

- 'Ledger' simply means 'book'.

- The **general ledger** is the accounting record which forms the complete set of ledger accounts for the organisation.

Each type of transaction has a ledger account in the general ledger. Ledger accounts are often called T-accounts because of how they look. An illustration of a bank ledger account follows below:

Bank

Details	Amount £	Details	Amount £
Sales	100	Purchases	75

Each ledger account has:

- Two sides, because each transaction has two effects

    - The left-hand side is the **debit** side.
    - The right-hand side is the **credit** side.

- A title, which explains which transaction it is recording eg bank, sales, purchases.

Remember the fundamental principle of double entry bookkeeping is the dual effect: **each and every transaction has two effects.**

So for every transaction that a business makes there must be:

- A debit entry in one ledger account.
- An equal and opposite credit entry in another ledger account.

The skill that you must acquire is to know which accounts to put the debit and credit entries into.

2 Double entry bookkeeping – general rules

There are some general rules for double entry bookkeeping which can help you to decide where debit and credit entries should be made in the ledger accounts:

(a) A **debit** entry represents:

   (i)   An increase in an asset
   (ii) An increase in expenses
   (iii) An increase in drawings
   (iv) A decrease in liabilities, income or capital

(b) A **credit** entry represents:

   (i)   An increase in a liability
   (ii) An increase in income
   (iii) An increase in capital
   (iv) A decrease in assets, expenses or drawings

A helpful way to remember this is to use the mnemonic DEAD CLIC:

Debits	Credits
(increase)	(increase)
Expenses	**L**iabilities
Assets	**I**ncome
Drawings	**C**apital

Assessment focus point

It is vitally important that you learn the general rules of double entry bookkeeping. Remembering the DEAD CLIC mnemonic is a good way to do this.

2.1 Double entry for cash transactions

We shall now look at some simple financial transactions to demonstrate the double entry principle. Students coming across double entry for the first time often have difficulty in knowing where to begin. A good starting point is the cash account, ie the ledger account in which receipts and payments of cash are recorded. The rules to remember about the cash account are as follows.

(a) A **cash payment** is a **credit entry** in the cash account. Here the **asset** (cash) **is decreasing**. Cash may be paid out, for example, to pay an expense (such as tax) or to purchase an asset (such as a machine). The **matching debit entry** is therefore made in the appropriate **expense** account or **asset** account.

(b) A **cash receipt** is a **debit entry** in the cash account. Here the **asset** (cash) **is increasing**. Cash might be received, for example, by a retailer who makes a cash sale. The **matching credit entry** would then be made in the **sales** account.

Illustration 1: Double entry for cash transactions

A business has the following transactions. What is the double entry for each transaction?

(a) A cash sale (ie a receipt) of £2

The two sides of the transaction are

(i)   Cash is received: **debit** entry in the cash account
(ii) Sales increase by £2: **credit** entry in the sales account

(b) Payment in cash of a rent bill totalling £150

The two sides of the transaction are

(i)   Cash is paid: **credit** entry in the cash account
(ii) Rent expense increases by £150: **debit** entry in the rent account

(c) Bought some goods for cash at £100

The two sides of the transaction are

(i)   Cash is paid: **credit** entry in the cash account
(ii) Purchases increase by £100: **debit** entry in the purchases account

(d) Bought a machine for cash at £200

The two sides of the transaction are

(i)   Cash is paid: **credit** entry in the cash account

(ii) Assets – in this case, machines – increase by £200: **debit** entry in machines account

2.2 Double entry for credit transactions

Not all transactions are settled immediately in cash. A business might purchase goods from its suppliers on credit terms, so that the suppliers would be **trade payables** of the business until settlement was made in cash. Equally, the business might grant credit terms to its customers, who would then be **trade receivables** of the business.

In the general ledger, **sales on credit** are posted to the **sales ledger control account** and purchases on credit are posted to the **purchases ledger control account**.

Illustration 2: Double entry for credit transactions

The following credit transactions have occurred. What is the double entry for each transaction?

(a)   The business sells goods on credit to a customer, Mr A, for £2,000.

The two sides of the transaction are

(i)   A trade receivable for £2,000 is created: **debit** entry in the sales ledger control account

(ii)   Sales increase by £2,000: **credit** entry in the sales account

(b)   The business buys goods on credit from supplier B for £100.

The two sides of the transaction are

(i)   A trade payable for £100 is created: **credit** entry in the purchases ledger control account

(ii)   Purchases increase by £100: **debit** entry in the purchases account

(c)   One month later, the business pays £100 in cash to supplier B.

The two sides of this new transaction are

(i)   Cash is paid: **credit** entry in the cash account

(ii)   The amount owing to trade payables is reduced: **debit** entry in the purchases ledger control account

(d)   A while later, Mr A pays in cash his debt of £2,000.

The two sides of the transaction are:

(i)   Cash is received: **debit** entry in the cash account

(ii)   The amount owed by trade receivables is reduced: **credit** entry in the sales ledger control account

Now try Activity 1 below. In each case you are required to complete the double entry, showing which account will be debited and which will be credited. You are also required to identify which elements of the financial statements are affected. The first two have been done for you.

Assessment focus point

A good way to approach a question on double entry is to follow these three steps.

For each transaction, you should:

(1)   Classify the transaction – what elements are affected?

(2)   Work out whether an increase or decrease to the element is required.

(3)   Use DEAD CLIC to work out whether that increase or decrease required is a debit or credit to the affected account.

Activity 1: Introduction to double entry

What is the double entry for each of the following?

Explain each entry in terms of the elements of the financial statements. The first two have been done for you.

	Transaction	Debit	Credit
(a)	Sales for cash	Cash **increase assets**	Sales **income**
(b)	Sales on credit	Sales ledger control **increase assets**	Sales **income**
(c)	Purchases for cash		
(d)	Purchases on credit		
(e)	Pay electricity bill using cash		
(f)	Receive cash from a credit customer		
(g)	Pay cash to a credit supplier		
(h)	Borrow money from the bank		

3 Entering transactions into a ledger account

In the ledger accounts, debits and credits are entered like this:

Asset account eg Bank

Details	Amount £	Details	Amount £
DEBIT		CREDIT	
(Increase)		(Decrease)	

Liability account eg Bank loan

Details	£	Details	£
DEBIT		CREDIT	
(Decrease)		(Increase)	

Capital account

Details	£	Details	£
DEBIT		CREDIT	
(Decrease)		(Increase)	

Expense account

Details	£	Details	£
DEBIT		CREDIT	
(Increase)		(Decrease)	

Income account

Details	£	Details	£
DEBIT		CREDIT	
(Decrease)		(Increase)	

Illustration 3: Entering a transaction into a ledger account

A business bought some goods for cash at £500.

The two sides of the transaction are

(i) Cash is paid: credit entry in the cash account

(ii) Purchases increase by £500: debit entry in the purchases account

This transaction is entered into the ledger accounts like this:

Cash

Details	Amount £	Details	Amount £
		Purchases	500

Purchases

Details	£	Details	£
Cash	500		

Note how the entry in the cash account is cross-referenced to the purchases account and vice-versa. This enables a person looking at one of the accounts to trace where the other half of the double entry can be found.

Now try the following activity.

Activity 2: Entering a transaction into a ledger account

A business sells goods for £200 to a customer who pays in cash. The dual effect of this transaction is an increase in cash and an increase in sales.

(a) Complete the table below to show the double entry required for this transaction.

Account		Debit ✓	Credit ✓
	▼		
	▼		

Picklist:

Cash
Sales

(b) Record this transaction in the ledger accounts below.

Cash

Details	Amount £	Details	Amount £

Sales

Details	Amount £	Details	Amount £

We will now look at the initial transactions of a small business owned by Ben Charles to illustrate the double entry of each transaction and how that transaction is recorded in the ledger accounts.

Illustration 4: Recording transactions in the general ledger accounts

(1) Ben Charles set up a business on 1 May with £10,000 in cash as the business's initial capital.

Cash has come into the business therefore we need to **debit** the cash account. The money paid in is from the owner of the business. It is therefore capital of the business so the **credit** entry is to the capital account.

Effect	Debit	Credit
Cash increases by £10,000	Cash £10,000	
Capital increases by £10,000		Capital £10,000

This transaction is recorded in Ben's ledger accounts like this:

Cash account

Details	Amount £	Details	Amount £
Capital	10,000		

Capital account

Details	Amount £	Details	Amount £
		Cash	10,000

The details column for each entry shows where the **other side** of the entry is.

In terms of the **accounting equation**, we see at this point that:

Assets (£10,000) – **Liabilities** (£0) = **Capital** (£10,000)

(2) Ben buys some goods for resale for £1,000 in cash.

Cash is going out of the business so we need to credit the cash account.

The payment was for goods for resale, which are known as purchases, an **expense account**, so we need to debit the purchases account.

Effect	Debit	Credit
Purchases of £1,000 have been made	Purchases £1,000	
Cash of £1,000 is paid out		Cash £1,000

This is entered into Ben's ledger accounts like this:

Cash

Details	Amount £	Details	Amount £
Capital	10,000	**Purchases**	**1,000**

Purchases

Details	Amount £	Details	Amount £
Cash	**1,000**		

(3) Ben buys some goods for resale for £2,000 on credit.

Again, these goods are purchases so we need to debit the purchases account.

The transaction is not for cash this time so there is no entry into the cash account; instead the credit entry is to the **purchases ledger control account** as it is a balance owed to a credit supplier (a balance owed to a supplier is a liability, so an increase is always a credit). The purchases ledger control account is the account in the general ledger where purchases made on credit are recorded.

Effect	Debit	Credit
Purchases of £2,000 have been made	Purchases £2,000	
A trade payable for £2,000 is created		Purchases ledger control £2,000

Purchases

Details	Amount £	Details	Amount £
Cash	1,000		
Purchases ledger control	**2,000**		

Purchases ledger control

Details	Amount £	Details	Amount £
		Purchases	2,000

(4) Ben pays rent for the business premises of £600 in cash.

Cash is going out of the business; therefore we need to credit the cash account.

The rent is an expense of the business so the rent account must be debited. An increase in expenses is always a debit entry in the expense ledger accounts.

Effect	Debit	Credit
A rent expense of £600 has been incurred	Rent £600	
Cash of £600 is paid out		Cash £600

Cash

Details	Amount £	Details	Amount £
Capital	10,000	Purchases	1,000
		Rent	**600**

Rent

Details	Amount £	Details	Amount £
Cash	600		

(5) Sales of £1,500 for cash are made by selling some of the goods.

Cash is coming into the business from these sales; therefore we need to debit the cash account.

The credit is to the sales account. Remember that an increase in income is always a credit entry.

Effect	Debit	Credit
Cash has increased by £1,500	Cash £1,500	
Sales of £1,500 have been made		Sales £1,500

Cash

Details	Amount £	Details	Amount £
Capital	10,000	Purchases	1,000
Sales	1,500	Rent	600

Sales

Details	Amount £	Details	Amount £
		Cash	1,500

(6) Sales of £1,800 are made on credit.

Again, we have a sale so the sales account must be credited.

This time, however, there is no cash coming in so it is not the cash account that is debited; instead the debit entry is made in the sales ledger control account. Remember that an increase in an asset such as a trade receivable is always a debit entry.

Effect	Debit	Credit
A trade receivable for £1,800 is created	Sales ledger control £1,800	
Sales of £1,800 have been made		Sales £1,800

Sales

Details	Amount £	Details	Amount £
		Cash	1,500
		Sales ledger control	**1,800**

Sales ledger control

Details	Amount £	Details	Amount £
Sales	**1,800**		

(7) Ben takes out £500 in cash from the business for his own living expenses.

Cash goes out of the business, so we must credit the cash account.

This is the owner taking money out of the business (**drawings**), so the drawings account must be debited.

Effect	Debit	Credit
Drawings of £500 have been made	Drawings £500	
Cash is decreased by £500		Cash £500

Cash

Details	Amount £	Details	Amount £
Capital	10,000	Purchases	1,000
Sales	1,500	Rent	600
		Drawings	**500**

Drawings

Details	Amount £	Details	Amount £
Cash	500		

(8) Ben pays his credit supplier £1,500 in cash.

Cash goes out of the business, so we must credit the cash account.

The money is being paid to Ben's credit supplier, and therefore it is reducing the trade payable balance. The purchases ledger control account must be debited to reflect this.

Effect	Debit	Credit
The amount of the trade payable is reduced by £1,500	Purchases ledger control £1,500	
Cash is reduced by £1,500		Cash £1,500

Cash

Details	Amount £	Details	Amount £
Capital	10,000	Purchases	1,000
Sales	1,500	Rent	600
		Drawings	500
		Purchases ledger control	**1,500**

Purchases ledger control

Details	Amount £	Details	Amount £
Cash	**1,500**	Purchases	2,000

(9) Ben's credit customer pays £1,800 in cash.

This is cash being received into the business so the cash account is debited.

The credit entry is to the sales ledger control account, as this receipt is reducing the amount that the trade receivable owes the business.

Effect	Debit	Credit
Cash is increased by £1,800	Cash £1,800	
The amount of the trade receivable is reduced by £1,800		Sales ledger control £1,800

Cash

Details	Amount £	Details	Amount £
Capital	10,000	Purchases	1,000
Sales	1,500	Rent	600
Sales ledger control	**1,800**	Drawings	500
		Purchases ledger control	1,500

Sales ledger control

Details	Amount £	Details	Amount £
Sales	1,800	**Cash**	**1,800**

As we have seen, cash transactions are recorded in the cash ledger account. However, most business operate a **business bank account**. All transactions that go through the business's bank account should be recorded in the **bank ledger account**. This includes cheques, direct debits and standing orders, as well as direct payments and receipts through the bank.

Activity 3: Recording transactions in the general ledger accounts

The following transactions took place during the first week of trading for Hampton:

(1) Started business by depositing £20,000 into the bank account
(2) Bought goods for resale and paid £250 by cheque
(3) Paid rent of £225 by cheque
(4) Sold goods for £657, customer paid in cash
(5) Paid rates £135 by cheque
(6) Sold goods on credit to a customer, J Henry, for £750
(7) Bought goods for resale on credit from C Bableton for £450
(8) Paid wages £75 cash

Record the transactions above in the general ledger accounts.

GENERAL LEDGER

Bank

Details	Amount £	Details	Amount £

Capital

Details	Amount £	Details	Amount £

Purchases

Details	Amount £	Details	Amount £

Rent

Details	Amount £	Details	Amount £

Sales

Details	Amount £	Details	Amount £

Cash

Details	Amount £	Details	Amount £

Rates

Details	Amount £	Details	Amount £

Sales ledger control

Details	Amount £	Details	Amount £

Purchases ledger control

Details	Amount £	Details	Amount £

Wages

Details	Amount £	Details	Amount £

4 Further practice at double entry bookkeeping

To understand double entry bookkeeping it is important to practise the DEAD CLIC mnemonic introduced earlier in the chapter.

Assessment focus point

In your assessment, you will either be asked to complete double entry in T-accounts as we saw earlier in the chapter, or you will be asked to use the tabular format, which is illustrated below. If a question requires you to use the tabular format, it will often ask for the 'journal entry', which is another way of asking for the double entry of the transaction.

Illustration 5: Tabular format for double entry

To record a cash sale of £100, the journal entry is:

Effect on elements	Account name	Amount £	Debit ✓	Credit ✓
Increase in asset	Cash	100	✓	
Increase in income	Sales	100		✓

Activity 4: Further practice at double entry bookkeeping

Required

Complete the following journal entries. Show the impact of each transaction on the elements of the financial statements. Then show the account name and amount and tick to indicate debit and credit entries.

(a) Credit sale of £200

Effect on elements	Account name	Amount £	Debit ✓	Credit ✓

(b) Cash purchase of £150

Effect on elements	Account name	Amount £	Debit ✓	Credit ✓

(c) Credit purchase of £500

Effect on elements	Account name	Amount £	Debit ✓	Credit ✓

(d) Capital contribution from the owner into the bank account of £1,000

Effect on elements	Account name	Amount £	Debit ✓	Credit ✓

BPP
LEARNING MEDIA

(e) Receipt of loan into the bank account of £2,000

Effect on elements	Account name	Amount £	Debit ✓	Credit ✓

(f) Drawings of £4,000 taken by the owner from the bank account

Effect on elements	Account name	Amount £	Debit ✓	Credit ✓

(g) Repayment of bank loan of £500

Effect on elements	Account name	Amount £	Debit ✓	Credit ✓

(h) Credit sale of £100

Effect on elements	Account name	Amount £	Debit ✓	Credit ✓

(i) Payment of wages in cash of £350

Effect on elements	Account name	Amount £	Debit ✓	Credit ✓

(j) Payment of rent from the bank account of £800

Effect on elements	Account name	Amount £	Debit ✓	Credit ✓

Chapter summary

- The general ledger is a collection of ledger accounts.

- A business's transactions are first entered into the books of prime entry. The books of prime entry are then totalled up and two entries will be made in the general ledger accounts with the total – this is called double entry bookkeeping.

- The dual effect is the basis of double entry bookkeeping: every transaction has two effects on a business.

- The two effects of each transaction are recorded in ledger accounts with a debit entry in one account and a credit entry in another account.

- A debit entry is an entry into the ledger on the left-hand side. A debit entry represents:

  - An increase in an asset
  - An item of expense
  - An increase in drawings
  - A decrease in liabilities, income or capital

- A credit entry is an entry into the ledger on the right-hand side. A credit entry represents:

  - An increase in a liability
  - An item of income
  - An increase in capital
  - A decrease in assets, expenses or drawings

- A helpful way to remember this is to use the mnemonic DEAD CLIC.

Keywords

- **Credit:** The credit side of a ledger account is the right-hand side
- **Debit:** The debit side of a ledger account is the left-hand side
- **Double entry bookkeeping:** A system of accounting where the two effects of each transaction are recorded
- **Drawings:** The money or goods that the owner takes out of the business
- **Dual effect:** Every transaction a business undertakes has two effects on the business
- **General ledger:** A collection of ledger accounts, where the double entry takes place for all the transactions of the business
- **Ledger accounts (or T-accounts):** The accounts in which each transaction is recorded – there will be a ledger account for each type of transaction, such as sales and purchases and for every type of asset and liability
- **Purchases ledger control account:** A general ledger account for credit suppliers, representing the total of all the accounts in the purchases ledger. Part of the double entry system
- **Sales ledger control account:** A general ledger account for credit customers, representing the total of all the accounts in the sales ledger. Part of the double entry system

1 What are the two effects of the following transactions?

   (a) Purchase of goods on credit

	✓
Increase expense	
Increase sales	
Increase trade payable	
Increase trade receivable	

   (b) Sale of goods on credit

	✓
Increase expense	
Increase sales	
Increase trade payable	
Increase trade receivable	

2 What are the two effects of the following transactions?

   (a) Receipt of money for sale of goods on credit

	✓
Increase cash	
Decrease cash	
Decrease trade receivable	
Increase trade receivable	

   (b) Payment to a credit supplier for purchase of goods on credit

	✓
Increase cash	
Decrease cash	
Decrease trade payable	
Increase trade payable	

3   For each of the following transactions, state which account should be debited and which account should be credited.

(a)   Purchase of goods on credit

Account name		Debit	Credit
	▼		
	▼		

(b)   Sale of goods on credit

Account name		Debit	Credit
	▼		
	▼		

(c)   Receipt of money for sale of goods on credit

Account name		Debit	Credit
	▼		
	▼		

(d)   Payment to a credit supplier

Account name		Debit	Credit
	▼		
	▼		

Picklist:

Bank
Purchases
Purchases ledger control
Sales
Sales ledger control

4   Identify the general ledger accounts that are debited and credited for each of the following transactions.

	Debit		Credit	
Money paid into the business bank account by the owner	▼		▼	
Purchases on credit	▼		▼	
Sales on credit	▼		▼	
Money taken out of the business (via the bank) by the owner	▼		▼	

5   The following transactions relate to a bookshop. Identify the general ledger accounts that are debited and credited for each of the transactions.

	Debit	Credit
Purchase of books on credit	▼	▼
Purchase of cash register using direct debit	▼	▼
Payment received from a credit customer via the bank account	▼	▼
Purchase of van using cheque	▼	▼

Picklist:

Bank
Cash
Cash register
Purchases
Purchases ledger control
Sales ledger control
Van

6   What are the journal entries for the following transactions?

(a)   Bought a machine on credit from A, cost £8,000

Account name	Debit £	Credit £
▼		
▼		

(b)   Bought goods on credit from B, cost £500

Account name	Debit £	Credit £
▼		
▼		

(c) Sold goods on credit to C, value £1,200

Account name		Debit £	Credit £
	▼		
	▼		

(d) Paid D (a credit supplier) £300 via cheque

Account name		Debit £	Credit £
	▼		
	▼		

Picklist:

Bank
Purchases
Purchases ledger control
Machine
Sales
Sales ledger control

7   What are the journal entries for the following transactions?

(a) Collected £180 in cash from E, a credit customer

Account name		Debit £	Credit £
	▼		
	▼		

(b) Paid wages £4,000 via bank transfer

Account name		Debit £	Credit £
	▼		
	▼		

(c) Paid rent of £700 to landlord G in cash

Account name		Debit £	Credit £
	▼		
	▼		

(d) Paid insurance premium £90 via direct debit

Account name		Debit £	Credit £
	▼		
	▼		

Picklist:

Bank
Cash
Insurance
Purchases
Purchases ledger control
Rent
Sales ledger control
Wages

8   A business has the following transactions on 7 April 20X7.
(a)   A cash sale of £60
(b)   Payment of a rent bill totalling £4,500 via direct debit
(c)   Buying some goods for cash at £300
(d)   Buying a car for £6,000 using a cheque

Show how these four transactions would be recorded in the ledger accounts below.

Bank

Details		Amount £	Details		Amount £
	▼			▼	
	▼			▼	
	▼			▼	

Cash

Details		Amount £	Details		Amount £
	▼			▼	
	▼			▼	
	▼			▼	

BPP
LEARNING MEDIA

Car

Details		Amount £	Details		Amount £
	▼			▼	
	▼			▼	
	▼			▼	

Purchases

Details		Amount £	Details		Amount £
	▼			▼	
	▼			▼	
	▼			▼	

Rent

Details		Amount £	Details		Amount £
	▼			▼	
	▼			▼	
	▼			▼	

Sales

Details		Amount £	Details		Amount £
	▼			▼	
	▼			▼	
	▼			▼	

Picklist:

Bank
Cash
Car
Purchases
Rent
Sales

9 What are the journal entries for the following transactions?

(a) Paid capital of £7,000 into bank

Account name	Debit £	Credit £
▼		
▼		

(b) Paid rent of £3,500

Account name	Debit £	Credit £
▼		
▼		

(c) Purchased goods for resale on credit for £5,000

Account name	Debit £	Credit £
▼		
▼		

(d) Took out a loan of £1,500 from the bank

Account name	Debit £	Credit £
▼		
▼		

Picklist:

Bank
Bank loan
Capital
Cash
Purchases
Purchases ledger control
Rent

10 What are the journal entries for the following transactions?

(a) Sales of £10,000 for cash

Account name		Debit £	Credit £
	▼		
	▼		

(b) Sales of £2,500 on credit

Account name		Debit £	Credit £
	▼		
	▼		

(c) Paid interest of £100 on bank loan via direct debit

Account name		Debit £	Credit £
	▼		
	▼		

(d) Drawings of £1,500 withdrawn from the bank

Account name		Debit £	Credit £
	▼		
	▼		

Picklist:

Bank
Bank loan
Cash
Drawings
Interest
Sales
Sales ledger control

Double entry bookkeeping (Part 2)

7

Learning outcomes

7.4	Demonstrate an understanding of the process of recording financial transactions
	• The ledgers: sales, purchases and general
	• The accounting equation: calculation of assets, liabilities and capital, dual effect of transactions
	• The classification of items: assets and liabilities
	• The classification of income and expenditure: capital income, capital expenditure, revenue income, revenue expenditure
7.2	**Total and balance ledger accounts**
	Students need to be able to:
	• Total and balance ledger accounts: balance carried down, balance brought down, debit balance, credit balance

Assessment context

Your understanding of double entry is a key skill which is needed to pass *Bookkeeping Transactions*. It was introduced in Chapter 6 and is studied further in Chapters 8 to 10.

The assessment will directly test double entry in two different ways. You could be asked to complete T-accounts by selecting an account name from a picklist (choice of account names) and entering the correct amount in the debit or credit column. You will then have to balance the T-account and show the closing amount.

Alternatively, you could be asked to enter the information in tabular format by selecting account names from a picklist and entering the relevant amount and ticks to indicate debit or credit entries.

Qualification context

Double entry bookkeeping is introduced in *Bookkeeping Transactions* and then developed in the Level 2 *Bookkeeping Controls* and Level 3 *Advanced Bookkeeping* courses. It is applied at Level 4 *Financial Statements of Limited Companies*.

Business context

Double entry is used to prepare financial statements which show the company's financial performance over the year and closing assets and liabilities. It is therefore essential in helping users of the financial statements to make business decisions.

Chapter overview

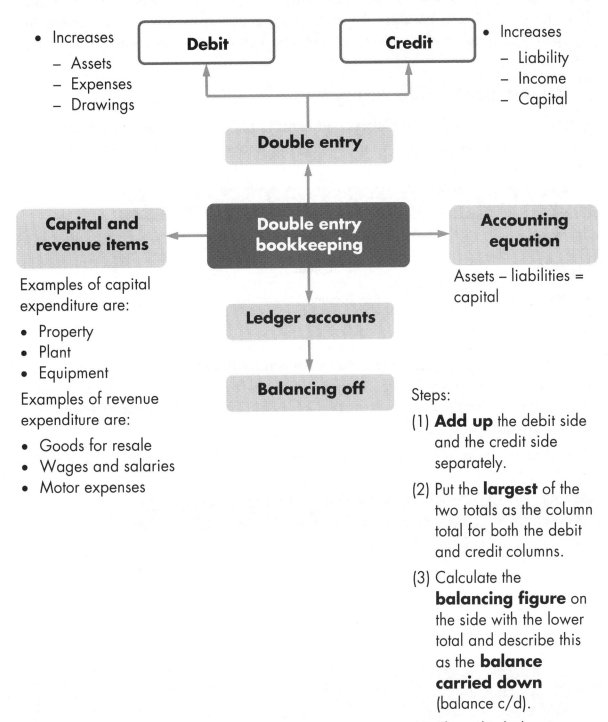

- Increases
  - Assets
  - Expenses
  - Drawings

Debit

Credit

- Increases
  - Liability
  - Income
  - Capital

Double entry

Capital and revenue items

Double entry bookkeeping

Accounting equation

Assets – liabilities = capital

Examples of capital expenditure are:

- Property
- Plant
- Equipment

Examples of revenue expenditure are:

- Goods for resale
- Wages and salaries
- Motor expenses

Ledger accounts

Balancing off

Steps:

(1) **Add up** the debit side and the credit side separately.

(2) Put the **largest** of the two totals as the column total for both the debit and credit columns.

(3) Calculate the **balancing figure** on the side with the lower total and describe this as the **balance carried down** (balance c/d).

(4) Show this balancing figure on the **opposite side**, below the totals line, and describe this figure as the **balance brought down** (balance b/d).

Introduction

In this chapter, we will continue to look at double entry bookkeeping and general ledger accounts, as well as the subsidiary ledgers – the sales and purchases ledgers. We will also consider the accounting equation, which we saw briefly in Chapter 4, before covering the difference between capital and revenue sales and expenses.

1 Recap of double entry

In Chapter 6, we introduced **debits** and **credits** and a useful way to remember the effect of debits and credits on the elements of financial statements, the mnemonic **DEAD CLIC**:

Debits	Credits
(increase)	(increase)
Expenses	**L**iabilities
Assets	**I**ncome
Drawings	**C**apital

We also looked at **ledger accounts** in the **general ledger** and considered how transactions are entered into ledger accounts by the use of double entry bookkeeping. Remember the example of Ben Charles's business (Chapter 6, Illustration 4):

Ben Charles set up in business on 1 May with £10,000 in cash as the business's initial capital.

Effect	Debit	Credit
Cash increases by £10,000	Cash £10,000	
Capital increases by £10,000		Capital £10,000

This transaction was recorded in Ben's general ledger accounts like this:

Cash account

Details	Amount £	Details	Amount £
Capital	10,000		

Capital account

Details	Amount £	Details	Amount £
		Cash	10,000

Once all of Ben's transactions are entered into his ledger accounts, the ledger accounts must be **balanced off**, so that we can know the total on each account.

2 Balancing off the ledger accounts

Periodically, usually monthly, it is necessary to balance off the ledger accounts so we know the balance on each account.

The steps to balance off a ledger account are:

Step 1   **Add up** the debit side and the credit side separately.

Step 2   Put the **largest** of the two totals as the column total for both the debit and credit columns.

Step 3   Calculate the **balancing figure** on the **side with the lower total and describe this as the balance carried down** (balance c/d).

Step 4   Show this balancing figure on the **opposite side**, below the totals line, and describe this figure as the **balance brought down** (balance b/d).

Assessment focus point

In your assessment, AAT uses 'balance b/f' to describe the **opening balance** on an account, and 'balance c/d' and 'balance b/d' are used to **balance off** the account. In practice however, you may see 'balance b/f' and 'balance b/d' used interchangeably.

Illustration 1: Balancing off a ledger account

We will illustrate the balancing off process by using Ben Charles's cash ledger account for his initial period of trading.

Cash

Details	Amount £	Details	Amount £
Capital	10,000	Purchases	1,000
Sales	1,500	Rent	600
Sales ledger control	1,800	Drawings	500
		Purchases ledger control	1,500

Step 1 Total both the debit and the credit columns, making a note of the totals for each.

Debit column total £13,300
Credit column total £3,600

Step 2 Put the largest of the two totals as the column total for both the debit and credit columns, leaving at least one empty line at the bottom of each column.

Cash

Details	Amount £	Details	Amount £
Capital	10,000	Purchases	1,000
Sales	1,500	Rent	600
Sales ledger control	1,800	Drawings	500
		Purchases ledger control	1,500
Total	13,300	Total	13,300

BPP LEARNING MEDIA

Step 3 Calculate the balancing figure on the **side with the lower total**. In this case, in the credit column, put in £(13,300 – 3,600) = £9,700. Describe this as the **balance carried down** (balance c/d).

Cash

Details	Amount £	Details	Amount £
Capital	10,000	Purchases	1,000
Sales	1,500	Rent	600
Sales ledger control	1,800	Drawings	500
		Purchases ledger control	1,500
		Balance c/d	**9,700**
Total	13,300	Total	13,300

Step 4 Show this balancing figure on the opposite side, below the totals line, and describe this figure as the balance brought down (balance b/d).

Cash

Details	Amount £	Details	Amount £
Capital	10,000	Purchases	1,000
Sales	1,500	Rent	600
Sales ledger control	1,800	Drawings	500
		Purchases ledger control	1,500
		Balance c/d	9,700
Total	13,300	Total	13,300
Balance b/d	**9,700**		

The brought down balance is showing us that we have an asset (a debit balance) of £9,700 of cash in the cash account. In the next period, we open up the cash account with a balance b/f of £9,700.

Now we will balance all the other accounts for Ben Charles in the same way.

Capital account

Details	Amount £	Details	Amount £
Balance c/d	10,000	Cash	10,000
Total	10,000	Total	10,000
		Balance b/d	10,000

The balance b/d is on the credit side, which makes sense because capital is a credit balance. This shows there is capital of £10,000 at the period end.

Sales

Details	Amount £	Details	Amount £
		Cash	1,500
Balance c/d	3,300	Sales ledger control	1,800
Total	3,300	Total	3,300
		Balance b/d	3,300

This shows that sales totalled £3,300 in the period. The balance b/d is on the credit side, which makes sense because income is a credit balance.

Purchases

Details	Amount £	Details	Amount £
Cash	1,000		
Trade payables	2,000	Balance c/d	3,000
Total	3,000	Total	3,000
Balance b/d	3,000		

This shows that purchases totalled £3,000 in the period. The balance is on the debit side, which makes sense because expenses are debit balances.

Rent

Details	Amount £	Details	Amount £
Cash	600	Balance c/d	600
Total	600	Total	600
Balance b/d	600		

This shows that the rent expense for the period was £600.

Drawings

Details	Amount £	Details	Amount £
Cash	500	Balance c/d	500
Total	500	Total	500
Balance b/d	500		

This shows that the owner's drawings (ie Ben's drawings) for the period totalled £500.

Purchases ledger control

Details	Amount £	Details	Amount £
Cash	1,500	Purchases	2,000
Balance c/d	500		
Total	2,000	Total	2,000
		Balance b/d	500

The balance b/d is on the credit side of the account, showing that the balance is a liability. This shows that Ben still owes his credit supplier £500 at the end of the period.

Sales ledger control

Details	Amount £	Details	Amount £
Sales	1,800	Cash	1,800
		Balance c/d	0
Total	1,800	Total	1,800
Balance b/d	0		

This shows that Ben's credit customer owes nothing at the end of the period.

Assessment focus point

In your assessment you are highly likely to be asked to balance off an account. Try the following activities to make sure you know how to do it.

Activity 1: Balancing off

The following information has been posted to the cash account below.

Balance off the cash account to determine the amount of cash held at the end of January.

Cash

Details	Amount £	Details	Amount £
Sales	500	Purchases	300
Sales	500	Telephone	50

Activity 2: Balancing off ledger accounts 1

Using the accounts for Hampton that were prepared in Chapter 6, balance off the ledger accounts. Show both the balance carried down and the balance brought down.

GENERAL LEDGER

Bank

Details	Amount £	Details	Amount £
Capital	20,000	Purchases	250
		Rent	225
		Rates	135

Capital

Details	Amount £	Details	Amount £
		Bank	20,000

Purchases

Details	Amount £	Details	Amount £
Bank	250		
Purchases ledger control	450		

Rent

Details	Amount £	Details	Amount £
Bank	225		

Sales

Details	Amount £	Details	Amount £
		Cash	657
		Sales ledger control	750

Cash

Details	Amount £	Details	Amount £
Sales	657	Wages	75

Rates

Details	Amount £	Details	Amount £
Bank	135		

Sales ledger control

Details	Amount £	Details	Amount £
Sales	750		

Purchases ledger control

Details	Amount £	Details	Amount £
		Purchases	450

Wages

Details	Amount £	Details	Amount £
Cash	75		

If we include **dates** in the ledger accounts, the date of the balance brought down is **one day after** the date of the balance carried down.

Activity 3: Balancing off ledger accounts 2

The following two accounts are in the general ledger at the close of business on 31 August.

Required

Use the picklist below to:

(a) **Insert the balance carried down together with date and details**

(b) **Insert the totals**

(c) **Insert the balance brought down together with date and details**

Electricity

Date 20XX	Details	Amount £	Date 20XX	Details		Amount £
01 Aug	Balance b/f	4,265			▼	
25 Aug	Bank	245			▼	
	Total			Total		
		▼			▼	

Discounts allowed

Date 20XX	Details	Amount £	Date 20XX	Details		Amount £
01 Aug	Balance b/f	2,500			▼	
22 Aug	Sales ledger control	300			▼	
	Total			Total		
	▼				▼	

Picklist:

Balance b/d
Balance c/d
Bank
Discounts allowed
Electricity
Sales ledger control

3 Subsidiary ledgers: sales and purchases ledgers

The ledger accounts that we have been considering so far in this chapter are all kept together in one **ledger** known as the **general ledger**.

There are also two other types of ledger, known as the **subsidiary ledgers**. These are the **sales ledger** and the **purchases ledger**, which we looked at briefly in Chapter 2.

The big difference between the general ledger and the subsidiary ledgers is that **no double entry** takes place in the subsidiary ledgers. The accounts in the sales ledger and the purchases ledger are not part of the double entry system of the general ledger, but completely separate 'memorandum' accounts. They just give information.

We have already come across the sales ledger and purchases ledger in previous chapters. Remember that:

- The **sales ledger** is a collection of ledger accounts for each individual credit customer of the business

- The **purchases ledger** is a collection of ledger accounts for each individual credit supplier of the business

Illustration 2: Recording information in the sales ledger

A business makes a sale of £400 on credit to Horwich Ltd (invoice 452).

The double entry in the general ledger for a sale on credit is:

- Credit the sales account
- Debit the sales ledger control account

Therefore the double entry in the general ledger accounts will be as follows:

GENERAL LEDGER

Sales

Details	£	Details	£
		Sales ledger control	400

Sales ledger control

Details	£	Details	£
Sales	400		

The entry in the sales ledger would be as follows:

SALES LEDGER

Horwich

Details	£	Details	£
Invoice 452	400		

Now suppose that £300 is received from Horwich via BACS.

In the general ledger, money into the bank means a debit to the bank account and a credit to the sales ledger control account. In the sales ledger the individual account will also be credited with the amount received:

General ledger

Bank

Details	£	Details	£
Sales ledger control	300		

Sales ledger control

Details	£	Details	£
Sales	400	Bank	300

Sales ledger

Horwich

Details	£	Details	£
Invoice 452	400	Bank – BACS	300

You can see that, when an entry is made in the sales ledger control account, an entry is also made in the customer's individual account in the sales ledger. The same is true of the purchases ledger control account and the supplier's individual account in the purchases ledger.

Activity 4: Recording transactions in the sales and purchases ledgers

The following two transactions have been entered into the general ledger as follows:

- Sold goods on credit to a customer, J Henry, for £750 (invoice 346)

Account name	Amount £	Debit ✓	Credit ✓
Sales ledger control	750	✓	
Sales	750		✓

- Bought goods for resale on credit from C Bableton for £450 (invoice 8801)

Account name	Amount £	Debit ✓	Credit ✓
Purchases	450	✓	
Purchases ledger control	450		✓

Enter these transactions into the sales ledger and the purchases ledger.

SALES LEDGER

J Henry

Details	Amount £	Details	Amount £

PURCHASES LEDGER

C Bableton

Details	Amount £	Details	Amount £

4 The accounting equation

In Chapter 4, we introduced the **accounting equation** when we looked at the statement of financial position:

Assets – Liabilities = Capital

The equation can also be rearranged. For example:

Assets = Liabilities + Capital

Assets – Capital = Liabilities

Double entry bookkeeping, and therefore financial accounting, is based on the accounting equation.

Illustration 3: The accounting equation

Nicholas has the following statement of financial position as at 31 March 20XX:

	£
ASSETS	
Current assets	
Inventories	5,000
Trade receivables	15,000
Total assets	20,000
LIABILITIES	
Current liabilities	
Bank overdraft	8,000
Trade payables	5,000
	13,000
Net current assets	7,000
Net assets	7,000
CAPITAL	
Capital	5,000
Profit	4,000
Less drawings	(2,000)
Total capital	7,000

Expressing this as the accounting equation:

Assets   –   Liabilities   =   Capital
£20,000   –   £13,000   =   £7,000

Assessment focus point

The following activities show some of the ways the accounting equation could be tested in your assessment.

Activity 5: Accounting equation

Required

(a) Are the following statements true or false?

	True ✓	False ✓
Assets plus capital = liabilities		
Capital plus liabilities = assets		
Capital = assets plus liabilities		

(b) Insert the correct answer to each of the following questions.

Question	Answer £
If liabilities total £36,000 and capital totals £84,000, what is the amount of assets?	
If assets total £80,000 and liabilities total £64,000, what is the amount of capital?	
If capital totals £56,000 and assets total £108,000, what is the amount of liabilities?	

Activity 6: Accounting equation – J Emerald

Silver started a new business, J Emerald, on 1 October with the following assets and liabilities.

Assets and liabilities	£
Motor vehicle	30,400
Loan from bank	15,000
Inventories	11,200
Cash at bank	4,520

Required

(a) **Show the accounting equation on 1 October by inserting the appropriate figures.**

Assets £	Liabilities £	Capital £

On 8 October the new business had the following assets and liabilities.

Assets and liabilities	£
Motor vehicle	30,400
Loan from bank	15,000
Inventories	9,500
Cash at bank	5,200
Trade receivables	7,650
Trade payables	1,530

(b) **Show the accounting equation on 8 October by inserting the appropriate figures.**

Assets £	Liabilities £	Capital £

5 Capital and revenue transactions

Most of the payments that businesses make are for goods for manufacture or to resell, or for the day-to-day expenses of the business. However, on occasions there may be other types of payment.

Activity 7: Capital and revenue expenditure

Required

Give examples of the different types of expenditure (purchases) a business may incur.

The above types of expenditure will fall into one of two categories.

Type	Detail
Revenue expenditure	These are the ongoing expenses which the business must incur to operate its **day-to-day activities**. Examples include the purchase of goods for resale and bills such as rent, electricity and repairs to assets such as machinery. How much a business spends on these items will impact the level of profit it makes.
Capital expenditure	These are purchases of items that will be used in the business on a **continuing** basis. Examples include the purchase and/or improvement of machines, vehicles and office equipment. These are shown in the statement of financial position as non-current assets.

Likewise, income can be classified into one of two categories.

Type	Detail
Revenue income	The majority of a business's income will be generated from sales of goods or the provision of services. This will be classified as **revenue income**.
Capital income	Capital income includes receipts from: • Sales of non-current assets. For example property, plant and equipment. • Injections of cash (eg capital) by the owner of the business.

Activity 8: Capital and revenue income and expenditure

Required

Select one option in each instance below to show whether the item will be capital expenditure, revenue expenditure, capital income or revenue income.

	Capital expenditure ✓	Revenue expenditure ✓	Capital income ✓	Revenue income ✓
Purchase of raw materials that can be turned into goods for resale				
Receipt from the sale of an unused machine				
Sale of goods to a credit customer				
Purchase of a motor vehicle to be used by the sales director				

Chapter summary

- Balancing off the ledger accounts enables the business to know the balance on each account.

- The sales ledger and purchases ledger are subsidiary ledgers (not part of the general ledger) which contain a ledger account for each individual credit customer and credit supplier. They do not form part of the double entry system.

- The accounting equation is: assets – liabilities = capital. The accounting equation can be rearranged: assets = liabilities + capital, assets – capital = liabilities.

- It is important to distinguish between capital income and revenue income, and between capital expenditure and revenue expenditure.

Keywords

- **Balance carried down:** In the ledger account the term used to describe the balancing figure that makes the column with the smaller figure total the larger figure

- **Balance brought down:** The same figure as the balance carried down, but used on the opposite side of the account to the balance carried down; the balancing figure is described as the balance brought down

- **Capital expenditure:** On assets used in the long term ie in more than one period (non-current assets)

- **Capital income:** From sales of assets used in the long term

- **Revenue expenditure:** Payments for day-to-day running costs and purchases, including wages and interest paid to the bank

- **Revenue income:** Receipts from sales and other short-term income such as interest from the bank, rent and commission

- **Subsidiary ledgers:** The sales ledger and purchases ledger, which are memorandum ledgers that are not part of the general ledger, contain a ledger account for each individual credit customer or credit supplier. Not part of the double entry system

1 (a) **Complete the account below by:**

- **Inserting the balance carried down together with details.**
- **Inserting the totals.**
- **Inserting the balance brought down together with details.**

Sales ledger control

Details	£	Details	£
Sales	2,600	Bank	1,800
Sales	1,400	Bank	1,200
Sales	3,700	Bank	2,000
Sales	1,300	▼	
▼		▼	
Total		Total	
▼		▼	

Picklist:

Balance b/d
Balance c/d

(b) **What does the balance represent?**

Details	✓
The amount owed by credit customers	
The amount owed to credit customers	

2 The following account is in the general ledger at the close of day on 30 June.

Complete the account below by:

- **Inserting the balance carried down together with date and details.**
- **Inserting the totals.**
- **Inserting the balance brought down together with date and details.**

Sales ledger control

Date	Details	Amount £	Date	Details	Amount £
1 Jun	Balance b/d	1,209	28 Jun	Bank	3,287
30 Jun	Sales	6,298	30 Jun	Sales returns	786
▼	▼		▼	▼	
	Total			Total	
▼	▼		▼	▼	

Picklist:

1 Jul
30 Jun
Balance b/d
Balance c/d

3 A credit customer, James Daniels, buys goods from your business on credit for £1,000 including VAT (invoice 96) and later pays £800 by cheque. Record these transactions in his account in the sales ledger.

James Daniels

Details		£	Details		£
	▼			▼	
	▼			▼	

Picklist:

Bank
Cash
Invoice 96
Sales

4   Identify whether each of these items is capital expenditure, revenue expenditure, capital income or revenue income.

	Revenue expenditure ✓	Revenue income ✓	Capital expenditure ✓	Capital income ✓
Sale of goods to credit customers				
Cash sales				
Sale of delivery van				
Purchase of goods for resale				
Purchase of building				
Purchase of coffee for office from petty cash				

5   Which of the following is/are correct?

	✓
Capital = assets + liabilities	
Capital = liabilities − assets	
Assets = capital + liabilities	
Capital + assets = liabilities	

Maintaining the cash book

Learning outcomes

1.4	Demonstrate an understanding of the process of recording financial transactions
	• The role of the cash book: as a book of prime entry only, as a book of prime entry and as part of the double entry bookkeeping system
4.1	**Enter receipts and payments into a two-column analysed cash book**
	• The format of the cash book: date, details, cash, bank, analysis columns (including VAT)
	• The documents to use: direct debit/standing order schedule, remittance advice (including BACS), paying-in slip, cheque stub, cash receipt, receipts and payments listing
	• Calculate VAT amounts from net and total figures
	• Make entries in the cash book
4.3	**Total and balance the cash book and petty cash book**
	• Present totals and balances: column totals, balance carried down, balance brought down, debit balance, credit balance, date and details

Assessment context

In *Bookkeeping Transactions* we look at the two-column cash book in which the bank and cash are the main columns and VAT an analysis column. In the assessment, you may be required to complete the two-column cash book.

Qualification context

Completing the cash book is only studied in *Bookkeeping Transactions*. However, in subsequent units you will post the cash book totals to the ledgers. Therefore, it is important to understand this book of prime entry.

Business context

All businesses aim to utilise cash efficiently to help achieve the main objectives. Most transactions ultimately result in cash being received or paid, making the cash book one of the most important sources of accounting information.

Chapter overview

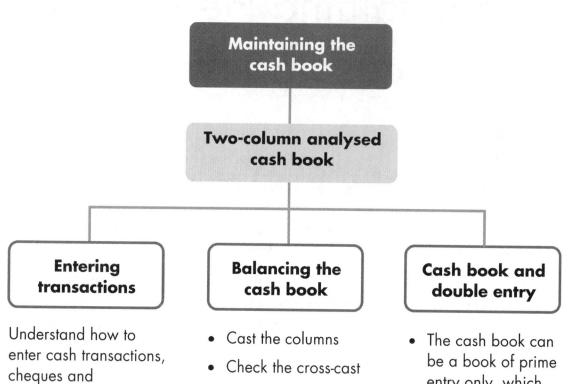

Maintaining the cash book

Two-column analysed cash book

Entering transactions

Understand how to enter cash transactions, cheques and automated receipts and payments

Balancing the cash book

- Cast the columns
- Check the cross-cast
- Reconcile the cash and bank totals with the analysis columns

Cash book and double entry

- The cash book can be a book of prime entry only, which means the cash and bank columns must be posted separately to the general ledger

- The cash book can be part of the double entry system, which means the cash and bank columns are not posted separately to the general ledger

Introduction

In Chapter 2 we saw a book of prime entry called the cash book. The cash book is vital for any business to ensure control over its cash, both when it is held on the premises (such as by a shop) and when it is in the bank account. In this chapter, we will look at how transactions are recorded in the cash book, and how the cash book is totalled and balanced off, and finally how the balances are posted to the general ledger.

1 The two-column cash book

The **cash book** is often referred to as the **two-column cash book** as there are two main columns:

- **Cash** – amount of money received or paid in cash

- **Bank** – amount of money received or paid through the bank (including **cheques**)

The other columns are **analysis** columns.

Having a cash book that contains columns for both cash and bank allows businesses to record all transactions properly, and therefore have control over them. It also enables transfers between the cash and bank account to be transparent.

The debit and credit side of the cash book combine to make one book.

> **Assessment focus point**
>
> In the assessment the cash book is often, though not always, split into the **cash book – debit side** (money in) and **cash book – credit side** (money out).

We will look at the format of the cash book and then enter transactions into the debit and credit sides.

Illustration 1: Cash book – debit side

Details	Cash £	Bank £	VAT £	Trade receivables £	Cash sales £	Sundry £
Balance b/f	400	1,000				
J Jones	600		100		500	
B Kindly		800		800		
Bank interest		100				100
F Feather		1,200		1,200		
I Glue	300		50		250	
Total	1,300	3,100	150	2,000	750	100

The cash book – debit side is the book used to record receipts into the business.

The figure in the 'Cash' column is the total (gross) amount of the receipt of notes and coin.

The figure in the 'Bank' column is the total (gross) amount of the receipts into the business's bank account, including cheques paid in.

The remaining columns are **analysis** columns.

The 'Trade receivables' column is the gross receipts from credit customers. When money is received from a **credit customer**, **no entry is made to the 'VAT'** column as the VAT was recorded when the original sales invoice was entered into the sales day book.

However, when **cash sales which include VAT** are made, the **VAT element** must be entered in the **VAT column**, and the net amount must be entered into the Cash sales column, so that the total of the Cash sales and VAT amounts is the figure in the Cash column.

The 'Sundry' column is the **net** amount of sundry income. The VAT element of sundry income is entered in the VAT column, if applicable.

Illustration 2: Cash book – credit side

Details	Cash £	Bank £	VAT £	Trade payables £	Cash purchases £	Sundry £
Mole Co		200				200
Adams	360		60		300	
Polly		3,000		3,000		
Oscar		4,000		4,000		
Fishers	90		15		75	
Total	450	7,200	75	7,000	375	200

There are many similarities between the cash book – credit side and the cash book – debit side.

The figure in the 'Cash' column is the total amount of the payments of notes and coin.

The figure in the 'Bank' column is the total value of the payments leaving the bank account by cheque, debit card or automated payment.

The remaining columns are **analysis** columns.

The 'Trade payables' column is the total amount paid to **credit suppliers**. When a payment is made to a credit supplier **no entry is made to the 'VAT'** column as the VAT was recorded when the original purchase invoice was entered into the purchases day book.

However, when **cash purchases** are made on which VAT is charged the **VAT element** is recorded in the **VAT column**, and the net amount is recorded in the 'Cash purchases' column, so that the total of the Cash purchases and VAT amounts is the figure in the Cash column.

The 'Sundry' column is the **net** amount of sundry expenses. The VAT element of sundry expenses is entered in the VAT column, if applicable.

Illustration 3: Cash book as one combined book

| | Debit side | | | | | | Credit side | | | | |
Details	Cash £	Bank £	VAT £	Trade receivables £	Cash sales £	Details	Cash £	Bank £	VAT £	Trade payables £	Cash purchases £
Balance b/f	400	1,000									
Bode	600		100		500	Right Ltd	360		60		300
Sarah		800		800		Tween		3,000		3,000	
Brook Co		1,200		1,200		MGNA		4,000		4,000	
Little	300		50		250	Aiden	90		15		75
Total	1,300	3,000	150	2,000	750	Total	450	7,000	75	7,000	375

The cash book above is simply the credit and debit sides of the cash book combined. There could also be additional analysis columns, such as 'Sundry', which we have not included here.

2 Documents used to update the cash book

When a transaction occurs, most businesses will not immediately record it in the cash book. Instead, they maintain **primary records** which **are financial documents** that are used to update the cash book on a regular basis.

The documents used to update the cash book include:

Receipts

- Cash receipts
- Paying-in slips
- Remittance advice notes
- Receipts listing (including list of automated receipts)

Payments

- Cheque book stubs
- Direct debit schedule
- Standing order schedule
- Remittance advice notes
- Payments listing (including list of automated payments)

These documents will be covered in detail in the *Bookkeeping Controls* course. For *Bookkeeping Transactions* you just need to be aware of them and that they are used to update the cash book.

2.1 Cheque book stub

A typical cheque and its **cheque book stub** (the part of the document that is retained by the business when writing out the cheque, as its primary record) is shown below, together with an indication of what each of the details on the face of the cheque means.

Illustration 4: Cheque

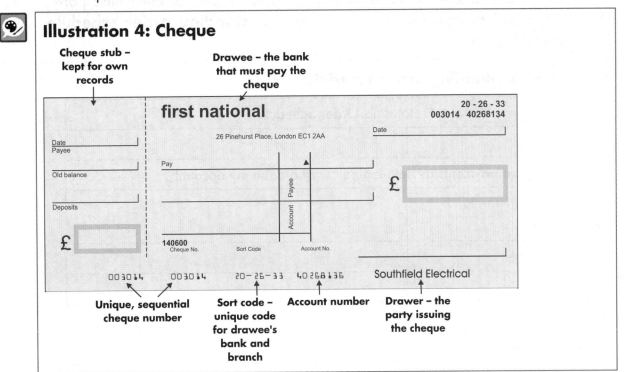

2.2 Paying-in slip stub

A typical paying-in slip plus the **paying-in slip stub** (to the left) is shown below.

Illustration 5: Paying-in slip

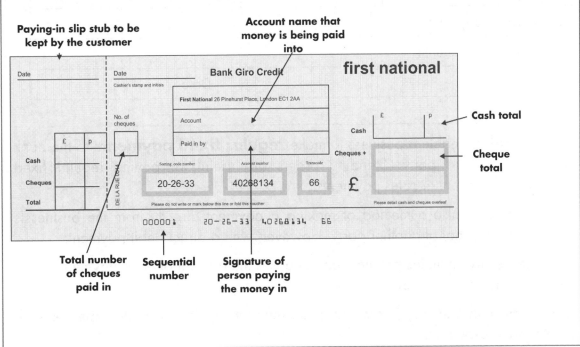

2.3 Standing order and direct debit schedule

Standing orders and **direct debits** are automated payments made through the bank.

A **standing order** is a method of making the same regular payment directly from a business's bank account to the bank account of a supplier or other third party. This is organised through the bank by filling in a **standing order schedule** (either paper or online).

Illustration 6: Standing order schedule

Standing Order Schedule		
To		
Please make the payments as detailed below and debit my account:		
Name of account to be debited		
Account number		
Payee details		
Name of payee		
Bank of payee		
Sort code of payee		
Account number of payee		
Amount of payment (in words)	£	
Date of first payment		
Frequency of payment		
Continue payments until		
Signature	Date	

Standing orders enable a business to make **regular fixed payments** to the bank account of a third party. Standing orders are useful for paying regular fixed amounts such as rent or rates payments.

Direct debit is also a method of making a payment directly from the business's bank account to that of another party. However, with a direct debit payment:

(a) The receiver initiates payment and chooses the amount of each payment

(b) The payments can vary in amount

As the payments can vary in amount, it is useful for regular, variable expenses such as telephone expenses.

To set up a direct debit the business must complete a **direct debit mandate**. This instructs its bank to pay the amounts the receiver asks for, on the dates the receiver requests payment.

Illustration 7: Direct debit mandate

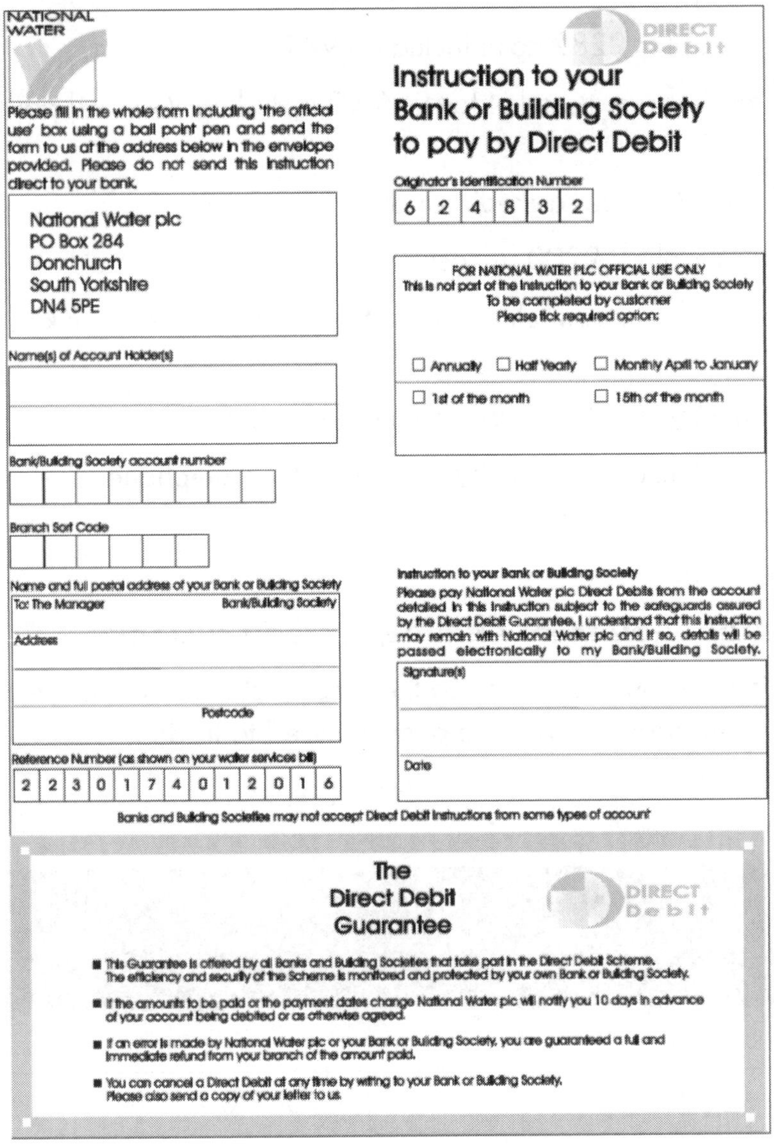
NATIONAL WATER

DIRECT Debit

Instruction to your Bank or Building Society to pay by Direct Debit

Please fill in the whole form including 'the official use' box using a ball point pen and send the form to us at the address below in the envelope provided. Please do not send this Instruction direct to your bank.

National Water plc
PO Box 284
Donchurch
South Yorkshire
DN4 5PE

Originator's Identification Number: 6 2 4 8 3 2

FOR NATIONAL WATER PLC OFFICIAL USE ONLY
This is not part of the Instruction to your Bank or Building Society
To be completed by customer
Please tick required option:

☐ Annually ☐ Half Yearly ☐ Monthly April to January
☐ 1st of the month ☐ 15th of the month

Name(s) of Account Holder(s)

Bank/Building Society account number

Branch Sort Code

Name and full postal address of your Bank or Building Society
To: The Manager Bank/Building Society
Address
Postcode

Reference Number (as shown on your water services bill): 2 2 3 0 1 7 4 0 1 2 0 1 6

Instruction to your Bank or Building Society
Please pay National Water plc Direct Debits from the account detailed in this Instruction subject to the safeguards assured by the Direct Debit Guarantee. I understand that this Instruction may remain with National Water plc and if so, details will be passed electronically to my Bank/Building Society.

Signature(s)

Date

Banks and Building Societies may not accept Direct Debit Instructions from some types of account

The Direct Debit Guarantee

- This Guarantee is offered by all Banks and Building Societies that take part in the Direct Debit Scheme. The efficiency and security of the Scheme is monitored and protected by your own Bank or Building Society.
- If the amounts to be paid or the payment dates change National Water plc will notify you 10 days in advance of your account being debited or as otherwise agreed.
- If an error is made by National Water plc or your Bank or Building Society, you are guaranteed a full and immediate refund from your branch of the amount paid.
- You can cancel a Direct Debit at any time by writing to your Bank or Building Society. Please also send a copy of your letter to us.

Businesses must keep an up-to-date **schedule of standing orders and direct debits** to check that the figures appearing on the bank statement are valid payments. This schedule is a primary record used to update the cash book.

3 Writing up the cash book

Now we have seen the format of the cash book, we will look at how transactions are entered into it, using the following illustration.

Illustration 8: Entering transactions into the two-column cash book

Zoe runs her own business and is registered for VAT. At the start of the day on 21 May, Zoe has £100 in cash and £850 in her bank account. Zoe makes the following transactions that day:

(1) Receives a cheque for £450 from Antoine, a credit customer

(2) Sells some goods to Bazzer for £282 cash including VAT

(3) Buys some goods for resale from a market for £56.40 including VAT and pays in cash

(4) Sends a cheque for £60 to Charlie, a credit supplier

(5) Pays Desmond, a credit supplier, £200 in cash

(6) Receives an automated payment from Ellie, a credit customer, into the bank account for £750

(7) Makes a payment of £40 by standing order for business rates

(8) Makes a payment of £36 (including VAT) by direct debit for telephone expenses

Let's take each transaction in turn.

(1) Receives a cheque for £450 from Antoine, a credit customer

This is treated as a receipt into the bank account, so the amount should be recorded in the **bank** column of the cash book – debit side and analysed to trade receivables.

Cash book – debit side

Details	Cash £	Bank £	VAT £	Cash sales £	Trade receivables £	Sundry income £
Balance b/f	100.00	850.00				
Antoine		450.00			450.00	

(2) Sells some goods to Bazzer for £282 cash including VAT

This is not a receipt straight into the bank account and so the gross amount is recorded in the **cash** column. It is analysed to **sales** (net amount: £282 × 100/120 = £235) and VAT (£282 × 20/120 = £47) in the cash book – debit side.

Cash book – debit side

Details	Cash £	Bank £	VAT £	Cash sales £	Trade receivables £	Sundry income £
Balance b/f	100.00	850.00				
Antoine		450.00			450.00	
Bazzer	282.00		47.00	235.00		

(3) Buys some goods for resale from a market for £56.40 including VAT and pays in cash

This gross amount is recorded in the **cash** column of the **credit side** of the cash book (as it is cash paid **out** of the business), and analysed to purchases (£56.40 × 100/120 = £47.00) and VAT (£56.40 × 20/120 = £9.40).

Cash book – credit side

Details	Cash £	Bank £	VAT £	Cash purchases £	Trade payables £	Sundry expenses £
Market	56.40		9.40	47.00		

(4) Sends a cheque for £60 to Charlie, a credit supplier

Writing out a cheque means that the money will come straight out of Zoe's bank account, so it is recorded in the **bank** column of the cash book – credit side.

Cash book – credit side

Details	Cash £	Bank £	VAT £	Cash purchases £	Trade payables £	Sundry expenses £
Market	56.40		9.40	47.00		
Charlie		60.00			60.00	

(5) Pays Desmond, a credit supplier, £200 in cash

This is again a payment out of cash, so we record this in the **cash** column on the credit side and analyse it to trade payables.

Cash book – credit side

Details	Cash £	Bank £	VAT £	Cash purchases £	Trade payables £	Sundry expenses £
Market	56.40		9.40	47.00		
Charlie		60.00			60.00	
Desmond	200.00				200.00	

(6) Receives an automated payment from Ellie, a credit customer, into the bank account for £750

The automated payment means that the money comes straight into Zoe's bank account. It is recorded in the **bank** column on the debit side and analysed to trade receivables.

Cash book – debit side

Details	Cash £	Bank £	VAT £	Cash sales £	Trade receivables £	Sundry income £
Balance b/f	100.00	850.00				
Antoine		450.00			450.00	
Bazzer	282.00		47.00	235.00		
Ellie		750.00			750.00	

(7) Makes a payment of £40 by standing order for business rates

A standing order payment means that the money comes straight out of Zoe's bank account. It is recorded in the **bank** column on the credit side and analysed in the expenses column.

Cash book – credit side

Details	Cash £	Bank £	VAT £	Cash purchases £	Trade payables £	Sundry expenses £
Market	56.40		9.40	47.00		
Charlie		60.00			60.00	
Desmond	200.00				200.00	
Rates		40.00				40.00

(8) Makes a payment of £36 (including VAT) by direct debit for telephone expenses

A direct debit payment means that the money comes straight out of Zoe's bank account. It is recorded in the **bank** column on the credit side. The VAT amount (36/6 = £6) is recorded in the VAT column and the net amount is analysed in the expenses column (£36 – £6 = £30).

Cash book – credit side

Details	Cash £	Bank £	VAT £	Cash purchases £	Trade payables £	Sundry expenses £
Market	56.40		9.40	47.00		
Charlie		60.00			60.00	
Desmond	200.00				200.00	
Rates		40.00				40.00
Telephone		36.00	6.00			30.00

Zoe can check the standing order and direct debit against her standing order and direct debit schedule.

Standing order and direct debit schedule

Date	Item	Detail	Company	Amount £
21 May	Standing order	Business rates	Trafford Council	40.00
Around 21st of each month*	Direct debit	Telephone	Tele Comm	Unknown**

* The date a direct debit is taken can vary, but the business will usually know the approximate date.

** The amount of the direct debit can vary each month.

Now try the following activities.

Activity 1: Cash book – debit side

There are four receipts to be entered in the debit side of the cash book during one week.

Cash sales listing

Customers paid in cash	Net £	VAT £	Gross £
Bumble	500	100	600
Ryan	140	28	168

Trade receivables listing

Credit customers paid by cheque	Amount paid £
AET	425
Elaine	5,600

Required

Record these transactions in the cash book – debit side.

Cash book – debit side

Details	Cash £	Bank £	VAT £	Trade receivables £	Cash sales £
▼					
▼					
▼					
▼					

Picklist:

AET
Bumble
Elaine
Ryan

Activity 2: Cash book – credit side

There are four payments to be entered in the credit side of the cash book during one week.

Cash purchases listing

Suppliers paid in cash	Net £	VAT £	Gross £
Daniel	130	26	156
Edgar	480	96	576

Trade payables listing

Credit suppliers paid by cheque	Amount paid £
Graham	150
Isaac	300

Required

Record these transactions in the cash book – credit side.

Cash book – credit side

Details	Cash £	Bank £	VAT £	Trade payables £	Cash purchases £
▼					
▼					
▼					
▼					

Picklist:

Daniel
Edgar
Graham
Isaac

4 Casting and cross-casting the cash book

In the examples seen so far, we have entered bank and cash receipts and payments in the cash book. However, for a business to be able to monitor and control the amount of money it has, both in the cash tills and in the bank account, the cash book should be totalled. This totalling process is also known as **casting**.

When casting any day book it is very easy to make errors in your additions. Therefore it is always advisable to **cross-cast** the day book as well. This means adding the analysis column totals to ensure that it adds back to the total column – if it does not then an error has been made. Once the day book has been cast and cross-cast the relevant amounts can be posted to the general ledger.

The next illustration shows how to cast and cross-cast the cash book.

Illustration 9: Casting and cross-casting the cash book

Taking Zoe's cash book from Illustration 7, we cast each column and ensure that, for each side of the cash book, the analysis columns added together are the same as the totals for the two cash and bank columns, **ignoring any balance brought forward**.

Step 1   Cast each column in the debit side of the cash book.

Cash book – debit side

Details	Cash £	Bank £	VAT £	Cash sales £	Trade receivables £	Sundry income £
Balance b/f	100.00	850.00				
Antoine		450.00			450.00	
Bazzer	282.00		47.00	235.00		
Ellie		750.00			750.00	
Totals	382.00	2,050.00	47.00	235.00	1,200.00	

Step 2 Cross-cast the cash book – debit side, making sure the brought forward balances are deducted from the cash and bank totals (so that they are not double counted in the totals).

Detail	£
Cash total	382.00
Less cash balance b/f	(100.00)
Bank receipts total	2,050.00
Less bank balance b/f	(850.00)
	1,482.00
VAT	47.00
Cash sales	235.00
Trade receivables	1,200.00
	1,482.00

Step 3 Cast each column in the cash book on the credit side.

Cash book – credit side

Details	Cash £	Bank £	VAT £	Cash purchases £	Trade payables £	Sundry expenses £
Market	56.40		9.40	47.00		
Charlie		60.00			60.00	
Desmond	200.00				200.00	
Rates		40.00				40.00
Telephone		36.00	6.00			30.00
Totals	256.40	136.00	15.40	47.00	260.00	70.00

Step 4 Cross-cast the cash book – credit side making sure any brought forward balances (there are none here) are deducted from the cash and bank totals.

Details	£
Cash total	256.40
Bank total	136.00
	392.40
VAT	15.40
Cash purchases	47.00
Trade payables	260.00
Sundry expenses	70.00
	392.40

Activity 3: Cash book – checking the cross-cast

There are four receipts to be entered in the debit side of Orion's cash book during one week.

Cash sales listing

Customers paid in cash	Net £	VAT £	Gross £
James	450	90	540
Pollard	205	41	246

Trade receivables listing

Credit customers paid by cheque	Amount paid £
Harvey	456
Rudson	2,055

(a) **Enter the details into the debit side of the cash book and total each column.**

Cash book – debit side

Details		Cash £	Bank £	VAT £	Trade receivables £	Cash sales £
Balance b/f		1,500				
	▼					
	▼					
	▼					
	▼					
Total						

Picklist:

Harvey
James
Pollard
Rudson

(b) **Check the cross-cast of the cash book – debit side.**

Cross-cast of cash book – debit side

Details	Amount £
Cash	
Less cash balance b/f	
Bank	
VAT	
Trade receivables	
Cash sales	

There are four payments to be entered in the credit side of the cash book during one week.

Cash purchases listing

Suppliers paid in cash	Net £	VAT £	Gross £
Horne	150	30	180
Meddly	50	10	60

Trade payables listing

Credit suppliers paid by cheque	Amount paid £
Adam	635
Timmons	4,600

(c) **Enter the details into the credit side of the cash book and total each column.**

Cash book – credit side

Details	Cash £	Bank £	VAT £	Trade payables £	Cash purchases £
Balance b/f		1,100			
▼					
▼					
▼					
▼					
Total					

Picklist:

Adam
Horne
Meddly
Timmons

(d) Check the cross-cast of the cash book – credit side.

Cross-cast of cash book – credit side

Details	Amount £
Cash	
Bank	
Less bank balance b/f	
VAT	
Trade payables	
Cash purchases	

4.1 Calculating the cash balance

A business will want to know the amount of cash it has both as cash in hand and in the bank. This can be calculated by subtracting the total cash or bank balance from the cash book – credit side from the total cash or bank balance from the cash book – debit side. This is best demonstrated with an illustration.

Illustration 10: Cash and bank balances

The totals from Zoe's cash book in Illustration 9 are shown below.

Cash book – debit side

Details	Cash £	Bank £	VAT £	Cash sales £	Trade receivables £	Sundry income £
Totals	382.00	2,050.00	47.00	235.00	1,200.00	

Cash book – credit side

Details	Cash £	Bank £	VAT £	Cash purchases £	Trade payables £	Sundry expenses £
Totals	256.40	136.00	15.40	47.00	260.00	70.00

Zoe's total amount of **cash** is calculated as

Cash	£
Total debits	382.00
Total credits	(256.40)
Cash total	125.60

Zoe's total **bank balance** is calculated as

Bank	£
Total debits	2,050.00
Total credits	(136.00)
Bank balance	1,914.00

A **positive** bank balance means that the business has an **asset** at the bank. A **negative** bank balance means that the business has an overdrawn bank balance (ie an **overdraft**), which is a **liability** to the bank.

The cash balance can only either be an **asset** (if it is a positive balance) or **nil**, if we have no cash. This is because we are dealing with actual notes and coin on the premises.

Assessment focus point

The next activity is similar to what you could expect to see in your assessment.

Activity 4: Maintaining and using the cash book

There are five payments to be entered in Jeremy Jackson's cash book.

Receipts

Received cash with thanks for goods bought. From Jeremy Jackson, a customer without a credit account. Net £160 VAT £32 Total £192 E Frank	Received cash with thanks for goods bought. From Jeremy Jackson, a customer without a credit account. Net £320 VAT £64 Total £384 G Jacob	Received cash with thanks for goods bought. From Jeremy Jackson, a customer without a credit account. Net £450 (No VAT) I Knight

Cheque book stubs

Pollard Ltd	Sure Motor Repairs
(Purchases ledger account FRA006)	(We have no credit account with this supplier)
£3,000	£96 including VAT
000168	000169

(a) Enter the details from the three receipts and two cheque book stubs into the credit side of the cash book shown below and total each column.

Cash book – credit side

Details	Cash £	Bank £	VAT £	Trade payables £	Cash purchases £	Motor expenses £
Balance b/f		6,600				
▼						
▼						
▼						
▼						
▼						
Total						

Picklist:

E Frank
G Jacob
I Knight
Pollard Ltd
Sure Motor Repairs

There are two automated receipts from credit customers to be entered in Jeremy Jackson's cash book:

K Rowlands £683
L Baldwin £476

(b) Enter the above details into the debit side of the cash book and total each column.

Cash book – debit side

Details		Cash £	Bank £	Trade receivables £
Balance b/f		1,256		
	▼			
	▼			
Total				

Picklist:

K Rowlands
L Baldwin

(c) Using your answers to (a) and (b) above, calculate the cash balance.

£ _____

(d) Using your answers to (a) and (b) above, calculate the bank balance. Use a minus sign if your calculations indicate an overdrawn bank balance, eg –123.

£ _____

(e) Will the bank balance calculated in (d) above be a debit or credit balance?

Debit/Credit

---

5 Posting the cash book to the general ledger

Once the cash book has been written up and totalled, the totals must be posted to the ledger accounts. The principles of this will be introduced in this section and then developed in later chapters.

An important difference between the cash book and other books of prime entry is that it can either be a book of prime entry **only**, or it can be **both** a book of prime entry **and** part of the general ledger.

5.1 Posting the cash book – book of prime entry only

If the cash book is a book of prime entry only, the totals of the cash and bank columns in the cash book will need to be posted to the cash account and bank account in the general ledger.

There will be a separate cash account and a separate bank account in the general ledger.

The tables below show where each of the columns in the cash book is posted in the general ledger.

Cash book – debit side

Cash £	Bank £	VAT £	Trade receivables £	Cash sales £	Sundry £
Post as a **debit** entry to cash account in the general ledger	Post as a **debit** entry to bank account in the general ledger	Post as **credit** entries to the relevant general ledger accounts			

Cash book – credit side

Cash £	Bank £	VAT £	Trade payables £	Cash purchases £	Sundry £
Post as a **credit** entry to cash account in the general ledger	Post as a **credit** entry to bank account in the general ledger	Post as **debit** entries to the relevant general ledger accounts			

5.2 Posting the cash book - part of the general ledger

In many businesses the cash book is treated as **both** a book of prime entry **and** part of the general ledger. This means that for **receipts**, the cash book is itself the debit side of the cash account and of the bank account in the general ledger, and for payments, the cash book is the credit side of the cash account and of the bank account in the general ledger.

The effect of this is that:

- There is no need to post debit and credit entries from the cash and bank columns to the general ledger

- There are no separate cash or bank control accounts in the general ledger

- The analysis columns are posted as normal

The tables below show where each of the columns in the cash book is posted in the general ledger if the cash book is both a book of prime entry and part of the general ledger.

Cash book – debit side

Cash £	Bank £	VAT £	Trade receivables £	Cash sales £	Sundry £
No posting required, as this is already the **debit** side of general ledger account for cash	No posting required, as this is already the **debit** side of general ledger account for bank	Post as **credit** entries to the general ledger accounts			

Cash book – credit side

Cash £	Bank £	VAT £	Trade payables £	Cash purchases £	Sundry £
No posting required, as this is already the **credit** side of general ledger account for cash	No posting required, as this is already the **credit** side of general ledger account for bank	Post as **debit** entries to the general ledger accounts			

Note that no separate posting has been made for the cash and bank columns. There is no need to post them to the general ledger as they are already included.

Assessment focus point

In your assessment it is likely that the information at the start of the assessment will say:

'The cash book and petty cash book should be treated as part of the double entry system unless the task instructions state otherwise.'

In practical terms this means that the cash and bank columns are already included in the general ledger. Therefore, if you are asked to make postings to the general ledger you will not need to post these columns as they will already be included. You will only need to post the other columns to the ledger.

However, task information may override this information to say:

'The cash book is a book of prime entry only.'

In this situation you need to post the cash and bank column totals to the ledgers, as well as posting the other columns.

5.3 Balancing off

If the cash book is part of the general ledger, we can balance off the cash book as we would any ledger account.

In the two-column cash book there are only two balances: for the cash account (cash in hand on the premises) and for the bank account.

The procedure for balancing off the cash book is the same as for any other general ledger account.

As we saw in Chapter 7, the steps to balance off a ledger account are:

Step 1 **Add up** the debit side and the credit side separately.

Step 2 Put the **largest** of the two totals as the column total for **both** the debit and credit columns.

Step 3 Calculate the **balancing figure** on the side with the lower total and describe this as the **balance carried down** (balance c/d).

Step 4 Show this balancing figure on the **opposite side**, below the totals line, and describe this figure as the **balance brought down** (balance b/d).

The only difference here is that we have two columns to balance off, the cash column and the bank column.

Unless it has a nil balance, the bank column may have either a debit or a credit balance brought down:

- A **debit balance brought down** means that the business has an **asset** at the bank; that is, it has a **positive bank balance**.

- A **credit balance brought down** means that the business has a **liability** to the bank; that is, it has a negative or **overdrawn bank balance**, or **overdraft**.

For the cash column there will only ever be either no balance or a debit balance because we are dealing with actual notes and coin on the premises.

Illustration 11: Balancing off the cash book

Returning to Zoe's cash book in Illustration 9 we will balance it off as follows:

- For the cash columns, the debit side total (£382.00) is greater than the credit side (£265.40), so the balance of £125.60 is carried down from the credit side to the debit side, where it is a **debit balance**.

- For the bank columns, the debit side total (£2,050.00) is greater than the credit side (£136.00), so the balance of £1,914.00 is carried down from the credit side to the debit side, where it is again a **debit balance**.

Cash book – debit side

Details	Cash £	Bank £	VAT £	Cash sales £	Trade receivables £	Sundry income £
Balance b/f	100.00	850.00				
Antoine		450.00			450.00	
Bazzer	282.00		47.00	235.00		
Ellie		750.00			750.00	
Totals	382.00	2,050.00	47.00	235.00	1,200.00	
Balance b/d	125.60	1,914.00				

Cash book – credit side

Details	Cash £	Bank £	VAT £	Cash purchases £	Trade payables £	Sundry expenses £
Market	56.40		9.40	47.00		
Charlie		60.00			60.00	
Desmond	200.00				200.00	
Rates		40.00				40.00
Telephone		36.00	6.00			30.00
Balance c/d	125.60	1,914.00				
Totals	~~256.40~~ 382.00	~~136.00~~ 2,050.00	15.40	47.00	260.00	70.00

As we have seen, the cash book can be a book of prime entry only, or it can be both a book of prime entry and part of the general ledger. We have also seen that the cash book can be presented as one combined book or as two separate books. The following illustration shows how the totals from a **combined** cash book that is **both** a book of prime entry **and** part of the general ledger are posted to the general ledger.

Assessment focus point

There was a question similar to Illustration 12 in both of the AAT sample assessments for *Bookkeeping Transactions*.

Illustration 12: Posting to the general ledger – combined cash book

The totals of Zoe's balanced-off cash book from Illustration 11 are shown below. The cash book is both a book of prime entry and part of the general ledger.

Cash book

Cash £	Bank £	VAT £	Cash sales £	Trade receivables £	Sundry income £	Cash £	Bank £	VAT £	Cash purchases £	Trade payables £	Sundry expenses £
382.00	2,050.00	47.00	235.00	1,200.00	0.00	382.00	2,050.00	15.40	47.00	260.00	70.00

Note the cash and bank totals on the debit side are **the same** as the cash and bank totals on the credit side because this cash book has been totalled and then **balanced off**.

To post these totals to the general ledger, we need to make the following entries:

Account name	Amount £	Debit ✓	Credit ✓
Sales ledger control	1,200.00		✓
Cash sales	235.00		✓
VAT	47.00		✓
Cash purchases	47.00	✓	
Purchases ledger control	260.00	✓	
Sundry expenses	70.00	✓	
VAT	15.40	✓	

The cash and bank totals do not need to be posted as they are already included in the general ledger.

Assessment focus point

The principles of posting to the general ledger introduced here will be expanded in the next two chapters. It is recommended that you study the next two chapters before attempting any assessment-style questions on this topic.

Chapter summary

- A two-column cash book includes a cash column and a bank column on each side, as well as analysis columns, and enables a business to fully record all transactions involving cash or the bank account.

- The cash book (debit side) is written up from cheques and cash received plus automated receipts.

- The cash book (credit side) is written up from the cheques and cash paid, and from the list of automated payments, including standing order and direct debit payments.

- Periodically, the cash book is cast and cross-cast to give the total receipts and payments for the period.

- The cash and bank balances can be found by subtracting the total credits for cash or bank from the total debits for cash or bank.

- The cash book is periodically posted to the general ledger. The cash book can be either a book of prime entry only, or it can be both a book of prime entry and part of the general ledger.

- If the cash book is a book of prime entry only, the cash and bank totals from the cash book – debit side and cash book – credit side are posted to the general ledger, along with the analysis columns.

- If the cash book is both a book of prime entry and part of the general ledger, only the analysis columns are posted to the general ledger.

- If the cash book is part of the general ledger, it can be balanced off in the same way as any other ledger account to give the cash and bank balances brought down.

BPP
LEARNING MEDIA

- **Casting:** An accounting term for adding up a column of figures

- **Cheque:** A customer's written order to their bank to pay a specified sum to a particular bank account

- **Cross-cast:** Adding up the totals of a number of columns to check that they add back to the overall total

- **Direct debit:** A method of making payments direct from the bank where payments are for variable amounts and/or varying time intervals

- **Overdraft:** A negative balance in the business's bank account, similar to a short-term loan as the business owes the bank that money; however, the bank can request payment of that money at any time

- **Primary records:** Receipts, invoices, remittances and other documents which are retained and used to update the cash book on a regular basis

- **Standing order:** Method of making regular payments directly from the bank account of the customer to the bank account of the supplier

- **Two-column cash book:** An analysed cash book containing cash and bank columns, plus analysis columns, including a VAT column

Test your learning

1   You work for Natural Productions. One of your duties is to write up the cash book. Natural Productions makes sales on credit to a number of credit customers and also has some cash sales from a small shop attached to the factory.

The cash and cheques received for the last week in January 20XX are given below. Note that all cheques are received from customers who have an account in the sales ledger.

23 Jan	£545.14 cheque from Hoppers Ltd
23 Jan	£116.70 cheque from Superior Products
24 Jan	£128.46 cash from cash sales including VAT
24 Jan	£367.20 automated payment from Esporta Leisure
25 Jan	£86.40 cash from cash sales including VAT
27 Jan	£706.64 cheque from Body Perfect
27 Jan	£58.80 cash from cash sales including VAT
27 Jan	£267.90 automated payment from Langans Beauty

You are required to:

(a)   Record these receipts in the cash book given below
(b)   Total the cash book and check that it cross-casts

Cash book – debit side

Date	Details	Cash £	Bank £	VAT £	Cash sales £	Trade receivables £

Cross-cast check:

	£
Trade receivables	
Cash sales	
VAT	
Total	
Cash receipts	
Bank receipts	
Total	

2   Most of the payments by Natural Productions are to credit suppliers but there are some cash purchases of materials from small suppliers, which include VAT.

The cheque payments and cash purchases (all of which include VAT) for the week ending 27 January 20XX are given below:

Date	Cheque number	Supplier	Amount £
23 Jan	002144	Trenter Ltd	1,110.09
23 Jan		Cash purchase	105.60
24 Jan	002145	W J Jones	246.75
24 Jan	002146	P J Phillips	789.60
24 Jan		Cash purchase	125.40
25 Jan	002147	Packing Supplies	305.45
26 Jan	002148	O & P Ltd	703.87
27 Jan		Cash purchase	96.00

You are required to:

(a)   Record these payments in the analysed cash book (credit side) given below
(b)   Total the credit side of the cash book and check that it cross-casts

Cash book – credit side

Date	Details	Cash £	Bank £	VAT £	Cash purchases £	Trade payables £

Cross-cast check:

	£
Trade payables	
Cash purchases	
VAT	
Total	
Cash payments	
Cheque payments	
Total	

3 There are five payments to be entered in Isdain Co's cash book.

Till receipts from suppliers for Isdain Co's cash purchases

Supplier: Klimt Supplies	**Supplier: Patel Trading**	**Supplier: TWE Ltd**
Received cash with thanks for goods bought.	Received cash with thanks for goods bought.	Received cash with thanks for goods bought.
Net £75 VAT £15 Total £90	Net £285 VAT £57 Total £342	Net £83 (No VAT)

Stubs from Isdain Co's cheque book

Payee: Western Industries (Purchases ledger account PL725) £4,278 Cheque number 256387	Payee: Mountebank Co For marketing leaflets (Isdain Co has no credit account with this supplier) £564 including VAT Cheque number 256388

(a) Enter the details of the three till receipts from suppliers and two cheque book stubs into the credit side of the cash book shown below. Total each column.

Cash book – credit side

Details	Cash £	Bank £	VAT £	Cash purchases £	Trade payables £	Marketing expenses £
Balance b/f		3,295				
Klimt Supplies						
Patel Trading						
TWE Ltd						
Western Industries						
Mountebank Co						
Total						

There are two automated payments received from credit customers to be entered in the cash book:

Vantage Ltd £1,278
Marbles Co £2,183

(b) Enter the above details into the debit side of the cash book and total each column.

Cash book – debit side

Details	Cash £	Bank £	Trade receivables £
Balance b/f	792		
Vantage Ltd			
Marbles Co			
Total			

(c) Using your answers to (a) and (b) above, calculate the cash balance.

£ [   ]

(d) Using your answers to (a) and (b) above, calculate the bank balance.

£ [   ]

(e) Is the bank balance calculated in (d) above a debit or credit balance?

	✓
Debit	
Credit	

Double entry for sales and trade receivables

Learning outcomes

1.2	Distinguish between prompt payment, trade and bulk discounts
	• How prompt payment discounts are recorded: discounts allowed or received account, sales or purchases ledger control account and VAT (value added tax) account in the general ledger
5.1	Transfer data from the books of prime entry to the ledgers
	• The books of prime entry: sales and sales returns daybooks, purchases and purchases returns daybooks, discounts allowed and discounts received daybooks, cash book, petty cash book
	• The ledgers: sales, purchases, general
	• That the sales and purchases ledger control accounts are part of the double entry system
	• Transfer data from books of prime entry to the relevant accounts in the ledgers
5.2	Total and balance ledger accounts
	• Total and balance ledger accounts: balance carried down, balance brought down, debit balance, credit balance

Assessment context

This chapter builds on your knowledge of double entry introduced in Chapters 6 and 7, focusing on recording sales and receivables in the general ledger. This topic is regularly tested in the assessment.

The assessment will test double entry directly in two different ways. You could be asked to complete T-accounts by selecting an account name from a picklist (choice of account names) and entering the correct amount in the debit or credit column. You will then have to balance the T-account and show the closing amount.

Alternatively, you could be asked to enter the information in tabular format by selecting account names from a picklist and entering the relevant amount and ticks to indicate debit or credit entries.

Qualification context

Double entry bookkeeping is introduced in *Bookkeeping Transactions* and then developed in the Level 2 *Bookkeeping Controls* and Level 3 *Advanced Bookkeeping* and *Final Accounts Preparation* courses. It is applied at Level 4 *Financial Statements of Limited Companies*.

Business context

Double entry is used to prepare financial statements which show the company's financial performance over the year and closing assets and liabilities. It is therefore essential in helping users of the financial statements to make business decisions.

Chapter overview

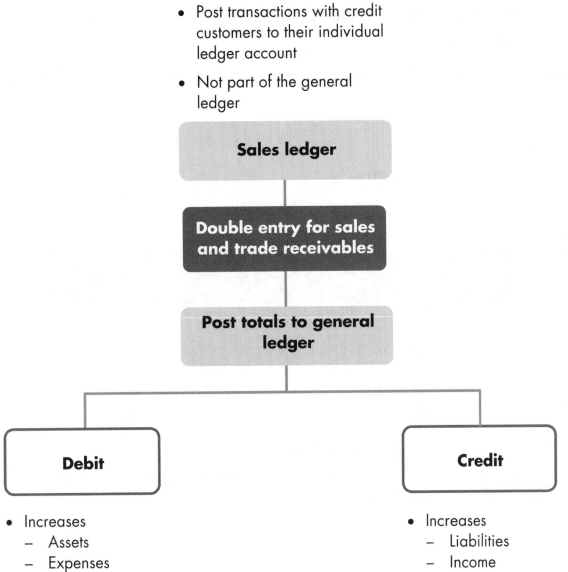

- Post transactions with credit customers to their individual ledger account
- Not part of the general ledger

Sales ledger

Double entry for sales and trade receivables

Post totals to general ledger

Debit

- Increases
  - Assets
  - Expenses
  - Drawings

Credit

- Increases
  - Liabilities
  - Income
  - Capital

Introduction

In this chapter we look at posting transactions for sales on credit recorded in the books of prime entry to the accounting records using double entry bookkeeping. We start off the chapter by recapping some of the basics of double entry and considering how this will be tested in your assessment.

1 Assessment focus: how double entry will be tested

There are two main ways in which knowledge of double entry is tested in the assessment:

- T-accounts
- Tabular format

1.1 Recap of T-accounts

As you saw in Chapter 6, this is a typical T-account:

Account name

Details	Amount £	Details	Amount £
▼		▼	
▼		▼	
▼		▼	
▼		▼	

To complete a T-account in your assessment:

(a) In the details column select the relevant **account name** from a drop down menu, known as a **picklist**

(b) Type the relevant **value** in the amounts column

(c) Balance off the T-account by **inserting totals** and showing the **balance carried down** (and also the **balance brought down** on the opposite side, if required)

1.2 Tabular format

The same knowledge of double entry may also be tested by completing a table. For example:

Account name	Amount £	Debit ✓	Credit ✓
▼			
▼			

To complete a tabular format question in your assessment, the approach is as follows:

(a) In the account name column select the relevant **account name** from a drop down menu, known as a **picklist**.

(b) Type the relevant **value** in the amounts column.

(c) Enter a **tick** in the debit or credit column as appropriate.

You will see plenty of examples of these formats in the remainder of the course.

2 Posting from the day books to the ledgers

In Chapters 6 and 7, we looked at double entry bookkeeping in the general ledger and the subsidiary sales and purchases ledgers for the transactions of a business. In those examples we entered each individual transaction directly into the ledger accounts.

However, in the real world, we have already entered each transaction into a book of prime entry, so there is no point then entering each transaction separately into the general ledger. Instead we enter the transactions into the books of prime entry and then enter the **totals** from the books of prime entry into the general ledger.

2.1 Accounting process

The first stage in the accounting process is to enter transactions into the books of prime entry.

TRANSACTION DOCUMENTS → BOOKS OF PRIME ENTRY → LEDGER ACCOUNTS

Four books of prime entry are relevant for sales and trade receivables:

- Invoices in respect of credit sales for a period are initially recorded in the **sales day book**.

- Credit notes in respect of credit sales are recorded in the **sales returns day book**.

- All receipts (including some that are not related to sales) are recorded in the **cash book – debit side**.

- Prompt payment discounts taken by credit customers are recorded in the **discounts allowed day book**.

The next stage in the accounting process is to **transfer** the details from the book of prime entry to the **accounting records**. In the case of the **sales day book**, this is to the:

- **Sales ledger** (where we will just be debiting the individual customer ledger accounts – the sales ledger is **not** part of the double entry bookkeeping system)

- General ledger (so we will be debiting the sales ledger control account and crediting the sales account).

It is common to refer to the process of transferring data into the ledgers as **posting** to the ledgers from the day books.

We will now look at the sales ledger and the sales ledger control account in more detail.

2.2 Subsidiary ledger: sales ledger

Key features of the sales ledger are that:

(a) It shows the business how much **each credit customer** owes it at any point in time.

(b) It is a separate **memorandum** ledger and not part of the double entry system. It is for information purposes only.

Illustration 1: Sales ledger

Stevenson Ltd sells to a credit customer named Jack & Co and maintains a sales ledger for this customer. This month it had four transactions with Jack & Co.

Jack & Co

Details	Amount £	Details	Amount £
Invoice 65	400	Credit note 45	150
Invoice 69	300	Bank	350

- Items on the debit side (left-hand side) increase the balance owed by the customer, eg invoices.
- Items on the credit side (right-hand side) decrease the balance owed by the customer, eg credit notes, prompt payment discounts, cash received.

2.3 Sales ledger control account

The **sales ledger control account** is an important **general ledger** account for sales, trade receivables and cash received.

Illustration 2: Sales ledger control account

Sales ledger control

Details	Amount £	Details	Amount £
Balance b/f	5,000	Bank	3,500
Sales	2,000	Sales returns	1,000
		Balance c/d	2,500
Total	7,000	Total	7,000
Balance b/d	2,500		

For a certain period (eg monthly) the sales ledger control account shows the **total sales** in a period, the **total sales returns** and **the total money received** from credit customers. The **balance owed** at the beginning and end of the period are also shown. Amounts owed by credit customers are an **asset** of the business, so the balance b/d is on the debit side of the account.

Assessment focus point

Remember, the DEAD CLIC mnemonic states that **assets** sit on the **debit** side of the T-account.

The sales ledger control account must be **reconciled** with the sales ledger on a regular basis. The total of the sales ledger should **equal** the balance brought down on the sales ledger control account.

The reconciliation process helps ensure that all transactions with credit customers are recorded accurately, and so it will be easier for management to identify errors.

2.4 VAT and double entry

Before we look at how the books of prime entry are posted to the ledger accounts, we need to consider the relationship between VAT and the accounting records.

Chapter 3 explained that a VAT-registered business must charge VAT on sales (outputs) and can reclaim VAT on purchases (inputs). This has implications for the accounting records.

Business documents such as invoices and credit notes need to show the net, VAT and gross amounts. The net, VAT and gross amounts also need to be included in the general ledger, as follows:

Amount	Account to post to
Net	Sales account or Purchases account
VAT	VAT control account
Gross	Sales ledger control or Purchases ledger control or Bank/Cash

The VAT on sales and purchases is posted to an account called the **VAT control account**.

- VAT on sales is **output tax** and is payable to HMRC, and is therefore a **liability** of the business. So it is **credited** to the VAT control account.

- VAT on purchases is **input tax** and is recoverable from HMRC, and is therefore **decreasing a liability** of the business. So it is **debited** to the VAT control account.

In summary:

Input tax	Output tax
Reclaimable from HMRC	Payable to HMRC
↓	↓
Decreases the liability	Increases the liability
To record a credit purchase with VAT:	**To record a credit sale with VAT:**
DEBIT Purchases	DEBIT Sales ledger control
DEBIT VAT control account	CREDIT VAT control account
CREDIT Purchases ledger control	CREDIT Sales

2.4.1 VAT control account

VAT is posted to a general ledger account called the **VAT control account**.

The purpose of the VAT control account is to record the VAT owed to HMRC (credit entry) and the VAT due from HMRC (debit entry).

Illustration 3: VAT control account

VAT control account

Details	Amount £	Details	Amount £
Purchases	1,200	Balance b/f	500
Bank	500	Sales	2,000
Balance c/d	800		
Total	2,500	Total	2,500
		Balance b/d	800

The VAT control account will usually have a balance b/d on the credit side, which is a **liability** and represents the amount owed to HMRC. This is because the business will usually be profitable and so the output tax charged on sales will be higher than the input tax reclaimable on purchases, and therefore VAT will be owed to HMRC.

Entries on the right-hand side of the account (the credit side) will **increase** the amount owed to HMRC, and entries on the left-hand side of the account (the debit side) will **decrease** the amount owed to HMRC.

The VAT control account must be **reconciled** with the company's **VAT records**. This will help ensure that all VAT transactions are recorded accurately and it will be easier for management to identify errors.

Activity 1: VAT and double entry

What will be the entries in the general ledger for each of the following?

(a) A business which is **not** registered for VAT sells goods on credit for £100.

Account name	Amount £	Debit ✓	Credit ✓
▼			
▼			

Picklist:

Cash
Sales
Sales ledger control
VAT

(b) A business which **is** VAT-registered sells goods on credit for £100 plus VAT. VAT is charged at 20%.

Account name		Amount £	Debit ✓	Credit ✓
	▼			
	▼			
	▼			

Picklist:

Cash
Sales
Sales ledger control
VAT

(c) A business which **is** VAT-registered sells goods for cash for £100 plus VAT. VAT is charged at 20%.

Account name		Amount £	Debit ✓	Credit ✓
	▼			
	▼			
	▼			

Picklist:

Cash
Sales
Sales ledger control
VAT

3 Posting the sales day book

As we saw at the start of the chapter, the first stage of the accounting process is to enter details of transaction documents into the **books of prime entry**. The next stage of the accounting process is to **transfer** the details from the book of prime entry to the **accounting records**. In the case of the sales day book, to the:

- **General ledger** (so we will be debiting the sales ledger control account and crediting the sales account)

- **Sales ledger**

In order to do this the sales day book must first be **cast** and **cross-cast**. Remember, cast means to add up the columns. In the case of the sales day book, cross-cast means to add up the totals of the VAT and net columns. If all the addition has been done correctly, then the totals of the VAT and net columns should equal the total of the gross column.

Illustration 4: Posting the sales day book

Shown below is the sales day book of Southwork Ltd. It has been cast and cross-cast.

Date 20XX	Customer	Invoice number	Customer code	Total £	VAT £	Net £
1 May	Grigsons Ltd	10356	SL 21	199.20	33.20	166.00
1 May	Hall & Co	10357	SL 05	105.60	17.60	88.00
1 May	Harris & Sons	10358	SL 17	120.00	20.00	100.00
2 May	Jaytry Ltd	10359	SL 22	309.60	51.60	258.00
	Totals			734.40	122.40	612.00

Cross-cast check:

Net	£612.00
VAT	£122.40
Total	£734.40

Posting to the general ledger

Now we want to post the totals from the sales day book into Southwork's general ledger. Remember, the general ledger is where the **double entry** takes place so let us consider the double entry required here. The sales day book represents the **sales on credit** that have been made by the business so:

- The **Net** column shows the total of credit sales – the business makes no profit out of charging VAT as it is paid over to HMRC, therefore the VAT is excluded from the sales total. The total of this column must be a **credit** entry in the **sales account**.

- The **VAT** column shows the amount of VAT that is owed as a liability to HMRC and as such is a **credit** entry in the **VAT control account**.

- The **Total** column shows the gross amount that the customer must pay to the business – the net total plus VAT. This is the amount of the trade receivable so the total of this column is a **debit** entry in the **sales ledger control account**.

We can now post the amounts from the sales day book to the general ledger.

GENERAL LEDGER

Sales ledger control

Details	Amount £	Details	Amount £
Sales	612.00		
VAT control	122.40		

Total: £734.40

Sales

Details	Amount £	Details	Amount £
		Sales ledger control	612.00

VAT control

Details	Amount £	Details	Amount £
		Sales ledger control	122.40

As always in double entry the total of the debit entries must equal the total of the credit entries:

DEBIT   (£612.00 + £122.40 =)   £734.40

CREDIT   (£612.00 + £122.40 =)   £734.40

Posting to the sales ledger

It is vitally important that we also post the individual invoice total amounts from the sales day book to the individual credit customer accounts in Southwork's **sales ledger**. Remember the sales ledger is a **subsidiary ledger** and is not part of the double entry system.

Step 1   Find the individual customer's account in the sales ledger.

Step 2   Enter the invoice total of the invoice, including VAT, on the **debit side** of the customer's account.

SALES LEDGER

Grigsons Ltd — SL 21

Details	£	Details	£
Invoice 10356	199.20		

Hall & Co — SL 05

Details	£	Details	£
Invoice 10357	105.60		

Harris & Sons — SL 17

Details	£	Details	£
Invoice 10358	120.00		

Jaytry Ltd — SL 22

Details	£	Details	£
Invoice 10359	309.60		

The individual customer accounts in this illustration are **coded**. Note how the codes match the customer codes in the sales day book.

A useful double check at this point is that the total of all the postings we made to the sales ledger is the same as the total of the postings to the sales ledger control account from the sales day book:

	Debit entries £	
Grigsons Ltd	199.20	
Hall & Co	105.60	Sales ledger
Harris & Sons	120.00	
Jaytry Ltd	309.60	
Sales ledger control	734.40	General ledger

Assessment focus point

The illustration above used the T-accounts format to post the double entry from the day book to the ledgers. The activity below uses the tabular format. Either could be used in your assessment, although the AAT sample assessments use the tabular format only.

For teaching purposes when using the T-account format in this Course Book, so that the double entry between the ledger accounts can be easily seen, the posting from the sales day book to the sales ledger control account has been split out into the net and VAT amounts. However, when using the tabular format, one single gross amount can be posted to the sales ledger control account. This is shown in the activity below.

Activity 2: Posting the sales day book

The following transactions all took place on 30 June and have been entered into the sales day book as shown below. No entries have yet been made into the ledger system.

Sales day book

Date 20XX	Details	Invoice number	Total £	VAT £	Net £
30 Jun	M Head	1032	3,600	600	3,000
30 Jun	G Irving	1033	3,102	517	2,585
30 Jun	K Tang	1034	5,988	998	4,990
30 Jun	L Harvey	1035	1,440	240	1,200
	Totals		14,130	2,355	11,775

(a) What will be the entries in the sales ledger?

Account name		Amount £	Debit ✓	Credit ✓
	▼			
	▼			
	▼			
	▼			

Picklist:

G Irving
K Tang
L Harvey

M Head
Purchases
Purchases ledger control
Purchases returns
Sales
Sales ledger control
Sales returns
VAT

(b) What will be the entries in the general ledger?

Account name		Amount £	Debit ✓	Credit ✓
	▼			
	▼			
	▼			

Picklist:

G Irving
K Tang
L Harvey
M Head
Purchases
Purchases ledger control
Purchases returns
Sales
Sales ledger control
Sales returns
VAT

Assessment focus point

A good way to approach this kind of question is to first work out what you should do with the total of the total column, and the rest of the answer flows from that. For example, in the activity above, the **total of the total column** is a **debit entry** in the general ledger as it represents an asset of the business. It then follows that:

- The **individual total amounts** in the total column should be posted as **debit entries** to the individual customer accounts in the **sales ledger**

- The **VAT and net amounts** must be **credit entries** in the general ledger, because total debit entries must always equal total credit entries

4 Posting the sales returns day book

In Chapter 3 we saw that the **sales returns day book** is a list of all the credit notes raised against sales which have been made on credit. Now we will look at posting the sales returns day book to the general and sales ledgers.

Illustration 5: Posting the sales returns day book

Shown below is Southwork Ltd's sales returns day book relating to the sales seen in Illustration 4. It has been cast and cross-cast.

Date 20XX	Customer	Credit note number	Customer code	Total £	VAT £	Net £
4 May	Grigsons Ltd	CN668	SL 21	72.00	12.00	60.00
5 May	Harris & Sons	CN669	SL 17	96.00	16.00	80.00
	Totals			168.00	28.00	140.00

Cross-cast check:

Net	£140.00
VAT	£28.00
Total	£168.00

Posting to the general ledger

In the general ledger the three column totals must be entered into the ledger accounts. The double entry is the reverse of that for a sale on credit, but let's consider the logic behind each entry:

- **Total:** As the customers have returned these goods they will no longer have to pay for them, so we must deduct the total of the gross amounts. As amounts owed by credit customers are decreased, this total is a **credit** entry in the sales ledger control account.

- **Net total:** This is the total of sales returns for the period which is effectively the reverse of a sale. Therefore a **debit** entry is required in the **sales returns ledger account** (not the sales account – we keep these separate).

- **VAT:** As these returned goods have not been sold, the VAT is no longer due to HMRC. Therefore a **debit** entry is made in the VAT control account.

We can now post the amounts into Southwork's general ledger accounts. The entries from the sales returns day book are shown in bold.

GENERAL LEDGER

Sales ledger control

Details	Amount £	Details	Amount £
Sales	612.00	**Sales returns**	**140.00**
VAT control	120.40	**VAT control**	**28.00**

Total: £168.00

Sales returns

Details	Amount £	Details	Amount £
Sales ledger control	140.00		

VAT control

Details	Amount £	Details	Amount £
Sales ledger control	28.00	Sales ledger control	120.40

Posting to the sales ledger

Now we must enter each individual credit note in the relevant customer's account in Southwork's sales ledger. The amount to be used is the **gross amount** and the customer's account must be **credited** with this figure to show that the customer no longer owes this amount.

Below are Southwork's sales ledger accounts. The entries from the sales returns day book are shown in bold.

SALES LEDGER

Grigsons Ltd   SL 21

Details	£	Details	£
Invoice 10356	199.20	**Credit note 668**	**72.00**

Harris & Sons   SL 17

Details	£	Details	£
Invoice 103568	120.00	**Credit note 669**	**96.00**

Again a useful double check is that the total of all the postings to the sales ledger from the sales returns day book is the same as the total of the postings to the sales ledger control account:

	Credit entries £	
Grigsons Ltd	72.00	Sales ledger
Harris & Sons	96.00	
Sales ledger control	168.00	General ledger

Activity 3: Posting the sales returns day book

The following transactions all took place on 30 June and have been entered into the sales returns day book as shown below. No entries have yet been made into the ledger system.

Sales returns day book

Date 20XX	Details	Credit note number	Total £	VAT £	Net £
30 Jun	F Fish	632	504	84	420
30 Jun	M Gordon	633	276	46	230
30 Jun	G Henry	634	744	124	620
30 Jun	R Left	635	696	116	580
	Totals		2,220	370	1,850

(a) **What will be the entries in the sales ledger?**

Account name	Amount £	Debit ✓	Credit ✓
▼			
▼			
▼			
▼			

Picklist:

F Fish

G Henry

M Gordon
Purchases
Purchases ledger control
Purchases returns
R Left
Sales
Sales ledger control
Sales returns
VAT

(b) What will be the entries in the general ledger?

Account name		Amount £	Debit ✓	Credit ✓
	▼			
	▼			
	▼			

Picklist:

F Fish
G Henry
M Gordon
Purchases
Purchases ledger control
Purchases returns
R Left
Sales
Sales ledger control
Sales returns
VAT

5 Cash book – debit side and double entry

In Chapter 8 we saw that when **money is received** by a business it is recorded in the book of prime entry known as the cash book. We also considered briefly how the cash book is posted to the ledgers. In this section we will consider in more detail how money received from cash customers and credit customers is included in the ledgers.

As we have seen, an important difference between the cash book and other books of prime entry is that it can either be a book of prime entry **only**, or it can be **both** a book of prime entry **and** part of the general ledger.

Assessment focus point

In your assessment it is likely that the information at the start of the assessment will say:

'The cash book and petty cash book should be treated as part of the double entry system unless the task instructions state otherwise.'

In practical terms this means that the cash and bank columns are already included in the general ledger. Therefore, if you are asked to make postings to the general ledger you will not need to post these columns as they will already be included. You will only need to post the other columns to the ledger.

However, task information may override this information to say:

'The cash book is a book of prime entry only.'

In this situation you need to post the cash and bank column totals to the ledgers, as well as posting the other columns.

5.1 Posting the cash book – debit side (book of prime entry only)

If the cash book is a book of prime entry only, the totals of the cash and bank columns in the cash book will need to be posted to the cash account and bank account in the general ledger.

There will be a separate cash account and a separate bank account in the general ledger.

The table below shows where each of the columns in the cash book – debit side is posted in the general ledger.

Cash book – debit side

Cash £	Bank £	VAT £	Trade receivables £	Cash sales £	Sundry £
Post as a **debit** entry to cash account in the general ledger	Post as a **debit** entry to bank account in the general ledger	Post as **credit** entries to the relevant general ledger accounts			

Note how the cash and bank columns are **posted** to the general ledger.

The illustration below shows how this works in practice.

Illustration 6: Posting the cash book – debit side (book of prime entry only)

Shown below is Southwork Ltd's cash book – debit side. In order to post receipts from the cash book to the ledgers, it must first be cast and cross-cast.

Date	Details	Ref	Cash £	Bank £	VAT £	Cash sales £	Trade rec'ables £	Sundry £
10 May	Grigsons Ltd	SL 21		114.48			114.48	
10 May	Jaytry Ltd	SL 22		278.64			278.64	
10 May	Cash sale		360.00		60.00	300.00		
10 May	Totals		360.00	393.12	60.00	300.00	393.12	

Posting to the general ledger

We can now make the postings to Southwork's general ledger, which contains accounts for cash and for bank since the cash book is a book of prime entry only. Below are Southwork's ledger accounts. The entries from the cash book are shown in bold.

GENERAL LEDGER

Cash account

Total: £360.00

Details	£	Details	£
Sales	**300.00**		
VAT control	**60.00**		

Bank account

Details	£	Details	£
Sales ledger control	**393.12**		

Sales ledger control

Details	£	Details	£
Sales	612.00	Sales returns	140.00
VAT control	120.40	VAT control	28.00
		Bank	**393.12**

Sales

Details	£	Details	£
		Sales ledger control	612.00
		Cash	**300.00**

Sales returns

Details	£	Details	£
Sales ledger control	140.00		

VAT control

Details	£	Details	£
Sales ledger control	28.00	Sales ledger control	120.40
		Cash	**60.00**

Posting to the sales ledger

We also need to enter each credit sales related receipt in the customers' accounts in Southwork's sales ledger. The amount for the receipt is the amount in the 'Trade receivables' column of the cash book and this must be entered in the credit side of the customer's ledger account, as it is a reduction in how much the customer owes us.

We do not post all the receipts in the cash book to the sales ledger: the two cash sales amounts (for the net sale and the related VAT) are **not** posted to the sales ledger as they are not related to credit customers.

SALES LEDGER

Grigsons Ltd   **SL 21**

Details	£	Details	£
Invoice 10356	199.20	Credit note 668	72.00
		Cash book	**114.48**

Jaytry Ltd   **SL 22**

Details	£	Details	£
Invoice 10359	309.60	**Cash book**	**278.64**

Assessment focus point

The illustration above used the T-accounts format to post the double entry from the cash book to the ledgers. The activity below uses the tabular format.

Activity 4: Posting the cash book – debit side (book of prime entry only)

Silver's cash book is a book of prime entry only. These are the totals of the columns in the debit side of the cash book at the end of the month.

Details	Cash £	Bank £	VAT £	Trade receivables £	Cash sales £	Rental income £
Totals	3,600	12,500	600	12,000	3,000	500

(a) What will be the entries in the general ledger?

Account name		Amount £	Debit ✓	Credit ✓
	▼			
	▼			
	▼			
	▼			
	▼			
	▼			

Picklist

Bank
Cash
Cash sales
K Scott
Rental income
Sales ledger control
Silver
VAT

One of the bank receipts to trade receivables was from K Scott for £300.

(b) What will be the entry in the sales ledger?

Sales ledger

Account name		Amount £	Debit ✓	Credit ✓
	▼			

Picklist:

Bank
Cash
Cash sales
K Scott
Rental income
Sales ledger control
Silver
VAT

5.2 Posting the cash book – debit side (part of the general ledger)

In many businesses the cash book is treated as **both** a book of prime entry **and** part of the general ledger. This means that for **receipts**, the cash book is itself the debit side of the cash account and of the bank account in the general ledger.

The effect of this is that:

*   There is no need to post a debit entry from the cash and bank columns to the general ledger

*   There are no separate cash or bank control accounts in the general ledger

*   The analysis columns are posted as normal

The table below shows where each of the columns in the cash book – debit side is posted in the general ledger if the cash book is both a book of prime entry and part of the general ledger.

Cash book – debit side

Cash £	Bank £	VAT £	Trade receivables £	Cash sales £	Sundry £
No posting required, as this is already the **debit** side of general ledger account for cash	No posting required, as this is already the **debit** side of general ledger account for bank	Post as **credit** entries to the general ledger accounts			

Remember that no posting is required for the cash and bank columns. The only entries you therefore need to make in the general ledger are **credit entries** for the analysis columns. This makes sense because the debit entries from the cash and bank columns are **already included** in the general ledger.

Try the following activity.

Activity 5: Posting the cash book – debit side (part of the general ledger)

Silver's cash book is both a book of prime entry and part of the double entry bookkeeping system. These are the totals of the columns in the debit side of the cash book at the end of the month.

Details	Cash £	Bank £	VAT £	Trade receivables £	Cash sales £	Rental income £
Totals	3,600	12,500	600	12,000	3,000	500

(a) What will be the entries in the general ledger?

Account name	Amount £	Debit ✓	Credit ✓
▼			
▼			
▼			
▼			

Picklist:

Bank
Cash
Cash sales
K Scott
Rental income
Sales ledger control
Silver
VAT

One of the bank receipts to trade receivables was from K Scott for £300.

(b) What will be the entry in the sales ledger?

Sales ledger

Account name	Amount £	Debit ✓	Credit ✓
▼			

Picklist:

Bank
Cash
Cash sales
K Scott
Rental income
Sales ledger control
Silver
VAT

6 Posting the discounts allowed day book

As we saw in Chapter 3, the **discounts allowed day book** is the book of prime entry used to record prompt payment discounts taken by credit customers. Now we will look at posting the discounts allowed day book to the general ledger and sales ledger.

In order to do this, the discounts allowed day book must first be **cast** and **cross-cast**.

Illustration 7: Posting the discounts allowed day book

Shown below is the discounts allowed day book of Southwork Ltd. It has been cast and cross-cast.

Date 20XX	Details	Credit note number	Customer code	Total £	VAT £	Net £
10 May	Grigsons Ltd	D23	SL21	12.72	2.12	10.60
10 May	S Jaytry Ltd	D24	SL22	30.96	5.16	25.80
	Totals			**43.68**	**7.28**	**36.40**

Cross-cast check:

Net	£36.40
VAT	£7.28
Total	£43.68

Posting to the general ledger

Now we want to post the totals from the discounts allowed day book into Southwork's general ledger. Remember, the general ledger is where the **double entry** takes place, so let us consider the double entry required here. The discounts allowed day book represents the prompt payment discounts taken by credit customers, so:

- The **Total** column shows the total amount of prompt payment discount, including VAT, taken by credit customers. As amounts owed by credit customers are decreased by this amount, the total of this column is a **credit** entry in the **sales ledger control account**.

- The **Net** column shows the net amount of prompt payment discount taken by credit customers. This is an expense of the business and the total of this column is posted as a **debit** entry in the **discounts allowed account**.

- The **VAT** column shows the VAT on the net discount taken and the total of this column is posted as a **debit** entry in the VAT control account, effectively cancelling out the original VAT charged.

We can now post the amounts from the discounts allowed day book to Southwork's general ledger. The entries from the discounts allowed day book are shown in bold.

GENERAL LEDGER

Sales ledger control

Details	£	Details	£
Sales	612.00	Sales returns	140.00
VAT control	120.40	VAT control	28.00
		Bank	393.12
		Discounts allowed	**36.40**
		VAT control	**7.28**

Total: £43.68 (for Discounts allowed 36.40 and VAT control 7.28)

VAT control

Details	£	Details	£
Sales ledger control	28.00	Sales ledger control	120.40
Sales ledger control	**7.28**	Cash	60.00

Discounts allowed

Details	£	Details	£
Sales ledger control	**36.40**		

Posting to the sales ledger

We also need to enter each prompt payment discount taken in the customers' accounts in Southwork's sales ledger. The gross amount of the discount allowed is posted to the credit side of the customer's account, as it reduces the amount owed by the customer.

SALES LEDGER

Grigsons Ltd SL 21

Details	£	Details	£
Invoice 10356	199.20	Credit note 668	140.00
	120.40	Cash book	114.48
		Credit note D23	**12.72**

Jaytry Ltd SL 22

Details	£	Details	£
Invoice 10359	309.60	Cash book	278.64
		Credit note D24	**30.96**

Assessment focus point

The illustration above used the T-accounts format to post the double entry from the discounts allowed day book to the ledgers. The activity below uses the tabular format.

Activity 6: Posting the discounts allowed day book

These are the totals of the discounts allowed day book at the end of the month.

Discounts allowed day book

Details	Total £	VAT £	Net £
Totals	600	100	500

(a) What will be the entries in the general ledger?

Account name		Amount £	Debit ✓	Credit ✓
	▼			
	▼			
	▼			

Picklist:

Discounts allowed
Discounts received
Purchases
Purchases ledger control
Purchases returns
Sales
Sales ledger control
Sales returns
VAT

One of the entries in the discounts allowed day book is for a credit note sent to K Smith for £20 plus VAT.

(b) What will be the entry in the sales ledger?

Account name		Amount £	Debit ✓	Credit ✓
▼				

Picklist:

Discounts allowed
Discounts received
K Smith
Purchases
Purchases ledger control
Purchases returns
Sales
Sales ledger control
Sales returns
VAT

Chapter summary

- The first stage of the accounting process is to enter details of transactions into the books of prime entry, eg sales and sales returns day books, cash book and discounts allowed day book.

- The second stage of the accounting process is to transfer details from the books of prime entry to the accounting records, ie the general ledger and sales ledger.

- The sales day book must be totalled and the totals entered into the ledger accounts in the general ledger.

- The gross amount of each individual sales invoice must also be entered into the individual credit customer's account in the sales ledger.

- The sales returns day book must also be totalled and posted to the general ledger and the sales ledger.

- The gross amount of each individual credit note must also be entered into the individual credit customer's account in the sales ledger.

- The cash book – debit side must be totalled and posted to the general ledger.

- Each receipt in the trade receivables column of the cash book – debit side must also be entered into the individual credit customer's account in the sales ledger.

- The discounts allowed day book must be totalled and the totals entered into the ledger accounts in the general ledger.

- The gross amount of each discount allowed must also be entered into the individual credit customer's account in the sales ledger.

Keywords

- **Discounts allowed account:** The account in the general ledger used to record prompt payment discounts taken by credit customers

- **Posting:** Transferring data from the books of prime entry (day books) into the ledgers

- **Sales ledger control account:** A general ledger account for trade receivables (credit customers), representing the total of all the accounts in the sales ledger

- **Sales returns account:** The account in the general ledger used to record customer returns

- **Subsidiary ledgers:** Sales and purchases ledgers that are not part of the general ledger and which contain a ledger account for each individual trade receivable or trade payable. Not part of the double entry system

1 Identify the general ledger accounts that the following totals from the sales day book will be posted to and whether they are a debit or a credit entry:

Sales day book total	Account name in general ledger	Debit ✓	Credit ✓
Gross			
VAT			
Net			

2 A credit note for £200 plus VAT has been issued to a customer. How much will be entered in the sales ledger control account in the general ledger and the customer's account in the sales ledger, and will these entries be debits or credits?

	Amount £	Debit ✓	Credit ✓
Sales ledger control account (general ledger)			
Customer's account (sales ledger)			

3 The cash book – debit side for a business acts as both a book of prime entry and as part of the general ledger. Total receipts for the last month are as follows:

Details	Cash £	Bank £	VAT £	Cash sales £	Trade receivables £
Totals	120.00	5,016.50	20.00	100.00	5,016.50

What entries will be posted to the general ledger? (tick debit or credit for each entry)

Account name	Amount £	Debit ✓	Credit ✓

4 From the sales day book and sales returns day book below, make the relevant entries in the general ledger and sales ledger accounts.

Sales day book

Date 20XX	Customer	Invoice number	Customer code	Gross £	VAT £	Net £
21 Sep	Dagwell Enterprises	56401	SL15	948.60	158.10	790.50
21 Sep	G Thomas & Co	56402	SL30	3,537.60	589.60	2,948.00
21 Sep	Polygon Stores	56403	SL03	1,965.60	327.60	1,638.00
21 Sep	Weller Enterprises	56404	SL18	1,152.00	192.00	960.00
				7,603.80	1,267.30	6,336.50

Sales returns day book

Date 20XX	Customer	Invoice number	Customer code	Gross £	VAT £	Net £
21 Sep	Whitehill Superstores	08650	SL37	356.40	59.40	297.00
23 Sep	Dagwell Enterprises	08651	SL15	244.80	40.80	204.00
				601.20	100.20	501.00

General ledger

Sales ledger control

Details	Amount £	Details	Amount £

Sales

Details	Amount £	Details	Amount £

Sales returns

Details	Amount £	Details	Amount £

VAT control

Details	Amount £	Details	Amount £

Sales ledger

Dagwell Enterprises   SL 15

Details	£	Details	£

G Thomas & Co   SL 30

Details	£	Details	£

Polygon Stores   SL 03

Details	£	Details	£

Weller Enterprises   SL 18

Details	£	Details	£

Whitehill Superstores   SL 37

Details	£	Details	£

5 A credit note related to a prompt payment discount for £40 plus VAT has been issued to a customer. What are the entries required to post this to the general ledger?

Account name	Amount £	Debit ✓	Credit ✓
▼			
▼			
▼			

Picklist:

Discounts allowed
Discounts received
Purchases
Purchases ledger control
Purchases returns
Sales
Sales ledger control
Sales returns
VAT

6 Below are the cash book – debit side and the discounts allowed day book. The cash book is part of the general ledger. From the cash book – debit side and discounts allowed day book below, make the relevant entries in the general ledger and sales ledger accounts.

Cash book – debit side

Date	Details	Ref	Cash £	Bank £	VAT £	Cash sales £	Trade receivables £
30 Jun	Cash sales		372.00		62.00	310.00	
30 Jun	H Henry	SLO115		146.79			146.79
30 Jun	P Peters	SLO135		221.55			221.55
30 Jun	K Kilpin	SLO128		440.30			440.30
30 Jun	Cash sales		300.76		50.12	250.64	
30 Jun	B Bennet	SLO134		57.80			57.80

Date	Details	Ref	Cash £	Bank £	VAT £	Cash sales £	Trade receivables £
30 Jun	S Shahir	SL0106		114.68			114.68
	Totals		672.76	981.12	112.12	560.64	981.12

Discounts allowed day book

Date	Details	Credit note number	Ref	Total £	VAT £	Net £
30 Jun	P Peters	D55	SL0135	6.85	1.14	5.71
30 Jun	S Shahir	D56	SL0106	3.55	0.59	2.96
	Totals			10.40	1.73	8.67

General ledger

VAT control   **GL 562**

Details	£	Details	£

Sales   **GL 049**

Details	£	Details	£

Sales ledger control   **GL 827**

Details	£	Details	£

Discounts allowed   **GL 235**

Details	£	Details	£

Sales ledger

H Henry   **SL 0115**

Details	£	Details	£

P Peters   **SL 0135**

Details	£	Details	£

K Kilpin   **SL 0128**

Details	£	Details	£

B Bennet   **SL 0134**

Details	£	Details	£

S Shahir   **SL 0106**

Details	£	Details	£

7 Post the cash book and discounts allowed day book below to the general ledger and sales ledger. The cash book is not part of the general ledger.

Cash book

Date	Details	Ref	Cash £	Bank £	VAT £	Cash sales £	Trade receivables £
20 May	G Gonpipe	SL55		332.67			332.67
20/5	Cash sales		672.00		112.00	560.00	
20/5	J Jimmings	SL04		127.37			127.37
20/5	N Nutely	SL16		336.28			336.28
20/5	T Turner	SL21		158.35			158.35
20/5	Cash sales		336.90		56.15	280.75	
20/5	R Ritner	SL45		739.10			739.10
			1,008.90	1,693.77	168.15	840.75	1,693.77

Discounts allowed day book

Date	Details	Credit note number	Ref	Total £	VAT £	Net £
20 May	J Jimmings	D08	SL04	6.70	1.11	5.59
20 May	N Nutely	D09	SL16	17.70	2.95	14.75
20 May	R Ritner	D10	SL45	38.90	6.48	32.42
	Totals			63.30	10.54	52.76

General ledger

Account name	Amount £	Debit ✓	Credit ✓
▼			
▼			
▼			
▼			
▼			
▼			

Picklist:

Bank
Cash
Cash sales
Discounts allowed
Discounts received
Purchases
Purchases ledger control
Purchases returns
Sales
Sales ledger control
Sales returns
Trade receivables
VAT

Sales ledger

Account name	Amount £	Debit ✓	Credit ✓
▼			
▼			
▼			
▼			
▼			

Picklist:

G Gonpipe
J Jimmings
N Nutely
R Ritner
T Turner

8 The following transactions all took place on 30 November and have been entered into the sales day book as shown below. No entries have yet been made into the ledger system.

Sales day book

Date 20XX	Details	Invoice number	Gross £	VAT £	Net £
30 Nov	Fries & Co	23907	2,136	356	1,780
30 Nov	Hussey Enterprises	23908	3,108	518	2,590
30 Nov	Todd Trading	23909	3,720	620	3,100
30 Nov	Milford Ltd	23910	2,592	432	2,160
	Totals		11,556	1,926	9,630

Make the required entries in the general ledger.

VAT control

Details	£	Details	£

Sales

Details	£	Details	£

Sales ledger control

Details	£	Details	£

Double entry for purchases and trade payables

10

Learning outcomes

1.2	Distinguish between prompt payment, trade and bulk discounts
	• How prompt payment discounts are recorded: discounts allowed or received account, sales or purchases ledger control account and VAT (value added tax) account in the general ledger.
5.1	Transfer data from the books of prime entry to the ledgers
	• The books of prime entry: sales and sales returns daybooks, purchases and purchases returns daybooks, discounts allowed and discounts received daybooks, cash book, petty cash book
	• The ledgers: sales, purchases, general
	• That the sales and purchases ledger control accounts are part of the double entry system.
	• Transfer data from books of prime entry to the relevant accounts in the ledgers
5.2	Total and balance ledger accounts
	• Total and balance ledger accounts: balance carried down, balance brought down, debit balance, credit balance

Assessment context

This chapter builds on your knowledge of double entry which was introduced in Chapters 6 and 7. The focus is now on recording purchases and payables. These topics are regularly tested in the assessment.

The assessment will directly test double entry in two different ways. You could be asked to complete T-accounts by selecting an account name from a picklist (choice of account names) and entering the correct amount in the debit or credit column. You will then have to balance the T-account and show the closing amount.

Alternatively, you could be asked to enter the information in tabular format by selecting account names from a picklist and entering the relevant amount and ticks to indicate debit or credit entries.

Qualification context

Double entry bookkeeping is introduced in *Bookkeeping Transactions* and then developed in the Level 2 *Bookkeeping Controls* and Level 3 *Advanced Bookkeeping* and *Final Accounts Preparation* courses. It is applied at Level 4 *Financial Statements of Limited Companies*.

Business context

Double entry is used to prepare financial statements which show the company's financial performance over the year and closing assets and liabilities.

Chapter overview

- Post transactions with credit suppliers to the individual ledger account
- Not part of the general ledger

Purchases ledger

Double entry for purchases and trade payables

Post totals to general ledger

Debit

- Increases
  - Assets
  - Expenses
  - Drawings

Credit

- Increases
  - Liabilities
  - Income
  - Capital

Introduction

In the last chapter we looked at how transactions for sales and credit customers were posted from the day books to the ledgers. In this chapter we will move on to consider how transactions for purchases and credit suppliers recorded in the day books are posted to the ledgers.

1 Posting from the day books to the ledgers

As with sales and trade receivables, the first stage of the accounting process for purchases and trade payables is to enter details of transaction documents into the relevant books of prime entry.

TRANSACTION  BOOKS OF LEDGER
DOCUMENTS PRIME ENTRY ACCOUNTS

Four books of prime entry are relevant for purchases and trade payables:

- Invoices for purchases on credit that are received in a period are initially recorded in the **purchases day book**.

- Credit notes received in respect of credit purchases are recorded in the **purchases returns day book**.

- All payments (including some that are not related to purchases) are recorded in the **cash book**.

- Prompt payment discounts taken by the business are recorded in the **discounts received day book**.

The next stage of the accounting process is to transfer details from the books of prime entry to the accounting records. In the case of the purchases day book, this is to the:

- **Purchases ledger** (where we will just be crediting the individual supplier ledger accounts – the purchases ledger is **not** part of the double entry bookkeeping system)

- General ledger (so we will be **crediting** the **purchases ledger control account** and **debiting purchases** or some other **expense**)

We will now look at the purchases ledger and the purchases ledger control account in more detail.

1.1 Subsidiary ledger: purchases ledger

Key features of the purchases ledger are that:

(a) It shows the business how much is **owed** to each **credit supplier** at any point in time.

(b) It is a separate **memorandum** ledger and not part of the double entry system. It is for information purposes only.

Illustration 1: Purchases ledger

Tolberg Ltd buys on credit from a supplier called Higgs & Co and maintains a purchases ledger account for this supplier. This month it had four transactions with Higgs & Co:

Higgs & Co

Details	Amount £	Details	Amount £
Credit note CN56	50	Invoice 654	400
Bank	300	Invoice 701	800

- Items on the debit side (left-hand side) decrease the balance owed to suppliers, eg credit notes, prompt payment discounts, cash paid.

- Items on the credit side (right-hand side) increase the balance owed to the supplier, eg invoices.

1.2 Purchases ledger control account

The **purchases ledger control account** is an important **general ledger** account for purchases, credit suppliers and payments.

Illustration 2: Purchases ledger control account

Purchases ledger control

Details	Amount £	Details	Amount £
Bank	7,000	Balance b/f	6,000
Purchases returns	2,000	Purchases	12,000
Balance c/d	9,000		
Total	18,000	Total	18,000
		Balance b/d	9,000

For a certain period (eg monthly) the purchases ledger control account shows the **total credit purchases** in a period, the **total credit purchases returns** and the **total money paid** to credit suppliers. The balance owed at the beginning and end of the period are also shown.

Balances owed to suppliers are **liabilities** of the business, therefore the balance b/d is on the credit side of the account.

The purchases ledger control account must be **reconciled** with the purchases ledger on a regular basis. The total of the purchases ledger control account should equal the total of the purchases ledger.

This will help ensure that all transactions with credit suppliers are recorded accurately, and so it will be easier for management to identify errors.

2 Posting the purchases day book

As we saw at the start of the chapter, the first stage of the accounting process is to enter details of transaction documents into the **books of prime entry**. The next stage of the accounting process is to **transfer** the details from the book of prime entry to the **accounting records**. In the case of the purchases day book, this is to the:

- General ledger (so we will be **crediting** the **purchases ledger control account** and **debiting purchases** or some other **expense**)

- **Purchases ledger**

In order to do this the purchases day book must first be **cast** and **cross-cast**. Remember, cast means to add up the columns. In the case of the purchases day book, cross-cast means to add up the totals of the VAT and net columns. If all the addition has been done correctly, then the totals of the VAT and net columns should equal the total of the gross column.

Illustration 3: Posting the purchases day book

Shown below is the purchases day book of Northold Ltd. It has been cast and cross-cast.

Date 20XX	Supplier	Invoice number	Supplier code	Total £	VAT £	Purchases £	Telephone £	Stationery £
1 May	Haley Ltd	33728	PL 25	60.00	10.00			50.00
1 May	JJ Bros	242G	PL 14	1,440.00	240.00	1,200.00		
1 May	B Tel	530624	PL 06	154.00	24.00		130.00	
1 May	Shipley & Co	673	PL 59	4,800.00	800.00	4,000.00		
	Totals			6,454.00	1,074.00	5,200.00	130.00	50.00

Cross-cast check:

Purchases	£5,200.00
Telephone	£130.00
Stationery	£50.00
VAT	£1,074.00
Total	£6,454.00

Posting to the general ledger

Now we want to post the totals into Northold's general ledger. Remember, the general ledger is where double entry takes place so let us consider the **double entry** required here. The purchases day book represents the purchases on credit that have been made by the business, so:

- The **Total** column shows the amount that the business must pay to the supplier, including VAT. This is the amount of the trade payable, so the total of this column is a **credit** entry in the purchases ledger control account in the general ledger.

- The **VAT** column shows the amount of VAT that is reclaimable from HMRC (ie it is an asset) and as such the total of this column is a **debit** entry in the VAT control account.

- The **purchases**, **telephone** and **stationery** columns show the cost to the business of the goods it has acquired and the expenses it has incurred – the business does not suffer VAT as a cost as it is paid back by HMRC, so VAT is excluded from the purchases and expenses totals. The totals of these columns must be **debit** entries in the relevant general ledger accounts.

We can now post the amounts from the purchases day book to the general ledger.

GENERAL LEDGER

Purchases ledger control

Details	£	Details	£
		Purchases	5,200.00
		Telephone	130.00
		Stationery	50.00
		VAT control	1,074.00

Total: £6,454.00

Purchases

Details	£	Details	£
Purchases ledger control	5,200.00		

Telephone

Details	£	Details	£
Purchases ledger control	130.00		

Stationery

Details	£	Details	£
Purchases ledger control	50.00		

VAT Control

Details	£	Details	£
Purchases ledger control	1,074.00		

Posting to the purchases ledger

We have completed the double entry in the general ledger for credit purchases, so we now need to post the invoice totals to the individual payable accounts in Northold's **purchases ledger**. Remember, the purchases ledger is a subsidiary ledger and is not part of the double entry system.

Step 1   Find the individual supplier's account in the purchases ledger.

Step 2   Enter the invoice total of the invoice (ie including VAT) on the credit side of the supplier's account.

PURCHASES LEDGER

Haley Ltd   **PL 25**

Details	£	Details	£
		Invoice 33728	60.00

JJ Bros   **PL 14**

Details	£	Details	£
		Invoice 242G	1,440.00

B Tel   **PL 06**

Details	£	Details	£
		Invoice 530624	154.00

Shipley & Co   **PL 59**

Details	£	Details	£
		Invoice 673	4,800.00

The individual supplier accounts in this illustration are **coded**. Note how the codes match the supplier codes in the purchases day book.

A useful double check at this point is that the total of all the postings we have just made to the purchases ledger is the same as the total of the credit postings to the purchases ledger control account from the purchases day book:

	Credit entries £	
Haley Ltd	60.00	
JJ Bros	1,440.00	Purchases ledger
B Tel	154.00	
Shipley & Co	4,800.00	
Purchases ledger control	6,454.00	General ledger

🔍 **Assessment focus point**

The illustration above used the T-accounts format to post the double entry from the day book to the ledgers. The activity below uses the tabular format. Either could be used in your assessment, although the AAT sample assessment uses the tabular format only.

For teaching purposes when using the T-account format in this Course Book, so that the double entry between the ledger accounts can be easily seen, the posting from the day book to the purchases ledger control account has been split out into the net and VAT amounts. However, when using the tabular format, one single gross amount can be posted to the purchases ledger control account. This is shown in the activity below.

Activity 1: Posting the purchases day book

The following transactions all took place on 31 July and have been entered into the purchases day book as shown below. No entries have yet been made into the ledger system.

Purchases day book

Date 20XX	Details	Invoice number	Total £	VAT £	Net £
31 Jul	Edith	K451	4,020	670	3,350
31 Jul	Eddie	7429	4,728	788	3,940
31 Jul	Amber	MK425	5,100	850	4,250
31 Jul	John	64	8,778	1,463	7,315
	Totals		22,626	3,771	18,855

(a) What will be the entries in the purchases ledger?

Account name		Amount £	Debit ✓	Credit ✓
	▼			
	▼			
	▼			
	▼			

(b) What will be the entries in the general ledger?

Account name		Amount £	Debit ✓	Credit ✓
	▼			
	▼			
	▼			

Picklist:

Amber
Edith
Eddie
John
Purchases
Purchases ledger control
Purchases returns
Sales
Sales ledger control
Sales returns
VAT

3 Posting the purchases returns day book

In Chapter 3 we saw that the **purchases returns day book** is a list of all the credit notes received for purchases made on credit. Now we will look at posting the purchases returns day book to the general and purchases ledgers.

Illustration 4: Posting the purchases returns day book

Shown below is Northold's purchases returns day book. It has been cast and cross-cast.

Date 20XX	Supplier	Credit note number	Supplier code	Total £	VAT £	Purchases £	Telephone £	Stationery £
4 May	Haley Ltd	CN783	PL25	24.00	4.00			20.00
5 May	JJ Bros	C52246	PL14	69.60	11.60	58.00		
				93.60	15.60	58.00		20.00

Cross-cast check:

Purchases	£58.00
Stationery	£20.00
VAT	£15.60
Total	£93.60

Posting to the general ledger

In the general ledger the column totals must be entered into the ledger accounts. The double entry is the reverse of that for a purchase on credit, but let's consider the logic behind each entry:

- **Total**: As the business has returned these goods to suppliers it will no longer have to pay for them, so we must deduct the total of this column from the amount owed to suppliers. As trade payables are decreased, the total of this column is a **debit** entry in the purchases ledger control account.

- **VAT total**: As the cost of these returned goods has not been incurred, the VAT is no longer reclaimable from HMRC. Therefore a **credit** entry is made in the VAT control account.

The **purchases** and **stationery** totals are a reduction in the cost to the business of the goods it has returned – again VAT is excluded.

- The total in the purchases column is a **credit** entry in the purchases returns account.

- The total in the stationery column is a **credit** entry in the stationery returns account.

We can now post the amounts to Northold's ledger accounts. The entries from the purchases returns day book are shown in bold.

GENERAL LEDGER

Purchases ledger control

Details	£	Details	£
Purchases returns	**58.00**	Purchases	5,200.00
Stationery returns	**20.00**	Telephone	130.00
VAT control	**15.60**	Stationery	50.00
		VAT control	1,074.00

Total: £93.60

Purchases returns

Details	£	Details	£
		Purchases ledger control	**58.00**

Stationery returns

Details	£	Details	£
		Purchases ledger control	**20.00**

VAT control

Details	£	Details	£
Purchases ledger control	1,074.00	**Purchases ledger control**	**15.60**

Posting to the purchases ledger

Now we must enter each individual credit note in the supplier's account in Northold's purchases ledger. The amount to be used is the **credit note total** and the supplier's account must be **debited** with this figure to show that the business no longer owes the supplier this amount.

PURCHASES LEDGER

Haley Ltd   PL 25

Details	£	Details	£
Credit note 783	24.00	Invoice 33728	60.00

JJ Bros   PL 14

Details	£	Details	£
Credit note C52246	69.60	Invoice 242G	1,440.00

Again, a useful double check is that the total of all the postings to the purchases ledger from the purchases returns day book is the same as the total of the debit postings to the purchases ledger control account.

	Debit entries £	
Haley Ltd	24.00	Purchases ledger control
JJ Bros	69.60	
Purchases ledger control	93.60	General ledger

Activity 2: Posting the purchases returns day book

The following transactions all took place on 31 July and have been entered into the purchases returns day book as shown below. No entries have yet been made into the ledger system.

Purchases returns day book

Date 20XX	Details	Credit note number	Total £	VAT £	Net £
31 Jul	Jacob	HJ8	408	68	340
31 Jul	Mandy	84	48	8	40
31 Jul	Clarence	NH4	816	136	680
	Totals		1,272	212	1,060

Required

(a) What will be the entries in the purchases ledger?

Account name	Amount £	Debit ✓	Credit ✓
▼			
▼			
▼			

(b) What will be the entries in the general ledger?

Account name	Amount £	Debit ✓	Credit ✓
▼			
▼			
▼			

Picklist:

Clarence
Jacob
Mandy
Purchases
Purchases ledger control
Purchases returns
Sales
Sales ledger control
Sales returns
VAT

4 Cash book – credit side and double entry

In Chapter 8 we saw that when payments are made by a business they are recorded in the book of prime entry known as the two-column cash book.

We will now look at how money paid to cash suppliers and credit suppliers is included in the ledger. As we have seen, the cash book can either be a book of prime entry only, or it can be part of the general ledger.

Assessment focus point

In your assessment it is likely that the information at the start of the assessment will say:

'The cash book and petty cash book should be treated as part of the double entry system unless the task instructions state otherwise.'

In practical terms this means that the cash and bank columns are already included in the general ledger. Therefore, if you are asked to make postings to the general ledger you will not need to post these columns as they will already be included. You will only need to post the other columns to the ledger.

However, task information may override this information to say:

'The cash book is a book of prime entry only.'

In this situation you need to post the cash and bank column totals to the ledgers, as well as posting the other columns.

4.1 Posting the cash book – credit side (book of prime entry only)

If the cash book is a book of prime entry only, the totals of the cash and bank columns in the cash book will need to be posted to the cash account and bank account in the general ledger.

There will be a separate cash account and a separate bank account in the general ledger.

The table below shows where each of the columns in the cash book – credit side is posted in the general ledger.

Cash book – credit side

Cash £	Bank £	VAT £	Trade payables £	Cash purchases £	Sundry £
Post as a **credit** entry to cash account in the general ledger	Post as a **credit** entry to bank account in the general ledger	Post as **debit** entries to the relevant general ledger accounts			

Note how the cash and bank columns are **posted** to the general ledger.

Illustration 5: Posting the cash book – credit side (book of prime entry only)

Northold's cash book is shown below. In order to post payments from the cash book to the ledgers, the cash book must first be cast and cross-cast.

Date	Details	Ref	Cash £	Bank £	VAT £	Cash purchases £	Trade payables £	Petty cash £
10 May	Haley Ltd	PL 25		31.20			31.20	
10 May	Shipley & Co	PL 59		4,600.00			4,600.00	
10 May	Cash purchase		204.00		34.00	170.00		
10 May	Petty cash			150.00				150.00
	Totals		204.00	4,781.20	34.00	170.00	4,631.20	150.00

Posting to the general ledger

The easiest way to see how the postings are made in the general ledger is to show the relevant general ledger account name beneath each cash book total, with an indication of whether the posting is a debit entry or a credit entry:

	Date	Details	Cash £	Bank £	VAT £	Cash purchases £	Trade payables £	Petty cash £
		Totals	204.00	4,781.20	34.00	170.00	4,631.20	150.00
General ledger account		Debit entry			VAT	Purchases	Purchases ledger control	Petty cash
		Credit entry	Cash	Bank				

We can then make the postings to Northold's general ledger:

GENERAL LEDGER

Cash

Details	£	Details	£	
		Purchases	**170.00**	Total: £204.00
		VAT	**34.00**	

Bank

Details	£	Details	£	
		Purchases ledger control	**4,631.20**	Total: £4,781.20
		Petty cash	**150.00**	

Purchases ledger control

Details	£	Details	£
Purchases returns	58.00	Purchases	5,200.00
Stationery returns	20.00	Telephone	130.00
VAT control	15.60	Stationery	50.00
Bank	**4,631.20**	VAT control	1,074.00

Purchases

Details	£	Details	£
Purchases ledger control	5,200.00		
Cash	**170.00**		

Purchases returns

Details	£	Details	£
		Purchases ledger control	58.00

Telephone

Details	£	Details	£
Purchases ledger control	130.00		

Stationery

Details	£	Details	£
Purchases ledger control	50.00		

Stationery returns

Details	£	Details	£
		Purchases ledger control	20.00

VAT control

Details	£	Details	£
Purchases ledger control	1,074.00	Purchases ledger control	15.60
Cash	**34.00**		

Petty cash*

Details	£	Details	£
Bank	150.00		

* Note we shall see more about petty cash, the petty cash book and the petty cash account in the general ledger in Chapter 11.

Posting to the purchases ledger

We also need to enter each credit purchases related payment in the suppliers' accounts in Northold's purchases ledger. The amount for the payment is the amount in the 'Trade payables' column and this must be entered in the **debit** side of the purchases ledger account, as it is a reduction in how much Northold owes.

PURCHASES LEDGER

Haley Ltd   PL 25

Details	£	Details	£
Credit note 783	24.00	Invoice 33728	60.00
Cash book	**31.20**		

Shipley & Co		PL 59	
Details	**£**	**Details**	**£**
Cash book	**4,600.00**	Invoice 673	4,800.00

Assessment focus point

The illustration above used the T-accounts format to post the double entry from the cash book to the ledgers. The activity below uses the tabular format.

Activity 3: Posting the cash book – credit side (book of prime entry only)

Silver's cash book is a book of prime entry only. These are the totals of the columns in the credit side of the cash book at the end of the month.

Details	Cash £	Bank £	VAT £	Trade payables £	Cash purchases £	Bank charges £
Totals	1,920	8,300	320	8,000	1,600	300

(a) What will be the entries in the general ledger?

Account name		Amount £	Debit ✓	Credit ✓
	▼			
	▼			
	▼			
	▼			
	▼			
	▼			

One of the bank payments to trade payables was to H Henry for £500.

(b) What will be the entry in the purchases ledger?

Account name		Amount £	Debit ✓	Credit ✓
	▼			

Picklist:

Bank
Bank charges
Cash
Cash purchases
H Henry
Purchases ledger control
Silver
VAT

4.2 Posting the cash book – credit side (part of the general ledger)

As we saw in Chapter 8, in many businesses the cash book is treated as **both** a book of prime entry **and** part of the general ledger. This means that for **payments**, the cash book is itself the credit side of the cash account and of the bank account in the general ledger. The effect of this is that:

- There is no need to post credit entries for the total payments from the cash book shown in the cash and bank columns

- There is no cash account or bank account in the general ledger

Cash book – credit side

Cash £	Bank £	VAT £	Trade payables £	Cash purchases £	Sundry £
No posting required, as this is already the **credit** side of general ledger account for cash	No posting required, as this is already the **credit** side of general ledger account for bank	Post as **debit** entries to the general ledger accounts			

Note that no posting is required for the cash and bank columns. The only entries you therefore need to make in the general ledger are **debit entries** for the analysis columns. This makes sense because the credit entries from the cash and bank columns are **already included** in the general ledger.

Try the following activity.

Activity 4: Posting the cash book – credit side (part of the general ledger)

Silver's cash book is both a book of prime entry and part of the double entry bookkeeping system. These are the totals of the columns in the credit side of the cash book at the end of the month.

Details	Cash £	Bank £	VAT £	Trade payables £	Cash purchases £	Bank charges £
Totals	1,920	8,300	320	8,000	1,600	300

(a) What will be the entries in the general ledger?

Account name		Amount £	Debit ✓	Credit ✓
	▼			
	▼			
	▼			
	▼			

One of the bank payments to trade payables was to H Henry for £500.

(b) What will be the entry in the purchases ledger?

Account name		Amount £	Debit ✓	Credit ✓
	▼			

Picklist:

Bank
Bank charges
Cash
Cash purchases
H Henry
Purchases ledger control
Silver
VAT

The activity demonstrates that the cash and bank columns are not posted to the general ledger because they already form part of the double entry bookkeeping system. To put it another way, they are already included and therefore do not need to be posted again!

5 Posting the discounts received day book

As we saw in Chapter 3, when a business chooses to take a prompt payment discount offered by a credit supplier, that supplier must then send a credit note to the business, showing the discount and the related VAT. These credit notes are recorded in **the discounts received day book**. Now we will look at posting the discounts received day book to the general ledger and purchases ledger.

In order to do this, the discounts received day book must first be **cast** and **cross-cast**.

Illustration 6: Posting the discounts received day book

Shown below is the discounts received day book of Northold Ltd. It has been cast and cross-cast.

Date 20XX	Details	Supplier code	Credit note number	Total £	VAT £	Net £
10 May	Shipley & Co	PL 59	CN56	240.00	40.00	200.00
10 May	Haley Ltd	PL 25	C102	4.80	0.80	4.00
	Totals			244.80	40.80	204.00

Cross-cast check:

Net	£204.00
VAT	£40.80
Total	£244.80

Posting to the general ledger

Now we want to post the totals from the discounts received day book into Northold's general ledger. Remember, the general ledger is where the **double entry** takes place, so let us consider the double entry required here. The discounts received day book represents the prompt payment discounts from credit suppliers, so:

- The **Total** column shows the total amount of prompt payment discount including VAT taken from credit suppliers. As amounts owed to credit suppliers are decreased by this amount, the total of this column is a **debit** entry in the **purchases ledger control account**.

- The **Net** column shows the net amount of prompt payment discount taken from credit suppliers. This is income of the business and the total of this column is posted as a **credit** entry in the **discounts received account**.

- The **VAT** column shows the VAT on the net discount taken and the total of this column is posted as a **credit** entry in the VAT control account, effectively cancelling out the original VAT payable.

We can now post the amounts from the discounts received day book to Northold's general ledger. The entries from the discounts received day book are shown in bold.

GENERAL LEDGER

Purchases ledger control

Details	£	Details	£
Purchases returns	58.00	Purchases	5,200.00
Stationery returns	20.00	Telephone	130.00
VAT control	15.60	Stationery	50.00
Bank	4,631.20	VAT control	1,074.00
Discounts received	**204.00**		
VAT	**40.80**		

Total: £244.80

Discounts received

Details	£	Details	£
		Purchases ledger control	**204.00**

VAT control

Details	£	Details	£
Purchases ledger control	1,074.00	Purchases ledger control	15.60
Cash	34.00	**Purchases ledger control**	**40.80**

Posting to the purchases ledger

We also need to enter each prompt payment discount taken in the suppliers' accounts in Northold's purchases ledger. The gross amount of the discount received is posted to the debit side of the supplier's account, as it reduces the amount owed to the supplier.

PURCHASES LEDGER

Haley Ltd   **PL 25**

Details	£	Details	£
Credit note 783	24.00	Invoice 33728	60.00
Cash book	31.20		
Credit note C102	**4.80**		

Shipley & Co   **PL 59**

Details	£	Details	£
Cash book	4,600.00	Invoice 673	4,800.00
Credit note CN 56	**240.00**		

Activity 5: Posting the discounts received day book

These are the totals of the discounts received day book at the end of the month.

Discounts received day book

Details	Total £	VAT £	Net £
Totals	600	100	500

(a)   What will be the entries in the general ledger?

Account name	Amount £	Debit ✓	Credit ✓
▼			
▼			
▼			

Picklist:

Discounts allowed
Discounts received
Purchases
Purchases ledger control

Purchases returns
Sales
Sales ledger control
Sales returns
VAT

One of the entries in the discounts received day book is for a credit note received from R Jones for £20 plus VAT.

(b) What will be the entry in the purchases ledger?

Account name		Amount £	Debit ✓	Credit ✓
▼				

Picklist:

Discounts allowed
Discounts received
Purchases
Purchases ledger control
Purchases returns
R Jones
Sales
Sales ledger control
Sales returns
VAT

Chapter summary

- The first stage of the accounting process is to enter details of transactions into the books of prime entry, eg for purchases: purchases day book, purchases returns day book, cash book – credit side and discounts received day book.

- The second stage is to transfer details from the books of prime entry to the accounting records, ie the general ledger and purchases ledger.

- The purchases day book must be totalled and the totals entered into the ledger accounts in the general ledger.

- The gross amount of each individual purchase invoice must be entered into the individual supplier's account in the purchases ledger.

- The purchases returns day book must be totalled and posted to the general ledger and the purchases ledger.

- The cash book – credit side must be totalled and posted to the general ledger (only debit entries if the cash book is part of the general ledger as well as a book of prime entry).

- Each cash payment in the trade payables column of the cash book must be entered into the individual supplier's account in the purchases ledger.

- The discounts received day book must be totalled and the totals entered into the ledger accounts in the general ledger.

- The gross amount of each discount received must also be entered into the individual credit supplier's account in the purchases ledger.

- **Purchases ledger:** Collection of ledger accounts for individual credit suppliers (not part of the double entry system – a subsidiary ledger)

- **Purchases ledger control account:** Total trade payables account in the general ledger

Test your learning

1 Identify the general ledger accounts that the following totals from the purchases day book will be posted to, and whether they are a debit or a credit entry.

Purchases day book total	Account name	Debit ✓	Credit ✓
Gross			
VAT			
Net			

2 A credit note for £600 plus VAT has been received from a supplier. How much will be entered in the purchases ledger control account in the general ledger and the supplier's account in the purchases ledger, and will this entry be a debit or a credit?

	Amount £	Debit ✓	Credit ✓
Purchases ledger control account (general ledger)			
Supplier's account (purchases ledger)			

3 From the purchases day book and purchases returns day book below, make the relevant entries in the general ledger and purchases ledger accounts.

Purchases day book

Date	Supplier	Invoice number	Supplier code	Total £	VAT £	Net £
16 Oct	Herne Industries	46121	PL15	864.00	144.00	720.00
15 Oct	Bass Engineers	663211	PL13	460.80	76.80	384.00
12 Oct	Southfield Electrical	56521	PL20	2,008.80	334.80	1,674.00
				3,333.60	555.60	2,778.00

Purchases returns day book

Date	Supplier	Credit note number	Supplier code	Total £	VAT £	Net £
20 Oct	Southfield Electrical	08702	PL20	120.00	20.00	100.00
20 Oct	Herne Industries	4502	PL15	132.00	22.00	110.00
				252.00	42.00	210.00

GENERAL LEDGER

Purchases ledger control

Details	Amount £	Details	Amount £

Purchases

Details	Amount £	Details	Amount £

Purchases returns

Details	Amount £	Details	Amount £

VAT control

Details	Amount £	Details	Amount £

PURCHASES LEDGER

Herne Industries   PL 15

Details	Amount £	Details	Amount £

Bass Engineers   PL 13

Details	Amount £	Details	Amount £

Southfield Electrical   PL 20

Details	Amount £	Details	Amount £

4   Post from the cash book below to the general ledger and purchases ledger accounts. The cash book is **not** part of the double entry system.

Details	Ref	Cash £	Bank £	VAT £	Cash purchases £	Trade payables £
P Products Ltd	PL23		241.58			241.58
Jason Bros	PL36		336.29			336.29
P Taylor		255.24		42.54	212.70	
R R Partners	PL06		163.47			163.47
Troyde Ltd	PL14		183.57			183.57
O L Simms		119.40		19.90	99.50	
F Elliott	PL20		263.68			263.68
		374.64	1,188.59	62.44	312.20	1,188.59

GENERAL LEDGER

VAT control   GL 100

Details	Amount £	Details	Amount £

Purchases   GL 200

Details	Amount £	Details	Amount £

Purchases ledger control   GL 300

Details	Amount £	Details	Amount £

Cash   GL 550

Details	Amount £	Details	Amount £

Bank   GL 600

Details	Amount £	Details	Amount £

PURCHASES LEDGER

R R Partners **PL 06**

Details	Amount £	Details	Amount £

Troyde Ltd **PL 14**

Details	Amount £	Details	Amount £

F Elliott **PL 20**

Details	Amount £	Details	Amount £

P Products Ltd **PL 23**

Details	Amount £	Details	Amount £

Jason Bros **PL 36**

Details	Amount £	Details	Amount £

5   The following transactions all took place on 30 November and have been entered into the purchases day book as shown below. No entries have yet been made into the ledger system.

Purchases day book

Date 20XX	Details	Invoice number	Total £	VAT £	Net £
30 Nov	Lindell Co	24577	2,136	356	1,780
30 Nov	Harris Rugs	829	5,256	876	4,380
30 Nov	Kinshasa Music	10/235	2,796	466	2,330
30 Nov	Calnan Ltd	9836524	2,292	382	1,910
	Totals		12,480	2,080	10,400

Make the required entries in the general ledger.

VAT control

Details	Amount £	Details	Amount £

Purchase

Details	Amount £	Details	Amount £

Purchases ledger control

Details	Amount £	Details	Amount £

Accounting for petty cash 11

Learning outcomes

1.4	**Demonstrate an understanding of the process of recording financial transactions**
	• The role of the petty cash book: as a book of prime entry only, as a book of prime entry and as part of the double entry bookkeeping system
4.2	**Enter receipts and payments into an analysed petty cash book**
	• The format of the petty cash book: date, details, amount, analysis columns (including VAT)
	• The documents to use: cash receipt, petty cash voucher
	• Calculate VAT amounts from net and total figures
	• Make entries in the petty cash book, including reimbursement, using the imprest and non-imprest systems
4.3	**Total and balance the cash book and petty cash book**
	• Present totals and balances: column totals, balance carried down, balance brought down, debit balance, credit balance, date and details
5.1	**Transfer data from the books of prime entry to the ledgers**
	• The books of prime entry: petty cash book
	• Transfer data from books of prime entry to the relevant accounts in the ledgers
5.2	**Total and balance ledger accounts**
	• Total and balance ledger accounts: balance carried down, balance brought down, debit balance, credit balance

Assessment context

Recording petty cash is one of the key areas of the syllabus and so is very examinable. You may be asked to complete petty cash vouchers, enter transactions into the petty cash book and restore the imprest amount. You may also be asked to post the petty cash book to the ledgers.

Qualification context

Petty cash is primarily tested in *Bookkeeping Transactions*. It is assumed knowledge for the other accounting courses.

Business context

All businesses have petty cash on their premises to pay for small items. It is essential for them to control this cash to prevent it being misappropriated.

Chapter overview

VAT must be shown as this can be reclaimed just like any other purchase

The petty cash box must be restored to the imprest set level

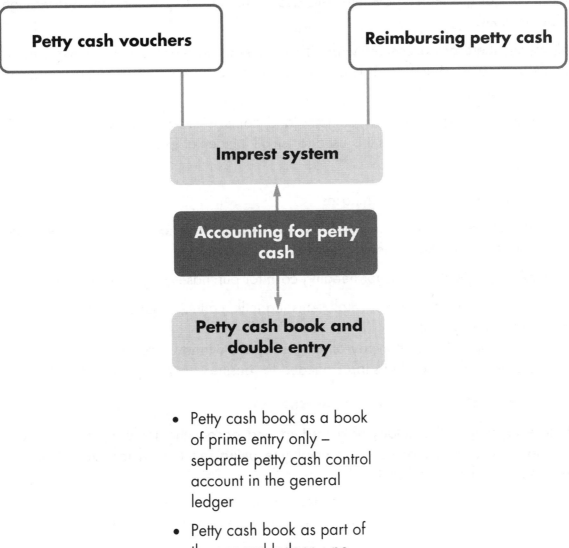

Petty cash vouchers

Reimbursing petty cash

Imprest system

Accounting for petty cash

Petty cash book and double entry

- Petty cash book as a book of prime entry only – separate petty cash control account in the general ledger

- Petty cash book as part of the general ledger – no separate petty cash control account in the general ledger

Introduction

In this chapter we consider all the procedures necessary for dealing with, and accounting for, petty cash.

1 Petty cash

Most businesses make the majority of payments from the bank account by cheque, debit card or automated payment. This avoids the need to pay for expenses through notes or coins.

However, there are occasions when it is necessary to make small payments using coins and notes. Therefore, it is convenient to have an amount of money set aside for this purpose.

This readily available amount of notes and coins is known as **petty cash**. It is referred to as 'petty' cash as it is used for small incidental expenses.

Petty cash is used to:

*   Make low-value cash purchases

*   Reimburse employees immediately for valid business expenses they have paid for, from their own money, on the business's behalf

Examples of typical reasons for needing cash for purchases might include:

*   Purchase of stationery or small items (eg milk, coffee) required in the office
*   Postage payments
*   Payment of casual, non-payroll wages, eg the window cleaner
*   Payment of taxi and bus fares needed for business travel by relevant staff

2 Petty cash claims process

Before looking at the details of recording and accounting for petty cash we will consider the overall process of an employee being reimbursed for expenditure by making a claim for petty cash.

Imagine you work in the accounts department of Southfield Electrical. You have been asked to go out to the local shop to buy more coffee for the office kitchen. This is how the petty cash claims process would work:

1. You go to the shop and buy a jar of coffee with your own money for £4.99.

2. You return to the office with the coffee and a shop till receipt for £4.99.

3. You go to the **petty cashier** and request that they fill out a **petty cash voucher** with the shop receipt attached.

4. You take the petty cash voucher to the person who told you to buy the coffee for authorisation.

5. You take the authorised petty cash voucher to the petty cashier and you are given £4.99 in return.

6. The petty cashier puts the petty cash voucher in the **petty cash box** and eventually records this in the **petty cash book**.

If, instead, money had been taken out of the petty cash box by you and taken to the shop to pay for the purchase, so you did not have to pay out your own cash at all, then the petty cash voucher would be completed in the same way, except that instead of being claimed by you it would be marked as paid to the shop. The till receipt would need to be authorised and attached in both cases.

2.1 Petty cash system

In outline, the petty cash system is operated by the petty cashier who:

- Writes out a cheque for a certain amount of cash to be withdrawn from the bank account

- Collects this amount as notes and coins from the bank

- Places the cash in a lockable **petty cash box**

- Physically looks after the petty cash box

- Deals with all **petty cash claims**

- Ensures that every payment from petty cash has a valid petty cash voucher

- Writes up the **petty cash book**, which is the book of prime entry for petty cash

- Regularly checks that the amount of notes and coins in the petty cash box is correct

- Tops up the amount of notes and coins in the petty cash box so there is always money available

Activity 1: Petty cash amount

Stationery has been purchased for £4.00 plus VAT at 20%.

Insert the amount that will be included as the total figure on the petty cash voucher.

£

3 Petty cash voucher

The key internal document for the proper functioning of a petty cash system is the **petty cash voucher**. This must be completed by the petty cashier and authorised before any cash can be paid out of the petty cash box.

Illustration 1: Petty cash voucher

Petty cash voucher	
Date: 4.12.XX	Number: PC436

Coffee for office kitchen Net £ 4.99 VAT £ 0.00 Gross £ 4.99	
Claimed by: *S Smith*	
Authorised by: *R Jones*	

There are a number of important points to note about this petty cash voucher:

- It is prepared by the petty cashier in response to a request from an employee who has a valid receipt for expenditure to be reimbursed.

- It has a sequential number entered by the petty cashier – 'PC436' – which ensures that all petty cash vouchers are accounted for.

- The details of the expense are clear – 'coffee for office kitchen' – and a till receipt (from the shop) should be attached.

- The amount of the expense is shown both net of VAT and gross, with VAT at 20% separated out where appropriate – in this case there is no charge for VAT.

- The voucher identifies the employee claiming the petty cash – 'S Smith'.

- Most importantly, the voucher is authorised by an appropriate member of staff – 'R Jones'.

Care must be taken to show the VAT incurred on an expense, where applicable, as this can be reclaimed just like any other purchase.

Activity 2: Petty cash voucher

The VAT rate is 20%. The following amount has been paid from petty cash:

100 sheets white cardboard for £20.00 plus VAT.

Complete the petty cash voucher below.

Petty cash voucher	
Date: 8.9.XX	Number: PC587
100 sheets white cardboard	
	£
Net	
VAT	
Gross	

4 Controlling petty cash – the imprest system

In order to ensure petty cash is secure and accurately recorded, most businesses operate an **imprest system** for petty cash. This is essentially a **float**.

The business will have a pre-set amount for its petty cash (the **float** or **imprest level**) and from this will make payments/reimburse expenses. Once funds have been depleted the petty cash box will be topped up to the imprest level.

The imprest system works like this:

(a) The business has a pre-set limit, say £50.

(b) As cash is withdrawn, it is replaced by a **petty cash voucher** of the equivalent amount.

(c) At any point in time, the total of cash plus the petty cash vouchers must equal the imprest amount:

cash (£) + vouchers (£) = imprest amount

(d) At the end of the week/month, the **petty cash book** is filled in from the vouchers.

(e) In order to restore the cash to the imprest amount, vouchers are withdrawn and replaced by cash of an equivalent amount, so:

top-up amount of cash = vouchers = money spent

(f) At the end of the period, therefore, you should be left with the imprest amount in the petty cash box.

Illustration 2: Imprest system

James and Co has an imprest system with an imprest amount of £50.

Details	£
Imprest amount	50
Amount in the petty cash box at the start of the month	50
Month spent during the month, as shown by the vouchers	(35)
Amount in the petty cash box at the end of the month	15

Question	£
What is the amount required to restore the petty cash box to the imprest amount at the end of the period?	35

The amount needed to top up the petty cash box to the imprest amount is the total of the vouchers for the period, £35.

Activity 3: Imprest system

Brian Ltd operates an imprest system to control its petty cash.

On the first day of each month cash is drawn from the bank account to restore the petty cash box to the imprest level.

A summary of petty cash transactions during July 20XX is shown below:

Opening balance 1 July 20XX	£37.50
Cash required on 1 July 20XX to restore cash to the imprest level	£52.50
Payments made from petty cash during July 20XX	£58.75

Required

Answer the following questions.

	£
What is the imprest amount at Brian Ltd?	
What is the amount of cash in the petty cash tin at 31 July 20XX?	

Activity 4: Restoring the petty cash

At the end of the month the cash in a petty cash box was £5.50. The imprest amount is £150.

Required

Complete the petty cash reimbursement document below to restore the imprest amount of £150.00.

Petty cash reimbursement		
Date		31.08.20XX
Amount required to restore the cash in the petty cash box	£	

4.1 Non-imprest petty cash system

We have concentrated so far on a petty cash system that has a fixed imprest amount. The petty cash box is always topped up to that amount at the end of each period. However, it is also possible to run a petty cash system without an imprest amount.

For example, it might be the business's policy to pay £50 into the petty cash box at the start of each week as this is a good estimate of the value of petty cash claims there are each week.

There are two potential problems with this system:

- If the claims in a week are more than £50 then the business may run out of cash in the petty cash box.

- If the claims are substantially less than £50 for a number of weeks then the amount of cash being held in the petty cash box will accumulate – this cash would be of more use in the business bank account than sitting unused in the petty cash box.

5 The petty cash book

The petty cash book is a **book of prime entry** and is used to **record the daily transactions concerning petty cash**.

It is very similar to the cash book in that there is a:

Debit side	records receipts of notes and coins into petty cash
Credit side	records payments of notes and coins from petty cash

Illustration 3: Petty cash book

Debit side		Credit side					
Details	Amount £	Details	Amount £	VAT £	Postage £	Travel £	Stationery £
Balance b/f	150.00	Tim's Taxi	11.00			11.00	
		Post Office	15.00		15.00		
		Smith Stationery	60.00	10.00			50.00
		Balance c/d	64.00				
	150.00		150.00	10.00	15.00	11.00	50.00

Points to note:

• The debit side is not analysed as it simply records the receipt of cash into the petty cash box.

• The credit side is analysed into the various types of petty cash expenditure incurred by the business.

• The credit side includes a VAT column as VAT-registered businesses can reclaim VAT on this expenditure.

Assessment focus point

The VAT rules are complex; however, your assessment will specify whether VAT is applicable or not.

5.1 Maintaining the petty cash book

At regular intervals the petty cash book will be written up from the petty cash vouchers that have been kept in the petty cash box. When the **petty cash float** is reimbursed or 'topped up' to the imprest amount there will also be an entry in the receipts side of the petty cash book for the cash paid in.

Illustration 4: Writing up the petty cash book

One of your duties at Southfield Electrical is to write up the petty cash book each week. At the start of the week, 4 October, the petty cash box was empty and the imprest amount of £100.00 was withdrawn from the bank in cash and placed in the petty cash box.

The petty cash vouchers for the week show the following details:

Voucher 0465   Stationery costing £5.64 including VAT

Voucher 0466 Train fare of £15.80 (no VAT)
Voucher 0467 Postage costs of £15.60 (no VAT)
Voucher 0468 Coffee for the office costing £3.85 (no VAT)
Voucher 0469 Copy paper £7.50 including VAT
Voucher 0470 Postage costs of £8.30 (no VAT)
Voucher 0471 Envelopes costing £2.82 including VAT
Voucher 0472 Train fare of £12.30 (no VAT)

The petty cash book will now be written up.

Petty cash book

Debit side RECEIPTS			Credit side PAYMENTS					ANALYSIS COLUMNS			
Date	Details	Total £	Date	Details	Voucher number	Total £	VAT £	Travel £	Post £	Stationery £	Office supplies £
4/10	Cash	100.00	8/10	Stationery	465	5.64	0.94			4.70	
			8/10	Train fare	466	15.80		15.80			
			8/10	Postage	467	15.60			15.60		
			8/10	Coffee	468	3.85					3.85
			8/10	Copy paper	469	7.50	1.25			6.25	
			8/10	Postage	470	8.30			8.30		
			8/10	Envelopes	471	2.82	0.47			2.35	
			8/10	Train fare	472	12.30		12.30			

Once the petty cash vouchers have been written up in the petty cash book they are filed in numerical sequence. The petty cash book is then totalled and balanced off.

The procedure for balancing off the petty cash book is the same as for any other general ledger account.

As we saw in Chapter 7, the steps to balance off a ledger account are:

Step 1 **Add up** the debit side and the credit side separately.

Step 2 Put the **largest** of the two totals as the column total for **both** the debit and credit columns. For the petty cash book, this will always be the receipts side, as we cannot take more out of the petty cash box than the amount of physical notes and coins in it.

Step 3 Calculate the **balancing figure** on the **side with the lower total and describe this as the balance carried down** (balance c/d).

Step 4 Show this balancing figure on the **opposite side**, below the totals line, and describe this figure as the **balance brought down** (balance b/d).

Petty cash book

Debit side RECEIPTS				Credit side PAYMENTS				ANALYSIS COLUMNS			
Details	Total £	Date	Details	Voucher number	Total £	VAT £	Travel £	Post £	Stationery £	Office supplies £
4 Oct	Cash	100.00	8 Oct	Stationery	465	5.64	0.94			4.70	
			8 Oct	Train fare	466	15.80		15.80			
			8 Oct	Postage	467	15.60			15.60		
			8 Oct	Coffee	468	3.85					3.85
			8 Oct	Copy paper	469	7.50	1.25			6.25	
			8 Oct	Postage	470	8.30			8.30		
			8 Oct	Envelopes	471	2.82	0.47			2.35	
			8 Oct	Train fare	472	12.30		12.30			
				Totals		71.81	2.66	28.10	23.90	13.30	3.85
				Balance c/d		28.19					
		100.00				100.00					
Balance b/d		28.19									

Activity 5: Writing up the petty cash book

This is a summary of petty cash payments made by Toby Ltd.

Tiger's Taxi paid £15.00 (no VAT)

Post Office paid 31.00 (no VAT)

Sara's Stationery paid £60.00 plus VAT

Required

Use the relevant drag items below to:

(a) Enter the above transactions in the petty cash book below

(b) Total the petty cash book and show the balance carried down

Each drag item can be used more than once. You may not need to use all the drag items.

Petty cash book

Debit side		Credit side						
Details	Amount £	Details		Amount £	VAT £	Postage £	Travel £	Stationery £
Balance b/f	200.00		▼					
			▼					
			▼					
			▼					
Total		Totals						

Picklist:

Balance c/d
Post Office
Sara's Stationery
Tiger's Taxi

The drag and drop choices are:

3.00	9.30	12.00	15.00	16.40
31.00	60.00	72.00	82.00	200.00

6 Posting the petty cash book to the general ledger

As with all the books of prime entry, the amounts in the petty cash book need to be included in the general ledger.

And, as we saw with the cash book, the petty cash book can be either part of the general ledger or a book of prime entry only.

> **Assessment focus point**
>
> In your assessment, it is your responsibility to check whether the petty cash book is part of the double entry system or not.
>
> The introductory screen to your assessment will probably include the following statement:
>
> **'The cash book and petty cash book should be treated as part of the double entry system unless the task instructions state otherwise.'**
>
> However, the task instructions may override this by stating something like 'the petty cash book is a book of prime entry only'.
>
> Make sure you know what is applicable to the task you are working on.

6.1 Posting the petty cash book to the general ledger (book of prime entry only)

If the petty cash book is a **book of prime entry only**, **all columns** are posted to the general ledger using the double entry bookkeeping system.

There will be a separate **petty cash control account** in the general ledger. This ledger account records receipts into the petty cash box and payments out of it. The petty cash control account forms part of the double entry system and should be agreed to the petty cash book and the cash in the petty cash box at regular intervals.

Illustration 5: Posting to the general ledger (book of prime entry only)

Petty cash book

Debit side		Credit side				
Details	Amount £	Details	Amount £	VAT £	Travel £	Office expenses £
Bank	100.00	Train fare	40.00		40.00	
		Stationery	60.00	10.00		50.00
	100.00		100.00	10.00	40.00	50.00

The credit and debit side of the petty cash book is posted to the general ledger:

Petty cash book – debit side

Account name	Amount £	Debit ✓	Credit ✓
Petty cash	100.00	✓	
Bank	100.00		✓

This entry represents the reimbursement of petty cash from the bank.

Petty cash book – credit side

Account name	Amount £	Debit ✓	Credit ✓
Petty cash	100.00		✓
VAT	10.00	✓	
Travel expenses	40.00	✓	
Office expenses	50.00	✓	

These entries represent the expenses paid out from petty cash.

Activity 6: Posting the petty cash book (book of prime entry only)

Harriet Ltd maintains a petty cash book as a book of prime entry only. The following transactions all took place on 31 July and have been entered in the petty cash book – credit side as shown below. No entries have yet been made in the general ledger.

Petty cash book – credit side

Date 20XX	Details	Amount £	VAT £	Office expenses £	Postage £	Travel £
31 Jul	Bus fare	25.00				25.00
31 Jul	Train fare	50.00				50.00
31 Jul	Lever arch files	108.00	18.00	90.00		
31 Jul	Post Office	16.00			16.00	
		199.00	18.00	90.00	16.00	75.00

What will be the FIVE entries in the general ledger?

General ledger

Account name		Amount £	Debit ✓	Credit ✓
	▼			
	▼			
	▼			
	▼			
	▼			

Picklist:

Balance b/d
Balance c/d
Bank
Bus fare
Lever arch files
Motor expenses
Office expenses
Petty cash
Petty cash book
Post Office

Postage
Train fare
Travel
VAT

6.2 Petty cash book as a book of prime entry AND part of the double entry system

We saw that the cash book often forms part of the general ledger. Similarly, it is common for the petty cash book to be both a book of prime entry and also part of the double entry system in the general ledger.

If the petty cash book is **both** a book of prime entry **and** part of the general ledger, the amounts columns on the debit and credit sides of the petty cash book form part of the general ledger account.

The effect of this is that:

(a)   There is no separate petty cash account in the general ledger

(b)   In respect of the **amounts** columns, the total received into petty cash (debit side) and the total paid out of petty cash (credit side) are **not** posted separately to the general ledger (as they are already included)

(c)   The analysis columns on the credit side of the petty cash book are posted as normal

(d)   Receipts from the bank account on the debit side of the petty cash book are posted as normal

This is illustrated in the next activity.

Activity 7: Posting the petty cash book (part of the general ledger)

Emily Ltd maintains a petty cash book as both a book of prime entry and part of the double entry accounting system. The following transactions all took place on 31 July and have been entered in the petty cash book as shown below. No entries have yet been made in the general ledger.

Petty cash book

Date 20XX	Details	Amount £	Date 20XX	Details	Amount £	VAT £	Motor expenses £	Office expenses £	Travel £
31 Jul	Balance b/f	92.00	31 Jul	Tea	8.90			8.90	
31 Jul	Bank	58.00	31 Jul	Bus fare	3.00				3.00
			31 Jul	Pens	18.00	3.00		15.00	
			31 Jul	Oil for car	14.40	2.40	12.00		
			31 Jul	Balance c/d	105.70				
		150.00			150.00	5.40	12.00	23.90	3.00

What will be the FIVE entries in the general ledger?

General ledger

Account name		Amount £	Debit ✓	Credit ✓
	▼			
	▼			
	▼			
	▼			
	▼			

Picklist:

Balance b/d
Balance c/d
Bank
Bus fare
Motor expenses
Office expenses
Oil for car
Pens
Petty cash
Petty cash book
Post Office
Postage
Tea
Travel
VAT

Chapter summary

- Most businesses will require small amounts of cash on the premises for the purchase of low-value items and the reimbursement of employees for business expenses.

- This cash is known as petty cash.

- The amount of notes and coins in the petty cash box is counted and reconciled to the balance on the petty cash book.

- An imprest system for petty cash is where the petty cash box is always topped up to the same amount, the imprest amount, at the end of each week or month.

- The petty cash vouchers must then be written up in the petty cash book.

- The petty cash book has a receipts (debit) side and a payments (credit) side and is normally part of the general ledger as well as being a book of prime entry – the payments side is analysed into columns for VAT and all the types of petty cash expense that the business normally deals with.

- When the petty cash vouchers have been written up into the petty cash book it must then be totalled and balanced.

- The double entry for the cash being paid into the petty cash box is a credit entry in the bank account and a debit entry in the petty cash book.

- The analysed payments side of the petty cash book is posted to the general ledger by debiting the VAT and analysis column totals to the relevant accounts in the general ledger.

- If the petty cash book is just a book of prime entry and not part of the double entry system then a separate petty cash account must be kept in the general ledger to record the receipts into the petty cash box and the total payments made; the VAT and analysis amounts are posted as usual.

Keywords

- **Imprest amount:** The amount to which the petty cash float is topped up at the end of a period of time

- **Imprest system:** A petty cash system whereby the petty cash box is always topped up to the same amount at the end of each week or month

- **Petty cash book:** The book of prime entry used to record the petty cash vouchers and any money paid into the petty cash box

- **Petty cash float:** The amount of cash held in the petty cash box at any one time

- **Petty cash voucher:** The document that must be completed and authorised before any cash can be paid out to an employee from the petty cash box

1   Complete the following explanation of how an imprest petty cash system works by selecting the appropriate choices in each case.

(a)   An imprest petty cash system is one where the amount of the topped-up petty cash float at the start of each period is:

Always the same

Sometimes the same

Never the same

(b)   Amounts that have been paid out for authorised expenditure are represented in the petty cash box by:

Notes and coin

Petty cash vouchers

(c)   At the end of the period the total of the

Notes and coin

Petty cash vouchers

in the petty cash box is the amount needed to restore the petty cash box to the imprest amount.

2   A petty cash system is run on the basis of having £150 in the petty cash box at the start of each week. At the end of one week the total of the vouchers in the petty cash box was £89.46. How much cash is required to restore the petty cash box to its imprest amount?

£

3   The petty cash system in your organisation is run on an imprest system with an imprest amount of £150.00. The petty cash float at the start of the week beginning 20 October was £150.00 and 8 petty cash vouchers were completed, authorised and paid on 24 October. The petty cash book analyses payments into VAT, postage, travel, sundry office expenses, and miscellaneous expenses.

The details of the petty cash vouchers are given below:

Voucher 771   Train fare (no VAT) £14.00
Voucher 772   Postage (no VAT) £18.60
Voucher 773   Envelopes (VAT receipt) £16.80
Voucher 774   Window cleaner (no VAT receipt) £20.00
Voucher 775   Pens and paper (VAT receipt) £18.90
Voucher 776   Postage (no VAT) £5.46

Voucher 777   Taxi fare (VAT receipt) £9.60

Voucher 778   Rewritable CDs for computers (VAT receipt) £28.20

You are required to:

(a)   Write up the petty cash book for these vouchers

(b)   Total and balance the petty cash book, bringing down the balance

(c)   Record the amount of cash paid into the petty cash box to restore it to the imprest amount

Petty cash book

RECEIPTS			PAYMENTS								
Date	Details	Amount £	Date	Details	Voucher number	Total £	VAT £	Post £	Travel £	Sundry office £	Misc £
20 Oct	Bank	150.00									
			Balance c/d								
	Total			Total							
Balance b/d											
Cash top-up											

4   This is a summary of petty cash payments made by a business.

Post Office paid	£12.60 (no VAT)
Motor Repair Workshop paid	£72.60 including VAT
Great Eastern Trains paid	£32.00 (no VAT)

The imprest amount for the business at the start of the month is £180.

Use the appropriate narrative from the picklist to complete the details column:

(a)   Enter the above transactions in the petty cash book.

(b)   Total the petty cash book and show the balance carried down.

Petty cash book

Debit side			Credit side				
Details	Amount £	Details	Amount £	VAT £	Postage £	Travel £	Motor expenses £
▼		▼					
▼		▼					
▼		▼					
▼		▼					
▼		▼					

Picklist:

Amount
Balance b/d
Balance c/d
Details
Great Eastern Trains
Motor expenses
Motor Repair Workshop
Postage
Post Office
Travel
VAT

5   A business has a petty cash system with an imprest amount of £50.00. During the week petty cash was paid out of the petty cash box totalling £41.30 and the remaining balance in the box was £8.70. How much cash is required to bring the petty cash box back to the imprest amount?

£	

Initial trial balance

12

Learning outcomes

5.3	Extract an initial trial balance
	• Use the general ledger to extract balances
	• The column to use in the trial balance: debit, credit
	• Transfer balances to the initial trial balance
	• Total and balance the initial trial balance

Assessment context

Tasks are likely to give you a list of account balances and year-end figures, and ask you to correctly list them in the debit or credit column and total the columns. Accuracy is a key skill which is tested here.

Qualification context

In *Bookkeeping Controls* you have to process journal adjustments before the trial balance can be prepared. In Level 3 *Advanced Bookkeeping* you will also be asked to process adjustments and produce a trial balance. In Level 3 *Final Accounts Preparation* and Level 4 *Financial Statements of Limited Companies* you will prepare accounts from a trial balance.

Business context

The trial balance is used to summarise business transactions and from this the financial statements are prepared.

Chapter overview

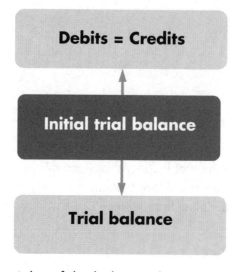

Debits = Credits

Initial trial balance

Trial balance

A list of the balances brought
down on each ledger account

Introduction

Throughout this course, we have been considering the accounting process.

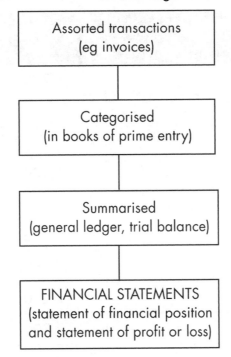

We have seen how business documents are categorised in the books of prime entry and how that information is then transferred from the books of prime entry and summarised in the general ledger. Now we need to extract a **trial balance** from the general ledger. The trial balance forms the basis of the financial statements.

1 The trial balance

A trial balance is drawn up by taking the **balance brought down** on each of the general ledger accounts and placing them in a **list**.

The list is divided into two columns, with one column for all the items with **debit balances** and another column for all the items with **credit balances**.

This is known as an **initial trial balance**.

Illustration 1: Trial balance

Trial balance as at 31 December 20XX

Account name	Debits £	Credits £
Bank	720	
Capital		500
Sales		2,200
Purchases	1,100	
Furniture	500	
Electricity	120	
Telephone	60	
Drawings	200	
Totals	2,700	2,700

The purpose of the trial balance is that it forms a check on the accuracy of the entries in the ledger accounts. **The total of the debit balances should equal the total of the credit balances**. If the **debits** in the trial balance **do not equal the credits** then this indicates that there has been an error in the double entry.

Only the ledger accounts in the **general ledger** are relevant to the preparation of the trial balance. The individual **sales** and **purchases ledger accounts** sit outside of the general ledger, and are not included in the trial balance.

Illustration 2: Initial trial balance

Below are Ben Charles's general ledger accounts.

GENERAL LEDGER

Bank

Details	Amount £	Details	Amount £
Capital	10,000	Purchases	1,000
Sales	1,500	Rent	600
Sales ledger control	1,750	Non-current assets	1,000
		Stationery	200
		Drawings	500
		Purchases ledger control	1,500
		Balance c/d	8,450
Total	13,250	Total	13,250
Balance b/d	8,450		

Capital

Details	Amount £	Details	Amount £
Balance c/d		Bank	10,000
Total	10,000	Total	10,000
		Balance b/d	10,000

Purchases

Details	Amount £	Details	Amount £
Bank	1,000		
Purchases ledger control	2,000	Balance c/d	3,000
Total	3,000	Total	3,000
Balance b/d	3,000		

Purchases ledger control

Details	Amount £	Details	Amount £
Bank	1,500	Purchases	2,000
Balance c/d	500		
Total	2,000	Total	2,000
		Balance b/d	500

Rent

Details	£	Details	£
Bank	600	Balance c/d	600
Total	600	Total	600
Balance b/d	600		

Sales

Details	£	Details	£
		Bank	1,500
Balance c/d	3,300	Sales ledger control	1,800
Total	3,300	Total	3,300
		Balance b/d	3,300

Sales ledger control

Details	£	Details	£
Sales	1,800	Bank	1,750
		Discount allowed	50
		Balance c/d	0
Total	1,800	Total	1,800
Balance b/d	0		

Non-current assets

Details	£	Details	£
Bank	1,000	Balance c/d	1,000
Total	1,000	Total	1,000
Balance b/d	1,000		

Stationery

Details	£	Details	£
Bank	200	Balance c/d	200
Total	200	Total	200
Balance b/d	200		

Drawings

Details	£	Details	£
Bank	500	Balance c/d	500
Total	500	Total	500
Balance b/d	500		

Discount allowed

Details	£	Details	£
Sales ledger control	50	Balance c/d	50
Total	50	Total	50
Balance b/d	50		

Now we will perform the next step in completing Ben Charles's accounts for the period by preparing a trial balance.

Step 1 List the balance brought down on each account as a debit or credit as appropriate.

	Debits £	Credits £
Bank	8,450	
Capital		10,000
Purchases	3,000	
Purchases ledger control		500
Rent	600	
Sales		3,300
Sales ledger control	0	
Non-current assets	1,000	
Stationery	200	
Drawings	500	
Discounts allowed	50	

Step 2 Total the debit column and the credit column and check that they are equal.

	Debits £	Credits £
Bank	8,450	
Capital		10,000
Purchases	3,000	
Purchases ledger control		500
Rent	600	
Sales		3,300
Sales ledger control	0	
Non-current assets	1,000	
Stationery	200	
Drawings	500	
Discounts allowed	50	
Totals	13,800	13,800

Activity 1: Initial trial balance

The general ledger T-accounts below are those that were prepared in an earlier chapter (Chapter 6) for a company called Hampton. Using the balances brought down in the general ledger T-accounts, you are required to prepare a trial balance.

GENERAL LEDGER

Bank

Details	Amount £	Details	Amount £
Capital	20,000	Purchases	250
		Rent	225
		Rates	135
		Balance c/d	19,390
	20,000		20,000
Balance b/d	19,390		

Capital

Details	Amount £	Details	Amount £
Balance c/d	20,000	Bank	20,000
	20,000		20,000
		Balance b/d	20,000

Purchases

Details	Amount £	Details	Amount £
Bank	250		
Purchases ledger control	450	Balance c/d	700
	700		700
Balance b/d	700		

Rent

Details	Amount £	Details	Amount £
Bank	225	Balance c/d	225
	225		225
Balance b/d	225		

Sales

Details	Amount £	Details	Amount £
		Cash	657
Balance c/d	1,407	Sales ledger control	750
	1,407		1,407
		Balance b/d	1,407

Cash

Details	Amount £	Details	Amount £
Sales	657	Wages	75
		Balance c/d	582
	657		657
Balance b/d	582		

Rates

Details	Amount £	Details	Amount £
Bank	135	Balance c/d	135
	135		135
Balance b/d	135		

Sales ledger control

Details	Amount £	Details	Amount £
Sales	750	Balance c/d	750
	750		750
Balance b/d	750		

Purchases ledger control

Details	Amount £	Details	Amount £
Balance c/d	450	Purchases	450
	450		450
		Balance b/d	450

Wages

Details	Amount £	Details	Amount £
Cash	75	Balance c/d	75
	75		75
Balance b/d	75		

Prepare the trial balance by placing the figures in the debit or credit column, as appropriate, and total each column.

Trial balance

Account name	Debit £	Credit £
Bank		
Capital		
Purchases		
Rent		
Sales		
Cash		
Rates		
Sales ledger control		
Purchases ledger control		
Wages		
Totals		

1.1 Balances to watch out for in your assessment

When you are given a set of general ledger T-accounts it is clear which side of the trial balance each balance should appear in: the same side as the **balance brought down** on the account.

However, in your assessment you will probably be given a list of balances and required to identify from their names whether they are debit or credit balances. You should watch out for the following, which students often get wrong.

Name of balance	Debit or credit balance?	Nature of balance
Inventory – of goods or materials held at any point in time	Debit	Asset
Bank overdraft	Credit	Liability
Bank **or** Cash **or** Petty cash	Debit	Asset
Loan	Credit	Liability
VAT owed to HMRC	Credit	Liability
VAT owed by HMRC	Debit	Asset
Capital	Credit	Capital
Drawings	Debit	Reduction in capital
Bank interest paid or bank charges	Debit	Expense
Bank interest received	Credit	Income

Assessment focus point

The illustration and activity above were preparation examples to enable you to see the process of transferring balances brought down in the general ledger to a trial balance. The activity below gives a list of balances and asks you to prepare a trial balance from that list. In your assessment, you could get a question that includes a combination of these techniques to form the trial balance.

Activity 2: Preparing a trial balance

Below is a list of balances to be transferred to the trial balance as at 31 March 20XX.

Required

Place the figures in the debit or credit column, as appropriate, and total each column.

Trial balance as at 31 March 20XX

Account name	Amount £	Debit £	Credit £
Motor vehicles	31,200		
Inventory	4,200		
Bank	18,260		
Sales ledger control	8,800		
Purchases ledger control	6,400		
Capital	80,000		
Sales	130,000		
Sales returns	10,000		
Purchases	84,000		
Purchases returns	5,400		
Bank charges	200		
Discounts allowed	1,800		
Discounts received	1,200		
Wages and salaries	43,600		
Rent and rates	12,400		
Telephone	2,040		
Electricity	5,100		
Office expenses	1,400		
Totals			

Tutorial note. The figure in the 'amount' column is the balance brought down on the T-account.

Chapter summary

- A trial balance is prepared by listing all the debit balances brought down and credit balances brought down and checking the totals of these balances to ensure that they agree.

- The purpose of the trial balance is that it forms a check on the accuracy of the entries in the ledger accounts.

Keyword

- **Initial trial balance:** A list of all the debit and credit balances brought down on the ledger accounts

1 Calculate and carry down the closing balances on each of the following accounts.

VAT account

	£		£
Purchases	3,778	Balance b/f	2,116
Bank	2,116	Sales	6,145

Sales account

	£		£
		Balance b/f	57,226
		Sales ledger control	42,895

Sales ledger control account

	£		£
Balance b/f	4,689	Bank	21,505
Sales	23,512	Discounts allowed	2,019

Purchases ledger control account

	£		£
Purchases returns	1,334	Balance b/f	2,864
Bank	13,446	Purchases	14,552
Discounts received	662		

2   Indicate whether each of the following balances would be shown as a debit balance or a credit balance in the trial balance.

	£	Debit balance ✓	Credit balance ✓
Discounts allowed	1,335		
Discounts received	1,013		
Purchases returns	4,175		
Sales returns	6,078		
Bank interest received	328		
Bank charges	163		

3   Given below are the balances on the ledger accounts of Thames Traders at 30 November 20XX. Prepare the trial balance as at 30 November 20XX, including totals.

	£	Debit £	Credit £
Motor vehicles	64,000		
Office equipment	21,200		
Sales	238,000		
Purchases	164,000		
Cash	300		
Bank overdraft	1,080		
Petty cash	30		

	£	Debit £	Credit £
Capital	55,000		
Sales returns	4,700		
Purchases returns	3,600		
Sales ledger control	35,500		
Purchases ledger control	30,100		
VAT (owed to HMRC)	12,950		
Telephone	1,600		
Electricity	2,800		
Wages	62,100		
Loan from bank	30,000		
Discounts allowed	6,400		
Discounts received	3,900		
Rent expense	12,000		
Totals			

4   Below is a list of balances to be transferred to the trial balance as at 30 June.

Place the figures in the debit or credit column, as appropriate, and total each column.

Account name	Amount £	Debit £	Credit £
Advertising	3,238		
Bank overdraft	27,511		
Capital	40,846		
Cash	689		
Discount allowed	4,416		
Discount received	2,880		
Hotel expenses	2,938		
Inventory	46,668		
Loan from bank	39,600		
Miscellaneous expenses	3,989		

Account name	Amount £	Debit £	Credit £
Motor expenses	7,087		
Motor vehicles	63,120		
Petty cash	720		
Purchases	634,529		
Purchases ledger control	110,846		
Purchases returns	1,618		
Rent and rates	19,200		
Sales	1,051,687		
Sales ledger control	405,000		
Sales returns	11,184		
Stationery	5,880		
Subscriptions	864		
Telephone	3,838		
VAT (owing to HM Revenue & Customs)	63,650		
Wages	125,278		
Totals			

5   Below are two ledger accounts and a partially completed trial balance.

Complete the trial balance by:

- Transferring the balances of the two general ledger accounts to the debit or credit column of the trial balance

- Entering the amounts shown against each of the other names into the debit or credit column of the trial balance

- Totalling both columns of the trial balance

Cash

Details	£	Details	£
Balance b/f	1,000.00	Cash payments	720.00
Cash receipts	240.00	Balance c/d	520.00
	1,240.00		1,240.00
Balance b/d	520.00		

VAT account

Details	£	Details	£
Sales returns	44.00	Balance b/f	1,500.00
Purchases	1,108.00	Sales	280.00
Cash	120.00	Cash	40.00
Balance c/d	640.00	Purchases returns	92.00
	1,912.00		1,912.00
		Balance b/d	640.00

Trial balance

Account name	Amount £	Debit £	Credit £
Cash			
Bank	9,320.00		
Sales ledger control	10,000.00		
Sales	21,650.00		
Sales returns	230.00		
VAT			
Discounts allowed	40.00		
Purchases ledger control	2,500.00		
Purchases	6,300.00		
Purchases returns	480.00		
Discounts received	140.00		
Capital	1,000.00		

CHAPTER 1 Business documentation

Activity 1: Cash or credit sale

	✓
A cash transaction	
A credit transaction	✓

Tutorial note. This is a credit transaction, as Cathy does not pay immediately; she has two weeks to make the payment.

Activity 2: Preparing an invoice

Garden Greats

16 Vash Lane, Elstree, KH3 9GH

VAT Registration No. 284 4924 93

INVOICE

Super Stores
42 The Pitch
Old Crabtree
Wellington GK34 9HL

Invoice no: 571

Customer account code:	SS454
Delivery note number:	39483
Date:	1 August 20XX

Quantity	Product code	Total list price £	VAT £	Gross £
200	F250	2,000.00	400.00	2,400.00

Tutorial note. The customer account code, the delivery note number, the quantity and the product code can all be taken directly from the delivery note. The remaining amounts must be calculated as follows:

		£
Total list price	200 × 10*	2,000.00
VAT	2,000.00 × 20%	400.00
Gross	2,000.00 + 400.00	2,400.00

*The list price was given below the delivery note: £10 per case

Activity 3: Coding an invoice

Toby Parts Ltd
31 Cannon Way, Amersham
Bucks HP8 3LD
VAT Registration No. 424 5242 42

INVOICE

Paving Co Ltd
24 George Street
Amersham
Bucks HP3 5BJ

Customer account code: PAV001

Date: 5 November 20XX

Invoice number: 694

Delivery note number: 43456

10 telephones @ £50	£500.00
VAT @ 20%	£100.00
Total	£600.00

Supplier code: | TOB51 | General ledger code: | GL119 |

Activity 4: Creating a code

Customer	Customer code
Docoa Ltd	Doc01
Jury Ltd	Jur03

Tutorial note. The first part of the code is the first three letters of the customer's name, so Doc and Jur in this case. The numerical part of the code depends on how many other customer names begin with the same letter. In the case of Docoa Ltd, there are no other customers with names beginning with D, therefore Docoa Ltd will be allocated 01. In the case of Jury Ltd, there are two other customers with names beginning with J, therefore Jury Ltd will be allocated 03.

CHAPTER 2 The books of prime entry

Activity 1: Sales day book

Sales day book

Date 20XX	Details	Invoice number	Customer code	Total £	VAT £	Net £	Sales type 1 £	Sales type 2 £
31 Aug	K Lead	2041	SL15	2,500 + 500 = 3,000	2,500/5 = 500	2,500	2,500	
31 Aug	O Ball	2042	SL02	300 + 60 = 360	300/5 = 60	300		300
31 Aug	P Reed	2043	SL10	665 + 133 = 798	665/5 = 133	665	665	
	Totals			4,158	693	3,465	3,165	300

Tutorial note. The analysis columns contain the net amounts. So you can calculate the VAT on the net amount by dividing the net amount by 5. The Total column is simply the gross amount = net + VAT.

Activity 2: Sales returns day book

Sales returns day book

Date 20XX	Details	Credit note number	Customer code	Total £	VAT £	Net £	Sales returns £
31 May	K Farm	751	SL08	350 + 70 = 420	350 / 5 = 70	350	350
31 May	S Fred	752	SL11	270	270 / 6 = 45	270 – 45 = 225	225
31 May	J Irons	753	SL07	200 × 6 = 1,200	200	1,200 – 200 = 1,000	1,000
	Totals			1,890	315	1,575	1,575

Tutorial note. This activity requires you to use the different figures you have been given to work out what the rest of the figures should be. For customer K Farm, you have been given the net amount in the sales returns analysis column. From this you can calculate VAT and then the total (or gross) amount. For customer S Fred, you have the gross amount, from which you can calculate VAT and then the net amount. Remember, the analysis column is the net amount. Finally for customer J Irons you have been given the VAT. To calculate the gross amount, multiply the VAT by six. Then you can subtract the VAT from the gross to give the net amount.

Activity 3: Purchases day book

Purchases day book

Date 20XX	Details	Invoice number	Supplier code	Total £	VAT £	Net £	Purchases £	Expenses £
28 Feb	Dill Ltd	5215	PL05	9,520 + 1,904 = 11,424	9,520 / 5 = 1,904	9,520		9,520
28 Feb	Neil Co	PO8214	PL17	130 + 26 = 156	130 / 5 = 26	130	130	
28 Feb	Elkin	SS852	PL33	5,240 + 1,048 = 6,288	5,420 / 5 = 1,048	5,240	5,240	
	Totals			17,868	2,978	14,890	5,370	9,520

Tutorial note. The analysis columns contain the net amount, so these figures can be used to populate the net column. The VAT and the Total (which is just the gross amount) can then be calculated from the net figure.

Activity 4: Purchases returns day book

Purchases returns day book

Date 20XX	Details	Credit note number	Supplier code	Total £	VAT £	Net £
31 Mar	Horace	NH94	PL01	120 + 24 = 144	120 / 5 = 24	120
31 Mar	Jameson	313	PL23	1,050	1,050 / 6 = 175	1,050 – 175 = 875
	Totals			1,194	199	995

Tutorial note. This activity requires you to again use the figures given to work out the remaining figures. For supplier Horace you have been given the net amount, so you can calculate VAT on the net amount in order to get the gross amount. For supplier Jameson, you need to calculate VAT from the gross amount in order to get the net amount.

Activity 5: Sales ledger

Sales ledger

Fred & Co

Details	Amount £	Details	Amount £
Invoice 121	3,425	Bank	1,952
Invoice 125	4,561	Credit note 31	553
	7,986		2,505

Tutorial note. Remember, entries on the left-hand side increase the amount owed by the customer, and entries on the right-hand side decrease the amount owed by the customer.

To calculate how much is owed by Fred & Co to Gregory & Sons, you should total the left-hand side of the account, and total the right-hand side of the account, then subtract the right-hand side total from the left-hand side total.

	£
How much does Fred & Co owe Gregory & Sons? (7,986 – 2,505)	5,481

Activity 6: Purchases ledger

Purchases ledger

Cyril & Co

Details	Amount £	Details	Amount £
Bank	4,250	Invoice 101	4,250
Credit note 87	1,032	Invoice 107	9,682
	5,282		13,932

Tutorial note. Remember, entries on the left-hand side decrease the amount the business owes the supplier, and entries on the right-hand side increase the amount the business owes the supplier.

To calculate how much Gregory & Sons owes Cyril & Co, you should total the left-hand side of the account, and total the right-hand side of the account, then subtract the left-hand side total from the right-hand side total.

	£
How much does Gregory & Sons owe Cyril & Co? (13,932 – 5,282)	8,650

CHAPTER 3 VAT and discounts

Activity 1: Calculating VAT on the net amount

Net £	VAT £	Gross £
100.00	100.00 × 20% = 20.00 Or 100.00 / 5 = 20.00	100.00 + 20.00 = 120.00
350.00	350.00 × 20% = 70.00 Or 350.00 / 5 = 70.00	350.00 + 70.00 = 420.00
3,898.34	3,898.34 × 20% = 779.66 Or 3,898.34 / 5 = 779.66	3,898.34 + 779.66 = 4,678.00
6,500.00	6,500.00 × 20% = 1,300.00 Or 6,500.00 / 5 = 1,300.00	6,500.00 + 1,300.00 = 7,800.00

Tutorial note. The VAT on item 3 (net amount £3,898.34) must be rounded down to 2 decimal places.

Activity 2: Calculating VAT from the gross amount

Net £	VAT £	Gross £
240.00 – 40.00 = 200.00	240.00 / 6 = 40.00	240.00
660.00 – 110.00 = 550.00	660.00 / 6 = 110.00	660.00
594.00 – 99.00 = 495.00	594.00 / 6 = 99.00	594.00
1,260.00 – 210.00 = 1,050.00	1,260.00 / 6 = 210.00	1,260.00

Activity 3: VAT and discounts

	£
List price	15,000.00
Trade discount	(4,000.00)
Sales price net of trade discount	11,000.00
VAT (11,000.00 / 5 = 2,200.00)	2,200.00
Gross (11,000.00 + 2,200.00 = 13,200.00)	13,200.00

Tutorial note. The prompt payment discount is not deducted from the amount shown on the invoice. It is instead shown in the terms section of the invoice.

Activity 4: VAT, discounts and business documentation

Car Parts R Us
14 Maze Road
Essex, UG1 7SG
VAT Registration No: 472 3591 71

INVOICE

Marcus Cars 3 Viewpoint Way Birmingham BH12 3LK	Customer account code:	MC001
	Invoice no:	5353
	Date:	9 August 20XX

Quantity	Product code	Total list price £	Net amount after discount £	VAT £	Gross £
1	9315	15,000.00	11,000.00	2,200.00	13,200.00

Payment terms: 10% discount if paid within 14 days
Otherwise, pay within 30 days.

Tutorial note. The net amount after discount is the amount after deducting the **trade discount** only, as calculated in Activity 3.

The VAT is calculated on the net amount after deducting the **trade discount**, as calculated in Activity 3.

The **gross amount** is the net amount plus VAT = 11,000.00 + 2,200.00 = 13,200.00

Activity 5: Discounts and credit notes

Amount	£
Net amount	1,100.00
VAT	220.00
Gross amount	1,320.00

Tutorial note. Remember the steps to calculate the amounts for the credit note:

Step	Method	Calculation	£
1	Calculate the discount taken. This is the gross amount on the credit note.	13,200.00 × 0.1	1,320.00
2	Calculate the VAT on the prompt payment discount taken.	1,320.00 × 20/120	220.00
3	Calculate the net amount.	1,320.00 – 220.00	1,100.00

Activity 6: Discounts and day books

Day book	Discounts allowed day book				
Date 20XX	Details	Credit note number	Total £	VAT £	Net £
10 Nov	Paving Co Ltd	105	12.00	2.00	10.00

Tutorial note. The credit note should be recorded in Toby Part Ltd's discounts allowed day book as it is a discount allowed to a customer.

The name of the customer (Paving Co Ltd) should be recorded in the Details column. The gross amount from the invoice should be recorded in the Total column, and the VAT and net amounts in those columns respectively.

CHAPTER 4 Recording credit sales

Activity 1: Business documentation

Stage	Process	Document
1	Quotation is requested for goods/services	Quotation
2	Order is placed	Customer order
3	Goods are despatched	Delivery note
4	Payment requested	Invoice
5	Goods may be returned to vendor*	Credit note
6	Payment	Remittance advice note

* This (of course!) does not happen with every sale.

Activity 2: Sales invoice

Invoice

Hugh Houghton

24 Bottrels Lane

Crewe CA3 DF

VAT Registration No. 482 4995 24

INVOICE

Elizabeth Elstree

89 Somerset Way

Moreton MK8 4JD

Customer account code: | ELI053

Delivery note number: | 84251

Invoice no: 1031 | Date: | 24 March 20XX

Quantity	Product code	Total list price £	Net amount after discount £	VAT £	Gross £
2,500	8321	750.00	605.62	121.12	726.74

Tutorial note. The customer account code, delivery number, quantity and product code can all be taken directly from the delivery note.

The remaining amounts must be calculated:

		£
Total list price	2,500 × £0.30 =	750.00
Trade discount	750.00 × 0.15 =	112.50
Net amount after trade discount	750.00 − 112.50 =	637.50
Bulk discount	637.50 × 0.05 =	31.88
Net after all discounts	637.50 − 31.88 =	605.62
VAT calculation	605.62 × 0.2 =	121.12
Gross	605.62 + 121.12 =	726.74

Activity 3: Credit note

Darren Dunn

482 The Lagger

Liverpool LI4 9MG

VAT Registration No. 424 5242 42

CREDIT NOTE

Jasper & Co
52 The Hilltop
Liverpool
LN8 8DW

Customer account code: JAS003

Date: 21 July 20XX

Credit note no: 454

Invoice no: 3567

Quantity	Product code	Total list price £	Net amount after discount £	VAT £	Gross £
5	5295	275.00	261.25	52.25	313.50

Tutorial note. The customer account code, quantity and product code are all given in the question and can be copied into the credit note.

The remaining amounts must be calculated:

		£
Total list price	5 × 55.00 =	275.00
Trade discount	275 × 0.05 =	(13.75)
		261.25
VAT calculation	261.25 × 20% =	52.25
Gross	261.25 + 52.25 =	313.50

Activity 4: Checking business documentation

(a)

	Yes ✓	No ✓
Is the product code on the invoice correct?		✓
Has the correct unit price per wheelbarrow been charged?	✓	
Has the correct trade discount been applied?		✓

Tutorial note. The product code on the delivery note is 841951; this code has been incorrectly included as 814951 on the invoice. Note the 4 and 1 have been mixed up.

The customer was entitled to receive a trade discount of 10% and a prompt payment discount of 5%. The invoice shows a discount of 5% as a trade discount, which is incorrect; it should be 10%. Remember that only the trade discount of 10% should be applied to the invoice; the prompt payment discount of 5% is included in the terms section only.

(b)

	£
What would be the VAT charge if the invoice was correct?	378.00
What would be the total amount charged if the invoice was correct?	2,268.00

Tutorial note. The amounts are calculated as follows:

		£
Total list price	35 × £60.00 =	2,100.00
Trade discount	2,100 × 0.1 =	210.00
Net amount after trade discount	2,100.00 – 210.00 =	1,890.00
VAT calculation	1,890.00 × 0.2 =	378.00
Gross	1,890.00 + 378.00 =	2,268.00

Activity 5: Checking the accuracy of customer receipts

(a)

Invoice 505

Tutorial note. The sales ledger account for Heidi Ltd shows a balance b/f of £6,000 and a receipt into the bank account for £6,000. So, these two items cancel each other out. By a process of trial and error you can work out that Invoice 505 has not been included:

	£
Invoice 501	1,200
Credit note 130	(450)
Total	750
Payment received	750

(b)

£	3,763.20

Tutorial note. If payment is received within 15 days, the customer can deduct the prompt payment discount of 2%: (3,200.00 + 640.00) × 0.98 = £3,763.20.

(c)

Net	£	64.00
VAT	£	12.80
Gross	£	76.80

Tutorial note. The amounts are calculated as follows:

		£
Gross amount	3,840.00 × 0.02 =	76.80
VAT	76.80/6 =	12.80
Net	76.80 – 12.80 =	64.00

(d)

£	3,840.00

Tutorial note. If the payment is not made within 15 days, the full amount of the invoice is due: 3,200.00 + 640.00 = £3,840.00.

CHAPTER 5 Recording credit purchases

Activity 1: Expenses: goods or services

(a) Goods – these are **physical items**

Car parts
Plastic to make toys
Stationery

(b) Services – there is **no physical item**

Cleaning services
Payroll work
Legal work

Activity 2: Accuracy of business documentation

	Yes ✓	No ✓
Is the purchase order number correctly included on the goods received note?	✓	
Has the correct quantity of aluminium sheets been delivered?		✓
Has the correct quantity of red plastic squares been delivered?		✓
Are the product codes correctly included on the goods received note?	✓	
Has the goods received note been signed to confirm the goods were checked on arrival?		✓

Tutorial note. Whales Way has mixed up the quantities of aluminium sheets and red plastic squares, and so has delivered the wrong quantity of both. The GRN has been signed by the person who received the goods, but not by the person who checked them.

Make sure that you read the question very carefully as it is easy to misread the question and so give the wrong answer.

Activity 3: Checking a statement of account

(a)

Which item is missing from the statement of account from Samuel Ltd?	Cheque for £4,200
Which item is missing from the supplier account in Peter Ltd's purchases ledger?	Invoice 408

Tutorial note. The best way to approach part (a) is to work through the statement of account and **tick off each item** that also appears in the purchases ledger. The remaining unticked items will enable you to answer the two questions in part (a).

(b)

	£
Assuming any differences between the statement of account from Samuel Ltd and the supplier account in Peter Ltd's purchases ledger are simply due to omission errors, what is the amount owing to Samuel Ltd?	2,700

Tutorial note. To answer part (b), you should work from the **closing balance** in the **supplier statement** and then add on or take off the missing amount:

	£
Closing balance	6,900
Missing payment	(4,200)
Amount owing	2,700

Activity 4: Reconciliation of a purchases ledger account and a supplier statement

(a)

	£
Balance on supplier's statement of account	4,317
Balance on supplier's account in purchases ledger *(900 + 2,342 + 725) – (750 + 150)	3,067
Difference (4,317 – 3,067) *	1,250

* Calculations are included for tutorial purposes and do not form part of the answer.

Tutorial note. To work out the balance on the supplier's account in the purchases ledger you need to add up the amounts on each side of the supplier's account. Remember that everything on the **left** side of the account **reduces** the total owed to the supplier, and everything on the **right** side of the account **increases** the total owed to the supplier.

(b)

Items	✓
Cheque for £750	
Invoice number 841	
Credit note number 76	
Invoice number 878	
Invoice number 891	✓

Tutorial note. The best way to approach part (b) is to work through the statement of account and **tick off each item** that also appears in the purchases ledger. The unticked items remaining will enable you to answer part (b). You can ignore the brought forward balance on the statement of account for the purposes of the ticking exercise.

Note that the difference identified in part (a) of £1,250 is the amount of the missing invoice 891 identified in part (b). This is a good way to check whether you have completed the reconciliation correctly.

Activity 5: Prompt payment discount

(a)

	✓
31 December 20XX	
15 December 20XX	✓
01 December 20XX	

Tutorial note. The terms of the PPD are for payment to be received within 14 days of the invoice date, which in this case was 1 December 20XX. So the payment must be received by 15 December.

(b)

£	749.70

Tutorial note. The prompt payment discount is 2%, so the total amount to be paid is calculated as: 765.00 × 0.98 = £749.70

(c)

Amount	£
Net amount	12.75
VAT	2.55
Gross amount	15.30

Tutorial note. Remember the steps from Chapter 3 on how to calculate the amounts to include on the credit note:

Step	Method	Calculation	£
1	Calculate the discount taken.	765.00 × 2%	15.30
2	Calculate the VAT on the prompt payment discount taken.	15.30 / 6	2.55
3	Calculate the net amount.	15.30 – 2.55	12.75

Activity 6: Authorisation

The purchase of raw materials costing £300 should be authorised by	line manager
The purchase of an item of machinery costing £49,999 should be authorised by	line manager plus finance director
The purchase of goods costing £3,500 should be authorised by	line manager plus manager from another department

Activity 7: BACS remittance advice note

(a)

	✓
Cardleys Bank plc	
HNB3 Bank plc	
Justin Jukes	
Rose Reed	✓

Tutorial note. Remember that the remittance advice is sent to the **supplier**, which in this case is Rose Reed.

(b)

	✓
31 January	
28 February	
31 March	
30 April	✓

Tutorial note. You might have thought that you would be preparing the remittance advice to accompany the payment made on 31 March shown in the ledger account. But that is not the case. You can see on the right-hand side of the ledger account an invoice dated 12 April, so the payment on 31 March has already been paid and a remittance advice will already have been sent. The remittance advice you are being asked to prepare is for the next month, ie 30 April. It will always be the case in your assessment that you are preparing the remittance advice for the payment **after the last payment** listed in the ledger account.

(c)

	✓
Invoice 4560	
Invoice 4591	✓
Invoice 5003	✓
Invoice 5115	
Credit note 56	
Credit note 67	

Tutorial note. The key piece of information from the question to help you with this answer is that Justin Jukes sends remittance advice notes to suppliers on **the last day of the month following the month of invoice**. So because you are preparing the remittance advice for **April**, it should include invoices from **March**: invoice 4591 and invoice 5003. There were no credit notes issued in April (remember credit notes are taken immediately) so there are none to include on the remittance advice.

(d)

	£
Total amount paid	5,326

Tutorial note. The total paid is:

	£
Invoice 4591	3,295
Invoice 5003	2,031
	5,326

CHAPTER 6 Double entry bookkeeping (Part 1)

Activity 1: Introduction to double entry

	Transaction	Debit	Credit
(a)	Sales for cash	Cash **increase assets**	Sales **Increase in income**
(b)	Sales on credit	Sales ledger control **increase assets**	Sales **increase in income**
(c)	Purchases for cash	Purchases **increase in expense**	Cash **decrease assets**
(d)	Purchases on credit	Purchases **increase in expense**	Purchases ledger control **increase liabilities**
(e)	Pay electricity bill using cash	Electricity **increase in expense**	Cash **decrease assets**
(f)	Receive cash from a credit customer	Cash **increase assets**	Sales ledger control **decrease assets**
(g)	Pay cash to a credit supplier	Purchases ledger control **decrease liabilities**	Cash **decrease assets**
(h)	Borrow money from the bank	Cash **increase assets**	Loan **increase liabilities**

Activity 2: Entering a transaction into a ledger account

(a)

Account	Debit ✓	Credit ✓
Cash	✓	
Sales		✓

(b)

Cash

Details	Amount £	Details	Amount £
Sales	200		

Sales

Details	Amount £	Details	Amount £
		Cash	200

Tutorial note. For each transaction, you should:

(1) Classify the transaction – what elements are affected?

(2) Work out whether an increase or decrease to the element is required

(3) Use DEAD CLIC to work out whether that increase or decrease required is a debit or credit to the affected account

Activity 3: Recording transactions in the general ledger accounts

Tutorial note. For each transaction, you should:

(1) Classify the transaction – what elements are affected?

(2) Work out whether an increase or decrease to the element is required

(3) Use DEAD CLIC to work out whether that increase or decrease required is a debit or credit to the affected account

The entries in the ledger accounts are shown below. To help you, the transactions and their required double entries are shown here:

(1)	Started business by depositing £20,000 into the bank account	DEBIT Bank	£20,000	
		CREDIT Capital		£20,000
(2)	Bought goods for resale and paid £250 by cheque	DEBIT Purchases	£250	
		CREDIT Bank		£250
(3)	Paid rent of £225 by cheque	DEBIT Rent	£225	
		CREDIT Bank		£225
(4)	Sold goods for £657, customer paid in cash	DEBIT Cash	£657	
		CREDIT Sales		£657
(5)	Paid rates £135 by cheque	DEBIT Rates	£135	
		CREDIT Bank		£135
(6)	Sold goods on credit to a customer, J Henry, for £750	DEBIT Sales ledger control	£750	
		CREDIT Sales		£750
(7)	Bought goods for resale on credit from C Bableton for £450	DEBIT Purchases	£450	
		CREDIT Purchases ledger control		£450
(8)	Paid wages £75 cash	DEBIT Wages	£75	
		CREDIT Cash		£75

Note that only actual cash (notes and coins) goes through the cash ledger account. Cheques are paid into the bank, therefore they are recorded in the business's bank account in the general ledger.

GENERAL LEDGER

Bank

Details	Amount £	Details	Amount £
Capital (1)	20,000	Purchases (2)	250
		Rent (3)	225
		Rates (5)	135

Capital

Details	Amount £	Details	Amount £
		Bank (1)	20,000

Purchases

Details	Amount £	Details	Amount £
Bank (2)	250		
Purchases ledger control (7)	450		

Rent

Details	Amount £	Details	Amount £
Bank (3)	225		

Sales

Details	Amount £	Details	Amount £
		Cash (4)	657
		Sales ledger control (6)	750

Cash

Details	Amount £	Details	Amount £
Sales (4)	657	Wages (8)	75

Rates

Details	Amount £	Details	Amount £
Bank (5)	135		

Sales ledger control

Details	Amount £	Details	Amount £
Sales (6)	750		

Purchases ledger control

Details	Amount £	Details	Amount £
		Purchases (7)	450

Wages

Details	Amount £	Details	Amount £
Cash (8)	75		

Tutorial note. The numbering is provided for teaching purposes only and does not form part of the answer.

Activity 4: Further practice at double entry bookkeeping

(a) Credit sale of £200

Effect on elements	Account name	Amount £	Debit ✓	Credit ✓
Increase in asset	Sales ledger control	200	✓	
Increase in income	Sales	200		✓

(b) Cash purchase of £150

Effect on elements	Account name	Amount £	Debit ✓	Credit ✓
Increase in expense	Purchases	150	✓	
Decrease in asset	Cash	150		✓

(c) Credit purchase of £500

Effect on elements	Account name	Amount £	Debit ✓	Credit ✓
Increase in expense	Purchases	500	✓	
Increase in liability	Purchases ledger control	500		✓

(d) Capital contribution from the owner into the bank account of £1,000

Effect on elements	Account name	Amount £	Debit ✓	Credit ✓
Increase in asset	Bank	1,000	✓	
Increase in capital	Capital	1,000		✓

(e) Receipt of loan into the bank account of £2,000

Effect on elements	Account name	Amount £	Debit ✓	Credit ✓
Increase in asset	Bank	2,000	✓	
Increase in liability	Bank loan	2,000		✓

(f) Drawings of £4,000 taken by the owner from the bank account

Effect on elements	Account name	Amount £	Debit ✓	Credit ✓
Increase in drawings	Drawings	4,000	✓	
Decrease in asset	Bank	4,000		✓

(g) Repayment of bank loan of £500

Effect on elements	Account name	Amount £	Debit ✓	Credit ✓
Decrease in liability	Bank loan	500	✓	
Decrease in asset	Bank	500		✓

(h) Credit sale of £100

Effect on elements	Account name	Amount £	Debit ✓	Credit ✓
Increase in asset	Sales ledger control	100	✓	
Increase in income	Sales	100		✓

(i)   Payment of wages in cash of £350

Effect on elements	Account name	Amount £	Debit ✓	Credit ✓
Increase in expense	Wages	350	✓	
Decrease in asset	Cash	350		✓

(j)   Payment of rent from the bank account of £800

Effect on elements	Account name	Amount £	Debit ✓	Credit ✓
Increase in expense	Rent	800	✓	
Decrease in asset	Bank	800		✓

CHAPTER 7 Double entry bookkeeping (Part 2)

Activity 1: Balancing off

Cash

Details	Amount £	Details	Amount £
Sales	500	Purchases	300
Sales	500	Telephone	50
		Balance c/d	650
	1,000		1,000
Balance b/d	650		

Tutorial note. You should follow the steps to balance off:

Step 1 **Add up** the debit side and the credit side separately. Here the debit side totals £1,000 and the credit side totals £350.

Step 2 Put the **largest** of the two totals as the column total for both the debit and credit columns. So here we need to put £1,000 as the total on both sides.

Step 3 Calculate the **balancing figure** on the **side with the lower total and describe this as the balance carried down** (balance c/d). So here, the credit side had the lower total. The balancing figure is £1,000 – £350 = £650. The balance c/d is £650.

Step 4 Show this balancing figure on the **opposite side**, below the totals line, and describe this figure as the **balance brought down** (balance b/d). So here, the balance b/d on the debit side is £650.

Activity 2: Balancing off ledger accounts 1

Tutorial note. In your assessment you will only have to balance off one or two accounts, and not the volume of accounts given here.

Note that even if a ledger account only contains one balance, you still need to balance it off.

GENERAL LEDGER

Bank

Details	Amount £	Details	Amount £
Capital	20,000	Purchases	250
		Rent	225
		Rates	135
		Balance c/d	19,390
	20,000		20,000
Balance b/d	19,390		

Capital

Details	Amount £	Details	Amount £
Balance c/d	20,000	Bank	20,000
	20,000		20,000
		Balance b/d	20,000

Purchases

Details	Amount £	Details	Amount £
Bank	250		
Purchases ledger control	450	Balance c/d	700
	700		700
Balance b/d	700		

Rent

Details	Amount £	Details	Amount £
Bank	225	Balance c/d	225
	225		225
Balance b/d	225		

Sales

Details	Amount £	Details	Amount £
Balance c/d	1,407	Cash	657
		Sales ledger control	750
	1,407		1,407
		Balance b/d	1,407

Cash

Details	Amount £	Details	Amount £
Sales	657	Wages	75
		Balance c/d	582
	657		657
Balance b/d	582		

Rates

Details	Amount £	Details	Amount £
Bank	135	Balance c/d	135
	135		135
Balance b/d	135		

Sales ledger control

Details	Amount £	Details	Amount £
Sales	750	Balance c/d	750
	750		750
Balance b/d	750		

Purchases ledger control

Details	Amount £	Details	Amount £
Balance c/d	450	Purchases	450
	450		450
		Balance b/d	450

Wages

Details	Amount £	Details	Amount £
Cash	75	Balance c/d	75
	75		75
Balance b/d	75		

Activity 3: Balancing off ledger accounts 2

Electricity

Date 20XX	Details	Amount £	Date 20XX	Details	Amount £
01 Aug	Balance b/f	4,265			
25 Aug	Bank	245	31 Aug	Balance c/d	4,510
	Total	4,510		Total	4,510
01 Sep	Balance b/d	4,510			

Discounts allowed

Date 20XX	Details	Amount £	Date 20XX	Details	Amount £
01 Aug	Balance b/f	2,500	31 Aug	Balance c/d	2,800
22 Aug	Sales ledger control	300			
	Total	2,800		Total	2,800
01 Sep	Balance b/d	2,800			

Tutorial note. The balance c/d date is the date the account is balanced off, ie the last day of the accounting period. So, in this case, it is 31 August. Remember the balance c/d must be **above** the total line. The balance b/d must be **below** the total line on the opposite side. The balance b/d date is the first day of the new accounting period, which is 1 September.

Activity 4: Recording transactions in the sales and purchases ledgers

SALES LEDGER

J Henry

Details	Amount £	Details	Amount £
Invoice 346	750		

PURCHASES LEDGER

C Bableton

Details	Amount £	Details	Amount £
		Invoice 8801	450

Tutorial note. The entries in the subsidiary ledgers mirror the entries in the general ledger. So, in the case of a sale to a credit customer, in the general ledger we would debit the sales ledger control account and credit sales. Because we have debited the sales ledger control account, we also need to debit the customer's individual account in the sales ledger.

Activity 5: Accounting equation

(a)

	True ✓	False ✓
Assets plus capital = liabilities (**Tutorial note.** Rearranging the equation: assets – liabilities = – capital, which is not true)		✓
Capital plus liabilities = assets (**Tutorial note.** Rearranging the equation: assets – liabilities = capital, which is true)	✓	
Capital = assets plus liabilities (**Tutorial note.** Rearranging the equation: assets – liabilities = – capital, which is not true)		✓

(b)

Question	Answer £
If liabilities total £36,000 and capital totals £84,000, what is the amount of assets? **Tutorial note.** Applying the accounting equation: assets – liabilities = capital Rearranging: assets = capital + liabilities assets = 84,000 + 36,000 = 120,000	120,000
If assets total £80,000 and liabilities total £64,000, what is the amount of capital? **Tutorial note.** Applying the accounting equation: assets – liabilities = capital 80,000 – 64,000 = capital capital = 16,000	16,000
If capital totals £56,000 and assets total £108,000, what is the amount of liabilities? **Tutorial note.** Applying the accounting equation: assets – liabilities = capital Rearranging: liabilities = assets – capital Liabilities = 108,000 – 56,000 = 52,000	52,000

Activity 6: Accounting equation – J Emerald

(a)

Assets £	Liabilities £	Capital £
46,120	15,000	31,120

Tutorial note.

Assets = 30,400 + 11,200 + 4,520 = 46,120

Liabilities = 15,000

Therefore, using the accounting equation: capital = assets – liabilities

Capital = 46,120 – 15,000 = 31,120

(b)

Assets £	Liabilities £	Capital £
52,750	16,530	36,220

Tutorial note.

Assets = 30,400 + 9,500 + 5,200 + 7,650 = 52,750

Liabilities = 15,000 + 1,530 = 16,530

Therefore, using the accounting equation: capital = assets – liabilities

Capital = 52,750 – 16,530 = 36,220

Activity 7: Capital and revenue expenditure

Expenditure

Wages

Rent, rates, electricity

Motor vehicle running expenses (petrol, road tax) and repairs

Postage and stationery

Property

Plant

Equipment

Tutorial note.

This is revenue expenditure

This is capital expenditure

Activity 8: Capital and revenue income and expenditure

	Capital expenditure ✓	Revenue expenditure ✓	Capital income ✓	Revenue income ✓
Purchase of raw materials that can be turned into goods for resale		✓		
Receipt from the sale of an unused machine			✓	
Sale of goods to a credit customer				✓
Purchase of a motor vehicle to be used by the sales director	✓			

CHAPTER 8 Maintaining the cash book

Activity 1: Cash book – debit side

Cash book – debit side

Details	Cash £	Bank £	VAT £	Trade receivables £	Cash sales £
Bumble	600		100		500
Ryan	168		28		140
AET		425		425	
Elaine		5,600		5,600	

Tutorial note. The cash and bank columns show the gross amounts received. For cash sales, VAT charged is analysed out. Remember, for trade receivables we do not analyse out the VAT as the VAT has already been recorded when the original sale was recorded in the sales day book. Note how the cheques are recorded in the bank column and cash is recorded in the cash column.

Activity 2: Cash book – credit side

Cash book – credit side

Details	Cash £	Bank £	VAT £	Trade payables £	Cash purchases £
Daniel	156		26		130
Edgar	576		96		480
Graham		150		150	
Isaac		300		300	

Tutorial note. The cash and bank columns show the gross amounts paid. For cash purchases, we analyse out the VAT charged. Remember, for trade payables we do not analyse out the VAT as the VAT has already been recorded when the original purchase was recorded in the purchases day book. Note how the cheques are recorded in the bank column and cash is recorded in the cash column.

Activity 3: Cash book – checking the cross-cast

(a) Cash book – debit side

Details	Cash £	Bank £	VAT £	Trade receivables £	Cash sales £
Balance b/f	1,500				
James	540		90		450
Pollard	246		41		205
Harvey		456		456	
Rudson		2,055		2,055	
Total	2,286	2,511	131	2,511	655

Tutorial note. As before, remember that:

- VAT is only analysed out on cash sales
- Cheques are entered in the bank column

(b) Cross-cast of cash book – debit side

Details	Amount £
Cash	2,286
Less cash balance b/f	(1,500)
Bank	2,511
	3,297
VAT	131
Trade receivables	2,511
Cash sales	655
	3,297

Tutorial note. What we have entered into the analysis column should total to the same amount of the cash and bank columns less any balances brought forward.

(c) Cash book – credit side

Details	Cash £	Bank £	VAT £	Trade payables £	Cash purchases £
Balance b/f		1,100			
Horne	180		30		150
Meddly	60		10		50
Adam		635		635	
Timmons		4,600		4,600	
Total	240	6,335	40	5,235	200

(d) Cross-cast of cash book – credit side

Details	Amount £
Cash	240
Bank	6,335
Less bank balance b/f	(1,100)
	5,475
VAT	40
Trade payables	5,235
Cash purchases	200
	5,475

Activity 4: Maintaining and using the cash book

(a) Cash book – credit side

Details	Cash £	Bank £	VAT £	Trade payables £	Cash purchases £	Motor expenses £
Balance b/f		6,600				
E Frank	192		32		160	
G Jacob	384		64		320	
I Knight	450				450	
Pollard Ltd		3,000		3,000		
Sure Motor Repairs		96	16			80
Total	1,026	9,696	112	3,000	930	80

Tutorial note. In this question you have been given five primary documents:

- **Three receipts** – the receipts are for payments to suppliers. Notice how the receipts state that Jeremy Jackson does **not have a credit account**, therefore these receipts must be for **cash purchases**, and so must be posted to the **cash** column of the cash book. As they are cash purchases, the VAT must be analysed out, where applicable. Notice that the receipt from I Knight does not have any VAT, presumably because I Knight is not registered for VAT. The net amounts are then analysed out to the cash purchases column.

- **Two cheque book stubs** – these are the cheque stubs from Jeremy Jackson's cheque book so represent payments he has made by cheque. **Cheques** are posted in the **bank** column of the cash book. One of the cheque stubs is to a credit supplier, Pollard Ltd, identified as such as the company has a **purchases ledger account code**. This amount should be analysed out to the trade payables column. There is therefore no VAT to analyse out on this payment as the VAT would have been recorded when the purchase was recorded in the purchases day book. The other cheque stub is for motor repairs, for which Jeremy Jackson has no credit account, so again the VAT must be analysed out: VAT = £96/6 = £16. The net £80 should be analysed out to the motor expenses column.

Once you have entered all the transactions into the cash book, you should cast and cross-cast the totals. This is a good check of whether you have entered the transactions correctly.

(b) Cash book – debit side

Details	Cash £	Bank £	Trade receivables £
Balance b/f	1,256		
K Rowlands		683	683
L Baldwin		476	476
Total	1,256	1,159	1,159

Tutorial note. The automated receipts should be recorded in the **bank** column of the cash book. The receipts are from credit customers, so the amounts must be analysed out into the trade receivables column.

Once you have entered all the transactions into the cash book, you should cast and cross-cast the totals. This is a good check of whether you have entered the transactions correctly.

(c)

£	230

Tutorial note. Total debits for cash 1,256 – total credits for cash 1,026 = 230

(d)

£	–8,537

Tutorial note. Total debits for bank 1,159 – total credits for bank 9,696 = –8,537

(e) Credit

Tutorial note. If Jeremy Jackson had a positive balance at the bank, this would be an **asset** of the business. This is usually what we would expect to see. However, in this case, the balance is negative, or overdrawn, so it is actually money that Jeremy Jackson owes the bank, and is therefore a liability. Using the mnemonic **DEAD CLIC** from Chapter 6, a liability is a **credit** balance.

Activity 1: VAT and double entry

(a)

Account name	Amount £	Debit ✓	Credit ✓
Sales ledger control	100	✓	
Sales	100		✓

Tutorial note. The business is not registered for VAT, so the business does not charge VAT on sales, so there are no entries for VAT in the general ledger.

(b)

Account name	Amount £	Debit ✓	Credit ✓
Sales ledger control	120	✓	
VAT	20		✓
Sales	100		✓

Tutorial note. The business is registered for VAT so can charge VAT on its sales. So the VAT must be analysed out in the ledger. The net amount of £100 should be posted to the sales account; as it is income, it is a credit entry. The VAT is calculated as £100 × 20% = £20; the VAT is a liability owed to HMRC, so it is also a credit entry. This is a sale on credit so the gross amount is posted to the sales ledger control account and is a debit as it is an asset of the business. Remember that total debits = total credits.

(c)

Account name	Amount £	Debit ✓	Credit ✓
Cash	120	✓	
VAT	20		✓
Sales	100		✓

Tutorial note. The business is registered for VAT so can charge VAT on its sales. So the VAT must be analysed out in the ledger. The net amount of £100 should be posted to the sales account; as it is income, it is a credit entry. The VAT is calculated as £100 × 20% = £20; the VAT is a liability owed to HMRC, so it is also a credit entry. The sale is a cash sale, so the gross amount is posted to the cash account and is a debit as it is an asset of the business. Remember that total debits = total credits.

Activity 2: Posting the sales day book

(a)

Account name	Amount £	Debit ✓	Credit ✓
M Head	3,600	✓	
G Irving	3,102	✓	
K Tang	5,988	✓	
L Harvey	1,440	✓	

Tutorial note. The gross amounts for each credit customer are posted to the sales ledger as a debit entry, as they are assets of the business.

(b)

Account name	Amount £	Debit ✓	Credit ✓
Sales ledger control	14,130	✓	
VAT	2,355		✓
Sales	11,775		✓

Tutorial note. The total gross amount is posted to the sales ledger control account as a debit as it is an asset of the business. Entries to the VAT and sales accounts are then credit entries as total debits must equal total credits. (Remember that this also makes sense because VAT is a liability of the business, it is owed to HMRC, so it must be a credit; sales are income of the business and so are also a credit.)

Activity 3: Posting the sales returns day book

(a)

Account name	Amount £	Debit ✓	Credit ✓
F Fish	504		✓
M Gordon	276		✓
G Henry	744		✓
R Left	696		✓

Tutorial note. Credit notes decrease the amounts owed by customers, so are credits in the sales ledger.

(b)

Account name	Amount £	Debit ✓	Credit ✓
Sales returns	1,850	✓	
VAT	370	✓	
Sales ledger control	2,220		✓

Tutorial note. Credit notes decrease an asset of the business (the amounts owed by customers) so the total of the gross column is a credit to sales ledger control. It then follows that the other entries are debit entries as debits must equal credits.

Activity 4: Posting the cash book – debit side (book of prime entry only)

(a)

Account name	Amount £	Debit ✓	Credit ✓
Bank	12,500	✓	
Cash	3,600	✓	
Cash sales	3,000		✓
Rental income	500		✓
Sales ledger control	12,000		✓
VAT	600		✓

Tutorial note. As the cash book is a book of prime entry only, we must post from the cash book to the cash and bank accounts in the ledger accounts. The entries are both debit entries as cash received is an asset of the business. It then follows that the other entries are credit entries as debits must equal credits. (Remember this also makes sense because cash sales and rental income are both income, so a credit is required in both of those. The sales ledger control account is an asset, a receipt of cash from a credit customer reduces that asset, so a credit entry is required. VAT is a liability as it is an amount owed to HMRC, therefore a credit entry is required.)

(b)

Account name	Amount £	Debit ✓	Credit ✓
K Scott	300		✓

Tutorial note. A receipt from a credit customer reduces the amount owed by that credit customer, so it reduces the asset; it is therefore a credit entry.

Activity 5: Posting the cash book – debit side (part of the general ledger)

(a)

Account name	Amount £	Debit ✓	Credit ✓
Cash sales	3,000		✓
Rental income	500		✓
Sales ledger control	12,000		✓
VAT	600		✓

Tutorial note. We don't need to debit cash or bank because the cash book is part of the general ledger and so the amounts are already included. It then follows that the other entries are credit entries as debits must equal credits. (Remember this also makes sense because cash sales and rental income are both income, so a credit is required in both of those accounts. The sales ledger control account is an asset, a receipt of cash from a credit customer reduces that asset, so a credit entry is required. VAT is a liability as it is an amount owed to HMRC, therefore a credit entry is required.)

The activity demonstrates that the cash and bank columns are not posted to the general ledger because they already form part of the double entry bookkeeping system. To put it another way, they are already included and therefore do not need to be posted again!

(b)

Account name	Amount £	Debit ✓	Credit ✓
K Scott	300		✓

Tutorial note. A receipt from a credit customer reduces the amount owed by that credit customer, so it reduces the asset; it is therefore a credit entry.

Activity 6: Posting the discounts allowed day book

(a)

Account name	Amount £	Debit ✓	Credit ✓
Discounts allowed	500	✓	
VAT	100	✓	
Sales ledger control	600		✓

Tutorial note. The gross amount is posted as a credit to the sales ledger control account as it is a reduction in the amount owed by credit customers. Debits must equal credits so the other entries must be debit entries, VAT to the VAT control account and the net discount to the discounts allowed account.

(b)

Account name	Amount £	Debit ✓	Credit ✓
K Smith	24		✓

Tutorial note. Discounts allowed are a reduction in the amount owed by credit customers, so are posted as a credit to the credit customer's (K Smith's) account. The amount to post is the gross amount as this is the total discount allowed to the customer: VAT = 20 × 0.2 = £4, gross amount = 20 + 4 = £24.

CHAPTER 10 Double entry for purchases and trade payables

Activity 1: Posting the purchases day book

(a)

Account name	Amount £	Debit ✓	Credit ✓
Edith	4,020		✓
Eddie	4,728		✓
Amber	5,100		✓
John	8,778		✓

Tutorial note. The names of the accounts here are taken from the details column in the purchases day book. As invoices owed to credit suppliers are liabilities of the business, we need to credit the suppliers' individual accounts. The amount posted to the supplier accounts is the gross amount of the invoice.

(b)

Account name	Amount £	Debit ✓	Credit ✓
Purchases	18,855	✓	
VAT	3,771	✓	
Purchases ledger control	22,626		✓

Tutorial note. Remember that the purchases day book records invoices received from credit suppliers, which are liabilities of the business. The gross total is therefore posted as a credit to the purchases ledger control account. The other entries must be debit entries as debits must at all times equal credits.

Activity 2: Posting the purchases returns day book

(a)

Account name	Amount £	Debit ✓	Credit ✓
Jacob	408	✓	
Mandy	48	✓	
Clarence	816	✓	

Tutorial note. The names of the accounts here are taken from the details column in the purchases returns day book. As credit notes from suppliers reduce the amounts owed to credit suppliers, and therefore reduce the liability, a debit entry is required in each supplier account.

(b)

Account name	Amount £	Debit ✓	Credit ✓
Purchases ledger control	1,272	✓	
VAT	212		✓
Purchases returns	1,060		✓

Tutorial note. Remember that the purchases returns day book records credit notes received from credit suppliers. Credit notes reduce the liability owed to each supplier. The gross total of the purchases returns day book is therefore posted as a debit to the purchases ledger control account. The other entries must be credit entries as credits must at all times equal debits.

Activity 3: Posting the cash book – credit side (book of prime entry only)

(a)

Account name	Amount £	Debit ✓	Credit ✓
Bank	8,300		✓
Bank charges	300	✓	
Cash	1,920		✓
Cash purchases	1,600	✓	
Purchases ledger control	8,000	✓	
VAT	320	✓	

Tutorial note. As the cash book is a book of prime entry only, we must post from the cash book to the cash and bank accounts in the ledger accounts. The entries are both credit entries, as cash paid out reduces the cash balance (asset) of the business. It then follows that the other entries are debit entries, as debits must equal credits.

(b)

Account name	Amount £	Debit ✓	Credit ✓
H Henry	500	✓	

Tutorial note. A payment to a credit supplier reduces the amount owed to that credit supplier, so it reduces the liability; it is therefore a debit entry.

Activity 4: Posting the cash book – credit side (part of the general ledger)

(a)

Account name	Amount £	Debit ✓	Credit ✓
Bank charges	300	✓	
Cash purchases	1,600	✓	
Purchases ledger control	8,000	✓	
VAT	320	✓	

Tutorial note. We don't need to credit cash or bank because the cash book is part of the general ledger and so the amounts are already included. It then follows that the other entries are debit entries as debits must equal credits.

The activity demonstrates that the cash and bank columns are not posted to the general ledger because they already form part of the double entry bookkeeping system. To put it another way, they are already included and therefore do not need to be posted again!

(b)

Account name	Amount £	Debit ✓	Credit ✓
H Henry	500	✓	

Tutorial note. A payment to a credit supplier reduces the amount owed to that credit supplier, so it reduces the liability; it is therefore a debit entry.

Activity 5: Posting the discounts received day book

(a)

Account name	Amount £	Debit ✓	Credit ✓
Discounts received	500		✓
VAT	100		✓
Purchases ledger control	600	✓	

Tutorial note. The gross amount is posted as a debit to the purchases ledger control account as it is a reduction in the amount owed to credit suppliers. Debits must equal credits so the other entries must be credit entries, VAT to the VAT control account and the net discount to the discounts received account.

(b)

Account name	Amount £	Debit ✓	Credit ✓
R Jones	24	✓	

Tutorial note. Discounts received are a reduction in the amount owed to credit suppliers, so are posted as a debit to the credit supplier's (R Jones's) account. The amount to post is the gross amount as this is the total discount allowed to the customer: VAT = 20 × 0.2 = £4, gross amount = 20 + 4 = £24.

CHAPTER 11 Accounting for petty cash

Activity 1: Petty cash amount

£	4.80

Tutorial note.

VAT = £4.00 × 0.2 = £0.80

Gross = £4.00 + £0.80 = £4.80

Activity 2: Petty cash voucher

Petty cash voucher	
Date: 8.9.XX	Number: PC587
100 sheets white cardboard	
	£
Net	20.00
VAT	4.00
Gross	24.00

Tutorial note. The question gives you the cost of the item excluding VAT, so you are given the net amount and must calculate the VAT and the gross amount.

VAT = £20.00 × 0.2 = £4.00
Gross = 20.00 + 4.00 = £24.00

If this was a real petty cash voucher, it would also need to include the signatures of the person making the claim and the person authorising the claim.

Activity 3: Imprest system

	£
What is the imprest amount at Brian Ltd?	90.00
What is the amount of cash in the petty cash tin at 31 July 20XX?	31.25

Tutorial note.

	£
Balance in petty cash tin at 1 July 20XX	37.50
Cash to restore imprest level	52.50
Imprest level	**90.00**
Less expenses paid during July 20XX	(58.75)
Balance in petty cash tin at 31 July 20XX	**31.25**

Activity 4: Restoring the petty cash

Petty cash reimbursement		
Date		31.08.20XX
Amount required to restore the cash in the petty cash box	£	144.50

Tutorial note. Remember this equation: cash (£) + vouchers (£) = imprest amount

The value of the vouchers is the value of the top-up required to restore the imprest amount. Applying this to the question:

5.50 + vouchers = £150.00

Therefore: vouchers = £150.00 – 5.50 = £144.50

Activity 5: Writing up the petty cash book

Debit side		Credit side					
Details	Amount £	Details	Amount £	VAT £	Postage £	Travel £	Stationery £
Balance b/f	200.00	Tiger's Taxi	15.00			15.00	
		Post Office	31.00		31.00		
		Sara's Stationery	72.00	12.00			60.00
		Balance c/d	82.00				
Total	200.00	Totals	200.00	12.00	31.00	15.00	60.00

Tutorial note. Cash payments reduce the amount of petty cash, therefore we need to enter the payments on the credit side of the petty cash book. The VAT on the payment to Sara's Stationery is calculated as $60 \times 0.2 = £12.00$. Once you have entered all the payments into the petty cash book, you then need to balance off the account. Remember the steps to balance off an account seen in Chapter 7:

Step 1 **Add up** the debit side and the credit side separately. Here, the debit side is £200 and the credit side is £108.

Step 2 Put the **largest** of the two totals as the column total for **both** the debit and credit columns. For the petty cash book, this will always be the receipts side, as we cannot take more out of the petty cash box than the amount of physical notes and coins in it. So the total to include is £200.

Step 3 Calculate the **balancing figure** on the **side with the lower total and describe this as the balance carried down** (balance c/d). Here, the balancing figure is 200 – 108 = £82.

Step 4 Show this balancing figure on the **opposite side**, below the totals line, and describe this figure as the **balance brought down** (balance b/d). The balance b/d, which is the opening balance for the next period, is £82. The balance b/d was not asked for in this question, but this step has been included here for completeness.

Activity 6: Posting the petty cash book (book of prime entry only)

Account name	Amount £	Debit ✓	Credit ✓
Petty cash	199.00		✓
Office expenses	90.00	✓	
Postage	16.00	✓	
Travel	75.00	✓	
VAT	18.00	✓	

Tutorial note. As the petty cash book is a book of prime entry only, we must post from the petty cash book to the petty cash account in the general ledger. The entry required is a credit entry as petty cash paid out reduces the petty cash balance (asset) of the business. It then follows that the other entries are debit entries as debits must equal credits.

Activity 7: Posting the petty cash book (part of the general ledger)

Account name	Amount £	Debit ✓	Credit ✓
Bank	58.00		✓
Motor expenses	12.00	✓	
Office expenses	23.90	✓	
Travel	3.00	✓	
VAT	5.40	✓	

Tutorial note. We don't need to credit the petty cash account in the general ledger because the petty cash book is part of the general ledger and so the amount is already included.

CHAPTER 12 Initial trial balance

Activity 1: Initial trial balance

Trial balance

Account name	Debit £	Credit £
Bank	19,390	
Capital		20,000
Purchases	700	
Rent	225	
Sales		1,407
Cash	582	
Rates	135	
Sales ledger control	750	
Purchases ledger control		450
Wages	75	
Totals	**21,857**	**21,857**

Tutorial note. Deciding whether a balance is a debit or credit balance is straightforward when you are given ledger accounts – if the balance b/d is on the debit side, you have a debit balance, and vice versa.

Activity 2: Preparing a trial balance

Trial balance as at 31 March 20XX

Account name	Amount £	Debit £	Credit £
Motor vehicles	31,200	31,200	
Inventory	4,200	4,200	
Bank	18,260	18,260	
Sales ledger control	8,800	8,800	
Purchases ledger control	6,400		6,400
Capital	80,000		80,000
Sales	130,000		130,000
Sales returns	10,000	10,000	
Purchases	84,000	84,000	
Purchases returns	5,400		5,400
Bank charges	200	200	
Discounts allowed	1,800	1,800	
Discounts received	1,200		1,200
Wages and salaries	43,600	43,600	
Rent and rates	12,400	12,400	
Telephone	2,040	2,040	
Electricity	5,100	5,100	
Office expenses	1,400	1,400	
Totals		**223,000**	**223,000**

Tutorial note. Preparing a trial balance from a list of balances requires a really good knowledge of debits and credits. Remember the DEAD CLIC mnemonic, and then work through each balance in turn applying DEAD CLIC. A good check of whether you have got the debits and credits right is whether or not the total of the debit column equals the total of the credit column.

Test your learning: answers

CHAPTER 1 Business documentation

1

	Cash ✓	Credit ✓
Purchase of a van with an agreed payment date in one month's time		✓
Sale of goods by credit card in a shop	✓	
Purchase of computer disks by cheque	✓	
Purchase of computer disks which are accompanied by an invoice		✓
Sale of goods which are paid for by cheque	✓	

2

	✓
An invoice	✓
A receipt	
A remittance advice	
A credit note	

3

	✓
An invoice	
A delivery note	
A remittance advice	
A credit note	✓

4

	✓
An invoice	
A delivery note	
A remittance advice	✓
A credit note	

5

Sale of goods for cash	Till receipt
Return of goods purchased on credit	Credit note
Reimbursement of employee for expense by cash	Petty cash voucher
Indication of which amounts that are owed are being paid	Remittance advice note

6

✓	Supplier code
	BEN41
	IMM56
✓	PRE62

CHAPTER 2 The books of prime entry

1

	£	Total	VAT	Net
Goods total	1,236.00			✓
VAT	247.20		✓	
Total	1,483.20	✓		

2 (a)

An invoice is entered on the	left	side of the customer's ledger account
A credit note is entered on the	right	side of the customer's ledger account

(b)

£	24.00

Tutorial note: Working 120 – 96 = 24

3

Total £	VAT £	Net £	Computers £	Printers £	Scanners £
1,560.00	260.00	1,300.00	800.00	300.00	200.00

Tutorial note: The amounts included in the analysis columns are the **net amounts**.

4 **Purchases day book**

Total £	VAT £	Net £	Purchases £	Expenses £
1,980.00	330.00	1,650.00	1,650.00	

Tutorial note: The business sells dishwashers, so the dishwashers on this invoice have been purchased in order to sell them on to customers. Therefore this invoice is recorded as purchases, and not expenses, of the business. Remember, expenses are overheads of the business, such as stationery and utilities.

5 **Sales day book**

Date	Customer	Invoice number	Customer code	Total £	VAT £	Net £
1 Jun	J Jepson	44263	SL34	141.60	23.60	118.00
2 Jun	S Beck & Sons	44264	SL01	384.00	64.00	320.00
3 Jun	Penfold Ltd	44265	SL23	196.80	32.80	164.00
4 Jun	S Beck & Sons	44266	SL01	307.20	51.20	256.00
4 Jun	J Jepson	44267	SL34	172.80	28.80	144.00
Total				1,202.40	200.40	1,002.00

Sales returns day book

Date	Customer	Credit note number	Customer code	Total £	VAT £	Net £
2 Jun	Scroll Ltd	3813	SL16	21.60	3.60	18.00
5 Jun	Penfold Ltd	3814	SL23	20.16	3.36	16.80
Total				41.76	6.96	34.80

6 Purchases day book

Date	Supplier	Invoice number	Supplier code	Total £	VAT £	Net £
6 Jun	YH Hill	224363	PL16	190.08	31.68	158.40
6 Jun	Letra Ltd	PT445	PL24	273.60	45.60	228.00
6 Jun	Coldstores Ltd	77352	PL03	189.60	31.60	158.00
Total				653.28	108.88	544.40

Purchases returns day book

Date	Supplier	Credit note number	Supplier code	Total £	VAT £	Net £
6 Jun	Letra Ltd	CN92	PL24	120.00	20.00	100.00
6 Jun	YH Hill	C7325	PL16	31.20	5.20	26.00
Total				151.20	25.20	126.00

7 Purchases day book

Date	Supplier	Invoice number	Supplier code	Total £	VAT £	Net £
16 Oct	Herne Industries	46121	PL15	864.00	144.00	720.00
15 Oct	Bass Engineers	663211	PL13	460.80	76.80	384.00
	Total			1,324.80	220.80	1,104.00

8   **Purchases returns day book**

Date	Supplier	Credit note number	Supplier code	Total £	VAT £	Net £
16 Oct	Southfield Electrical	08702	PL20	120.00	20.00	100.00
17 Oct	Herne Industries	CN4502	PL15	132.00	22.00	110.00
		Total		252.00	42.00	210.00

CHAPTER 3 VAT and discounts

1   (400 × 30) – (400 × 30 × 5/100) = £11,400 before bulk discount but after trade discount

11,400 – (11,400 × 10/100) = £10,260 net total after bulk discount

£	**10,260**

2   (a)   VAT = £378.00 × 20% (20/100)

£	**75.60**

(b)   VAT = £378.00 × 20/120 or 378.00/6

£	**63.00**

Net total = £378.00 – 63.00

£	**315.00**

3   (a)   VAT   =   £3,154.80 × 20/120 = £525.80

Net total   =   £3,154.80 – 525.80 = £2,629.00

(b)   VAT   =   £446.40 × 20/120 = £74.40

Net total   =   £446.40 – 74.40   = £372.00

(c)   VAT   =   £169.20 × 20/120 = £28.20

Net total   =   £169.20 – 28.20   = £141.00

Gross amount	VAT	Net amount
(a) £3,154.80	£525.80	£2,629.00
(b) £446.40	£74.40	£372.00
(c) £169.20	£28.20	£141.00

4 (a)

(i)	Total cost before discount	23 × £56.00	£1,288.00
(ii)	Trade discount	15% × £1,288.00	£193.20
(iii)	Net total	£1,288.00 – £193.20	£1,094.80
(iv)	VAT	20% × £1,094.80	£218.96
(v)	Gross total		£1,313.76

(b)

(i)	Net total	131.38 – 21.89	£109.49
(ii)	VAT	131.38/6	£21.89*
(iii)	Gross total	1,313.76 × 0.1	£131.38

* **Tutorial note.** The task instructions advised that we should round down VAT to the nearest penny.

5

£	**2,448.00**

Tutorial note.

	£
List price	2,400.00
Less discount £2,400.00 × 15/100	(360.00)
Net total	2,040.00
VAT: £2,040.00 × 20/100	408.00
Gross total	2,448.00

6

£	**2,280.96**

Tutorial note.

	£
List price	2,400.00
Less trade discount £2,400.00 × 10/100	(240.00)
	2,160.00
Less bulk discount £2,160.00 × 12/100	(259.20)
Net total	1,900.80
VAT: £1,900.80 × 20/100	380.16
Gross total	2,280.96

7

£	**2.21**

Tutorial note.

Credit note amounts	£
Net total	368.00
VAT £368 × 0.2	73.60
Gross total	441.60
Prompt payment discount taken 441.60 × 0.03	13.25
VAT 13.25/6 (rounded up)	2.21

CHAPTER 4 Recording credit sales

1

To inform the customer of the amount due for a sale	Invoice
To inform the supplier of the quantities required	Customer order
To inform the customer of the quantity delivered	Delivery note
To inform the customer that the invoiced amount was overstated	Credit note

2　(a)

	£
Price before discount 23 × £56.00	1,288.00
Trade discount 15% × £1,288.00	193.20
Net	1,094.80
VAT 20% × £1,094.80	218.96
Gross	1,313.76

(b)

	£
Net (39.41 – 6.57)	32.84
VAT (39.41/6)	6.57
Gross (1,313.76 × 0.03)	39.41

Tutorial note. There was no advice given in the task instruction for how to round the VAT. The answer above has rounded up the VAT, but credit would also be given if you rounded down the VAT.

3

	Description of error or omission
1	It is not dated.
2	There is no customer code.
3	The calculation of the total price of the tumble dryers is incorrect.
4	The calculation of the trade discount is incorrect.

Corrected figures

	£
Tumble dryers 21 × £180	3,780.00
Mixers	400.00
Goods total	4,180.00
Less 15% discount	627.00
Net total	3,553.00
VAT 20% × 3,553	710.60
Invoice total	4,263.60

4   Cheque from Quinn Ltd – the remittance advice has been correctly totalled but there has been an error made in writing the cheque as the cheque is for £770.80 rather than £770.08.

Cheque from T T Peters – the remittance advice has been incorrectly totalled and the cheque total should have been for £1,191.02.

5   By a process of trial and error you can find the invoices and credit note that total to £226.79.

Invoice/credit note number	£
30234	157.35
30239	85.24
CN2381	15.80
Total	226.79

6

Wendlehurst Trading					
VAT Registration No. 876983479					

Stroll In Stores

Customer account code: ST725
Delivery note number: 8973
Date: 1 Dec 20XX

Invoice No: 624

Quantity of cases	Product code	Total list price £	Net amount after discount £	VAT £	Gross £
600/12 = 50	TIG300	500.00	425.00	85.00	510.00

Tutorial note. The quantity of cases, product code, customer account code and delivery note number can all be taken from the delivery note.

The list price is calculated as: 50 cases × £10 = £500.00

The net amount after discount is the list price less the trade discount only: 500 – (500 × 15%) = £425.00

The VAT is calculated on the net amount after trade discount only (the PPD should not be deducted): 425.00 × 20% = £85.00

The gross amount is 425.00 + 85.00 = £510.00

CHAPTER 5 Recording credit purchases

1

To accompany goods being returned to a supplier	Returns note
To record for internal purposes the quantity of goods received	Goods received note
To request payment from a purchaser of goods	Invoice
To order goods from a supplier	Purchase order
To accompany payment to a supplier	Remittance advice note

2
- The invoice does not agree to the purchase order as only 70 Get Well cards were ordered. However, when the credit note is taken into account the invoice quantity is correct minus the credit note quantity.

- The unit price on the credit note is only £0.25 whereas the invoice (and order) price is £0.33.

3

	Yes ✓	No ✓
Has the correct purchase price of the printer paper been charged?	✓	
Has the correct trade discount been applied?		✓

	£
What should the corrected VAT amount be?	70.00
What should be the total amount charged?	420.00

Tutorial note. The correct amounts are calculated as:

Purchase price (80 × 20)	400.00
Trade discount (400 × 12.5%)	(50.00)
Net amount	350.00
VAT @ 20%	70.00
Total	420.00

4

£	**931.20**

Tutorial note. Payment = £960 × 0.97 = £931.20

5

1 December

Tutorial note. 23 Nov + 10 days = 3 Dec

3 Dec – 2 days = 1 Dec

CHAPTER 6 Double entry bookkeeping (Part 1)

1 (a) Purchase of goods on credit

Increase expense	✓
Increase sales	
Increase trade payable	✓
Increase trade receivable	

(b) Sale of goods on credit

Increase expense	
Increase sales	✓
Increase trade payable	
Increase trade receivable	✓

2 (a) Receipt of money for sale of goods on credit

Increase cash	✓
Decrease cash	
Decrease trade receivable	✓
Increase trade receivable	

(b) Payment to a credit supplier for purchase of goods on credit

Increase cash	
Decrease cash	✓
Decrease trade payable	✓
Increase trade payable	

3

(a) Purchase of goods on credit

Account name	Debit	Credit
Purchases	✓	
Purchases ledger control		✓

(b) Sale of goods on credit

Account name	Debit	Credit
Sales ledger control	✓	
Sales		✓

(c) Receipt of money for sale of goods on credit

Account name	Debit	Credit
Bank	✓	
Sales ledger control		✓

(d) Payment to a credit supplier

Account name	Debit	Credit
Purchases ledger control	✓	
Bank		✓

4

	Debit	Credit
Money paid into the business bank account by the owner	Bank	Capital
Purchases on credit	Purchases	Purchases ledger control
Sales on credit	Sales ledger control	Sales
Money taken out of the business (via the bank) by the owner	Drawings	Bank

5

	Debit	Credit
Purchase of books on credit	Purchases	Purchases ledger control
Purchase of cash register using direct debit	Cash register	Bank
Payment received from a credit customer via the bank account	Bank	Sales ledger control
Purchase of van using cheque	Van	Bank

Tutorial note. Payments made using cheques are classified as payments through the bank account.

6

(a) Bought a machine on credit from A, cost £8,000

Account name	Debit £	Credit £
Machine	8,000	
Purchases ledger control		8,000

(b) Bought goods on credit from B, cost £500

Account name	Debit £	Credit £
Purchases	500	
Purchases ledger control		500

(c) Sold goods on credit to C, value £1,200

Account name	Debit £	Credit £
Sales ledger control	1,200	
Sales		1,200

(d) Paid D (a supplier) £300

Account name	Debit £	Credit £
Purchases ledger control	300	
Bank		300

7

(a) Collected £180 in cash from E, a credit customer

Account name	Debit £	Credit £
Cash	180	
Sales ledger control		180

(b) Paid wages £4,000 via bank transfer

Account name	Debit £	Credit £
Wages	4,000	
Bank		4,000

(c) Paid rent of £700 to landlord G in cash

Account name	Debit £	Credit £
Rent	700	
Cash		700

(d) Paid insurance premium £90 via direct debit

Account name	Debit £	Credit £
Insurance	90	
Bank		90

8

Bank

Details	Amount £	Details	Amount £
		Rent (b)	4,500
		Car (d)	6,000

Cash

Details	Amount £	Details	Amount £
Sales (a)	60	Purchases (c)	300

Car

Details	Amount £	Details	Amount £
Bank (d)	6,000		

Purchases

Details	Amount £	Details	Amount £
Cash (c)	300		

Rent

Details	Amount £	Details	Amount £
Bank (b)	4,500		

Sales

Details	Amount £	Details	Amount £
		Cash (a)	60

9

(a) Paid capital of £7,000 into bank

Account name	Debit £	Credit £
Bank	7,000	
Capital		7,000

(b) Paid rent of £3,500

Account name	Debit £	Credit £
Rent	3,500	
Bank		3,500

(c) Purchased goods for resale on credit for £5,000

Account name	Debit £	Credit £
Purchases	5,000	
Purchases ledger control		5,000

(d) Took out a loan of £1,500 from the bank

Account name	Debit £	Credit £
Bank	1,500	
Bank loan		1,500

10

(a) Sales of £10,000 for cash

Account name	Debit £	Credit £
Cash	10,000	
Sales		10,000

(b) Sales of £2,500 on credit

Account name	Debit £	Credit £
Sales ledger control	2,500	
Sales		2,500

(c) Paid interest of £100 on bank loan via direct debit

Account name	Debit £	Credit £
Interest	100	
Bank		100

(d) Drawings of £1,500 withdrawn from the bank

Account name	Debit £	Credit £
Drawings	1,500	
Bank		1,500

1 (a) Sales ledger control

Details	Amount £	Details	Amount £
Sales	2,600	Bank	1,800
Sales	1,400	Bank	1,200
Sales	3,700	Bank	2,000
Sales	1,300		
		Balance c/d	4,000
Total	9,000	Total	9,000
Balance b/d	4,000		

(b)

	✓
The amount owed by credit customers	✓
The amount owed to credit customers	

2 Sales ledger control

Date	Details	Amount £	Date	Details	Amount £
1 Jun	Balance b/d	1,209	28 Jun	Bank	3,287
30 Jun	Sales	6,298	30 Jun	Sales returns	786
			30 Jun	Balance c/d	3,434
	Total	7,507		Total	7,507
1 Jul	Balance b/d	3,434			

3

James Daniels

Details	Amount £	Details	Amount £
Invoice 96	1,000	Bank	800

4

	Revenue expenditure ✓	Revenue income ✓	Capital expenditure ✓	Capital income ✓
Sale of goods to credit customers		✓		
Cash sales		✓		
Sale of delivery van				✓
Purchase of goods for resale	✓			
Purchase of building			✓	
Purchase of coffee for office from petty cash	✓			

5

	✓
Capital = assets + liabilities	
Capital = liabilities – assets	
Assets = capital + liabilities	✓
Capital + assets = liabilities	

Tutorial note. As assets – liabilities = capital, then assets = capital + liabilities

1 **Cash book – debit side**

Date	Details	Cash £	Bank £	VAT £	Cash sales £	Trade receivables £
23 Jan	Hoppers Ltd		545.14			545.14
23 Jan	Superior Products		116.70			116.70
24 Jan	Cash sales	128.46		21.41	107.05	
24 Jan	Esporta Leisure (auto)		367.20			367.20
25 Jan	Cash sales	86.40		14.40	72.00	
27 Jan	Body Perfect		706.64			706.64
27 Jan	Cash sales	58.80		9.80	49.00	
27 Jan	Langans Beauty (auto)		267.90			267.90
		273.66	2,003.58	45.61	228.05	2,003.58

Cross-cast check:

	£
Trade receivables	2,003.58
Cash sales	228.05
VAT	45.61
Total	2,277.24
Cash receipts	273.66
Bank receipts	2,003.58
Total	2,277.24

2 Cash book – credit side

Date	Details	Cheque No	Cash £	Bank £	VAT £	Cash purchases £	Trade payables £
23 Jan	Trenter Ltd	002144		1,110.09			1,110.09
23 Jan	Cash purchase		105.60		17.60	88.00	
24 Jan	W J Jones	002145		246.75			246.75
24 Jan	P J Phillips	002146		789.60			789.60
24 Jan	Cash purchase		125.40		20.90	104.50	
25 Jan	Packing Supp	002147		305.45			305.45
26 Jan	O & P Ltd	002148		703.87			703.87
27 Jan	Cash purchase		96.00		16.00	80.00	
			327.00	3,155.76	54.50	272.50	3,155.76

Cross-cast check:

	£
Trade payables	3,155.76
Cash purchases	272.50
VAT	54.50
Total	3,482.76
Cash payments	327.00
Cheque payments	3,155.76
Total	3,482.76

3 (a) **Cash book – credit side**

Details	Cash £	Bank £	VAT £	Cash purchases £	Trade payables £	Marketing expenses £
Balance b/f		3,295				
Klimt Supplies	90		15	75		
Patel Trading	342		57	285		
TWE Ltd	83			83		
Western Industries		4,278			4,278	
Mountebank Co		564	94			470
Total	515	8,137	166	443	4,278	470

(b) **Cash book – debit side**

Details	Cash £	Bank £	Trade receivables £
Balance b/f	792		
Vantage Ltd		1,278	1,278
Marbles Co		2,183	2,183
Total	792	3,461	3,461

(c) Cash balance £792 – £515

£	**277**

(d) Bank balance £3,461 – £8,137

£	**4,676**

(e) Bank balance calculated in (d) above: credit balance

	£
Debit	
Credit	✓

CHAPTER 9 Double entry for sales and trade receivables

1

Sales day book total	Account name in general ledger	Debit	Credit
Gross	Sales ledger control	✓	
VAT	VAT control		✓
Net	Sales		✓

2

	Amount £	Debit ✓	Credit ✓
Sales ledger control account (general ledger)	240 ((200 + (200 × 20%))		✓
Customer's account (sales ledger)	240		✓

3

Account name	Amount £	Debit ✓	Credit ✓
VAT control	20.00		✓
Sales	100.00		✓
Sales ledger control account	5,016.50		✓

4

Sales ledger control

Details	Amount £	Details	Amount £
Sales	6,336.50	Sales returns	501.00
VAT control	1,267.30	VAT control	100.20

Sales

Details	Amount £	Details	Amount £
		Sales ledger control	6,336.50

Sales returns

Details	Amount £	Details	Amount £
Sales ledger control	501.00		

VAT control

Details	Amount £	Details	Amount £
Sales ledger control	100.20	Sales ledger control	1,267.30

Sales ledger

Dagwell Enterprises   SL 15

Details	Amount £	Details	Amount £
Invoice 56401	948.60	Credit note 08651	244.80

G Thomas & Co   SL 30

Details	Amount £	Details	Amount £
Invoice 56402	3,537.60		

Polygon Stores   SL 03

Details	Amount £	Details	Amount £
Invoice 56403	1,965.60		

Weller Enterprises   SL 18

Details	Amount £	Details	Amount £
Invoice 56404	1,152.00		

Whitehill Superstores   **SL 37**

Details	Amount £	Details	Amount £
		Credit note 08650	356.40

5

Account name	Amount £	Debit ✓	Credit ✓
Discounts allowed	40	✓	
VAT	8	✓	
Sales ledger control	48		✓

6 **General ledger**

VAT control   **GL 562**

Details	Amount £	Details	Amount £
Sales ledger control	1.73	Cash	112.12

Sales   **GL 049**

Details	Amount £	Details	Amount £
		Cash	560.64

Sales ledger control   **GL 827**

Details	Amount £	Details	Amount £
		Bank	981.12
		Discounts allowed	8.67
		VAT	1.73

Discounts allowed   GL 235

Details	Amount £	Details	Amount £
Sales ledger control	8.67		

Sales ledger

H Henry   SL 0115

Details	Amount £	Details	Amount £
		Cash book	146.79

P Peters   SL 0135

Details	Amount £	Details	Amount £
		Cash book	221.55
		Credit note D55	6.85

K Kilpin   SL 0128

Details	Amount £	Details	Amount £
		Cash book	440.30

B Bennet   SL 0134

Details	Amount £	Details	Amount £
		Cash book	57.80

S Shahir   SL 0106

Details	Amount £	Details	Amount £
		Cash book	114.68
		Credit note D56	3.55

7 **General ledger**

Account name	Amount £	Debit ✓	Credit ✓
Bank	1,693.77	✓	
Cash	1,008.90	✓	
Discounts allowed	52.76	✓	
Cash sales	840.75		✓
Sales ledger control (1,693.77 + 63.30)	1,757.07		✓
VAT (168.15 – 10.54)	157.61		✓

Sales ledger

Account name	Amount £	Debit ✓	Credit ✓
G Gonpipe	332.67		✓
J Jimmings (127.37 + 6.70)	134.07		✓
N Nutely (336.28 + 17.70)	353.98		✓
T Turner	158.35		✓
R Ritner (739.10 + 38.90)	778.00		✓

8

VAT control

Details	Amount £	Details	Amount £
		Sales ledger control	1,926

Sales

Details	Amount £	Details	Amount £
		Sales ledger control	9,630

Sales ledger control

Details	Amount £	Details	Amount £
Sales	9,630		
VAT control	1,926		

CHAPTER 10 Double entry for purchases and trade payables

1

Purchase day book total	Account name	Debit ✓	Credit ✓
Gross	Purchases ledger control		✓
VAT	VAT control	✓	
Net	Purchases	✓	

2

	Amount £	Debit ✓	Credit ✓
Purchases ledger control account (general ledger)	720	✓	
Supplier's account (purchases ledger)	720	✓	

3

GENERAL LEDGER

Purchases ledger control

Details	Amount £	Details	Amount £
Purchases returns	210.00	Purchases	2,778.00
VAT control	42.00	VAT control	555.60

Purchases

Details	Amount £	Details	Amount £
Purchases ledger control	2,778.00		

Purchases returns

Details	Amount £	Details	Amount £
		Purchases ledger control	210.00

VAT control

Details	Amount £	Details	Amount £
Purchases ledger control	555.60	Purchases ledger control	42.00

PURCHASES LEDGER

Herne Industries   PL 15

Details	Amount £	Details	Amount £
Credit note 4502	132.00	Invoice 46121	864.00

Bass Engineers   PL 13

Details	Amount £	Details	Amount £
		Invoice 663211	460.80

Southfield Electrical   PL 20

Details	Amount £	Details	Amount £
Credit note 08702	120.00	Invoice 56521	2,008.80

4 GENERAL LEDGER

VAT control   GL 100

Details	Amount £	Details	Amount £
Cash	62.44		

BPP
LEARNING MEDIA

Purchases GL 200

Details	Amount £	Details	Amount £
Cash	312.20		

Purchases ledger control GL 300

Details	Amount £	Details	Amount £
Bank	1,188.59		

Cash GL 550

Details	Amount £	Details	Amount £
		Purchases	312.20
		VAT control	62.44

Bank GL 600

Details	Amount £	Details	Amount £
		Purchases ledger control	1,188.59

PURCHASES LEDGER

R R Partners PL 06

Details	Amount £	Details	Amount £
Cash book	163.47		

Troyde Ltd PL 14

Details	Amount £	Details	Amount £
Cash book	183.57		

F Elliott   **PL 20**

Details	Amount £	Details	Amount £
Cash book	263.68		

P Products Ltd   **PL 23**

Details	Amount £	Details	Amount £
Cash book	241.58		

Jason Bros   **PL 36**

Details	Amount £	Details	Amount £
Cash book	336.29		

5

VAT control

Details	Amount £	Details	Amount £
Purchases ledger control	2,080.00		

Purchases account

Details	Amount £	Details	Amount £
Purchases ledger control	10,400.00		

Purchases ledger control

Details	Amount £	Details	Amount £
		Purchases	10,400.00
		VAT control	2,080.00

CHAPTER 11 Accounting for petty cash

1   (a)   An imprest petty cash system is one where the amount of the topped-up petty cash float at the start of each period is:

> Always the same

(b)   Amounts that have been paid out for authorised expenditure are represented in the petty cash box by:

> Petty cash vouchers

(c)   At the end of the period the total of the

> Petty cash vouchers

in the petty cash box is the amount needed to restore the petty cash box to the imprest amount.

2 | £ | 89.46 |

Amount of vouchers = amount required to restore the imprest amount = £89.46

3   **Petty cash book**

RECEIPTS			PAYMENTS								
Date	Details	Amount £	Date	Details	Voucher number	Total £	VAT £	Post £	Travel £	Sundry office £	Misc £
20 Oct	Bank	150.00	24 Oct	Train fare	771	14.00			14.00		
			24 Oct	Postage	772	18.60		18.60			
			24 Oct	Envelopes	773	16.80	2.80			14.00	
			24 Oct	Window cleaner	774	20.00					20.00
			24 Oct	Pens/paper	775	18.90	3.15			15.75	
			24 Oct	Postage	776	5.46		5.46			
			24 Oct	Taxi fare	777	9.60	1.60		8.00		
			24 Oct	Computer disc	778	28.20	4.70			23.50	
						131.56	12.25	24.06	22.00	53.25	20.00
				Balance c/d		18.44					
	Total	150.00				150.00					
Balance b/d		18.44									
Cash top-up		131.56									

4 Petty cash book

Debit side		Credit side					
Details	Amount £	Details	Amount £	VAT £	Postage £	Travel £	Motor expenses £
Balance b/f	180.00	Post Office	12.60		12.60		
		Motor Repair Workshop	72.60	12.10			60.50
		Great Eastern Trains	32.00			32.00	
		Balance c/d	62.80				
	180.00		180.00	12.10	12.60	32.00	60.50

5

£	41.30

Amount of vouchers = amount required to restore the imprest amount = £41.30

CHAPTER 12 Initial trial balance

1

VAT account

Details	Amount £	Details	Amount £
Purchases	3,778	Balance b/f	2,116
Bank	2,116	Sales	6,145
Balance c/d	2,367		
	8,261		8,261
		Balance b/d	2,367

Sales account

Details	Amount £	Details	Amount £
		Balance b/f	57,226
Balance c/d	100,121	Sales ledger control	42,895
	100,121		100,121
		Balance b/d	100,121

Sales ledger control account

Details	Amount £	Details	Amount £
Balance b/f	4,689	Bank	21,505
Sales	23,512	Discounts allowed	2,019
		Balance c/d	4,677
	28,201		28,201
Balance b/d	4,677		

Purchases ledger control account

Details	Amount £	Details	Amount £
Purchases returns	1,334	Balance b/f	2,864
Bank	13,446	Purchases	14,552
Discounts received	662		
Balance c/d	1,974		
	17,416		17,416
		Balance b/d	1,974

2

	£	Debit balance ✓	Credit balance ✓
Discounts allowed	1,335	✓	
Discounts received	1,013		✓
Purchases returns	4,175		✓
Sales returns	6,078	✓	
Bank interest received	328		✓
Bank charges	163	✓	

3

	Debit £	Credit £
Motor vehicles	64,000	
Office equipment	21,200	
Sales		238,000
Purchases	164,000	
Cash	300	
Bank overdraft		1,080
Petty cash	30	
Capital		55,000
Sales returns	4,700	
Purchases returns		3,600
Sales ledger control	35,500	
Purchases ledger control		30,100
VAT (owed to HMRC)		12,950
Telephone	1,600	
Electricity	2,800	
Wages	62,100	
Loan from bank		30,000
Discounts allowed	6,400	
Discounts received		3,900
Rent expense	12,000	
Totals	374,630	374,630

4

Account name	Amount £	Debit £	Credit £
Advertising	3,238	3,238	
Bank overdraft	27,511		27,511
Capital	40,846		40,846

Account name	Amount £	Debit £	Credit £
Cash	689	689	
Discount allowed	4,416	4,416	
Discount received	2,880		2,880
Hotel expenses	2,938	2,938	
Inventory	46,668	46,668	
Loan from bank	39,600		39,600
Miscellaneous expenses	3,989	3,989	
Motor expenses	7,087	7,087	
Motor vehicles	63,120	63,120	
Petty cash	720	720	
Purchases	634,529	634,529	
Purchases ledger control	110,846		110,846
Purchases returns	1,618		1,618
Rent and rates	19,200	19,200	
Sales	1,051,687		1,051,687
Sales ledger control	405,000	405,000	
Sales returns	11,184	11,184	
Stationery	5,880	5,880	
Subscriptions	864	864	
Telephone	3,838	3,838	
VAT (owing to HM Revenue & Customs)	63,650		63,650
Wages	125,278	125,278	
Totals		1,338,638	1,338,638

5 Trial balance

Account name	Amount £	Debit £	Credit £
Cash	520.00	520.00	
Bank	9,320.00	9,320.00	
Sales ledger control	10,000.00	10,000.00	
Sales	21,650.00		21,650.00
Sales returns	230.00	230.00	
VAT	640.00		640.00
Discounts allowed	40.00	40.00	
Purchases ledger control	2,500.00		2,500.00
Purchases	6,300.00	6,300.00	
Purchases returns	480.00		480.00
Discounts received	140.00		140.00
Capital	1,000.00		1,000.00
		26,410.00	26,410.00

Synoptic assessment preparation

Certain *Bookkeeping Transactions* assessment objectives will be tested in the *AAT Foundation Certificate in Accounting* synoptic assessment. Therefore, at this stage in your studies, it is useful to consider the style of tasks you may see in the synoptic assessment.

However, it is recommended that the *AAT Foundation Certificate in Accounting* synoptic assessment is only taken when all other units have been completed.

Questions

1   Your workload for the coming week is shown in the table below. Your hours of work are 09.00 to 17.00 with an hour for lunch from 13.00 to 14.00. There is always a departmental meeting on a Monday afternoon at 16.00 which lasts for one hour. You are required to take notes at the meeting. Other weekly tasks you have to complete are as follows:

| Task | Task to be completed by: | | |
	Day	Time	Task Duration
Petty cash reconciliation	Friday	12:00	1 hour
Wages analysis	Tuesday	09:00	2 hours
Fixed (non-current) asset analysis	Monday	11:00	1 hour
Mail distribution	Every day	10:00	1 hour
Sales invoice processing	Thursday	17:00	3 hours
Cheque processing	Wednesday	12:00	2 hours

Your manager has left the following note on your desk:

Hi

I have an important meeting with the bank manager today. The meeting is to discuss gaining finance for the organisation and I need you to reconcile the bank statement. My meeting is at 16.00 so I will have to leave the office at 15.00. I think the job will take you about 2 hours to complete. It is vital I have this information for the meeting.

Thanks

(a) **Complete the To Do list below for MONDAY by selecting the appropriate tasks from the picklist provided.**

MONDAY To Do List		Order of task completion
	▼	First task
	▼	Second task
	▼	Third task
	▼	Fourth task
	▼	Fifth task

Picklist:

Bank statement reconciliation

Cheque processing

Departmental meeting

Fixed (non-current) asset analysis

Mail distribution

Petty cash reconciliation

Sales invoice processing

Wages analysis

(b) **Identify the TWO most likely impacts on your colleagues, your manager, or the organisation if you were unable to complete the bank reconciliation on time.**

Your manager would not be able to attend the meeting. ☐

Your manager would not have the necessary information
to support his discussions with the bank manager. ☐

The organisation may face financial difficulty if it does
not secure the finance required. ☐

Your colleagues would be unable to complete their work on time. ☐

2   On 10 July Silver received the following purchase order from Beard and Son. The goods were delivered the following day. The customer has been offered an 8% trade discount. You have been asked to complete the invoice to send to Beard and Son.

```
Beard and Son

Redcar Road

Wallington, WA15 0MX

Purchase order B392

Silver                                    10 July 20XX
14 High Street
Wallington
WA11 4GX

Please supply 85 units of product code BC765
```

Price list

Product code	Price per unit £
BC765	3.55
BD766	4.20
BE768	5.85
BF769	6.05

(a) Refer to the price list and complete the EIGHT boxes in the sales invoice below.

```
                        Silver

           14 High Street, Wallington, WA11 4GX

                  SALES INVOICE 336

Date: [              ▼]

To:  Beard and Son              Customer account code: BEA003

     Redcar Road

     Wallington, WA15 OMX       Purchase order no: [          ]
```

Quantity of units	Product code	Price each £	Total amount after trade discount £	VAT £	Total £

Your next task is to enter the invoice into the appropriate day book.

(b) Record the invoice in the appropriate day book by:

- selecting the correct day book title and
- making the necessary entries.

Day book:	▼

Picklist:

Cash book
Discounts allowed day book
Discounts received day book
Petty cash book
Purchases day book
Purchases returns day book
Sales day book
Sales returns day book

Customer	Customer code	Invoice number	Total £	VAT £	Net £
▼					

Picklist:

Beard and Son
Silver

After reviewing the purchases ledger, your colleague identified that Beard and Sons had an outstanding invoice. This is a draft of a letter to be addressed to Mr Beard, of Beard and Son, regarding the outstanding invoice.

(c) Review the draft letter and identify FIVE words which are spelled incorrectly, or are inappropriate. Click on a word to select it and click on the word again if you want to remove your selection.

> Deer Mr Beard
>
> Please find enclosed an invoice in respect of the Profesional IT Manual delivered last month.
>
> Our records show that this amount is still outstanding. Our terns of payment are strictly 30 days and therefore this invoice is overdue for payment.
>
> If their is any reason why the amount outstanding has not been paid you should contact the Accounts Department immediately. Alternatively you should ensure your payment in full settlement reaches us within 7 days of this letter.
>
> We look forward to hearing from you.
>
> Yours faithfully

3   You are preparing for the accounting month end at Silver. One of your tasks is to transfer the data from the sales returns day book to the ledgers. An extract from the sales returns day book is shown below.

Sales returns day book

Date 20XX	Details	Credit note number	Total £	VAT £	Net £
30 Sept	Web Designers	CN32	564	94	470

(a)   What will be the entry in the sales ledger?

Sales ledger

Account name	Amount £	Debit ✓	Credit ✓
▼			

Picklist:

Purchases
Purchases ledger control
Purchases returns
Sales
Sales ledger control
Sales returns
VAT
Web Designers

(b) **What will be the entries in the general ledger?**

General ledger

Account name		Amount £	Debit ✓	Credit ✓
	▼			
	▼			
	▼			

Picklist:

Purchases
Purchases ledger control
Purchases returns
Sales
Sales ledger control
Sales returns
VAT
Web Designers

The following is a partially completed email to inform Simon West (swest@silver.co.uk) of a meeting with James Bright (jbright@silver.co.uk) on Friday at 15.00 in the Green Room. The meeting is being held to discuss the new credit control procedures.

(c) **Complete the email by:**

- **Inserting the email address of the person it is going to**

- **Selecting the most appropriate words or phrases from the picklists.**

From:	AATstudent@silver.co.uk
To:	[ ]
Subject:	**(1)** [▼]

Hello Simon

There is a meeting planned with **(2)** [▼] at **(3)** [▼] on Friday in the **(4)** [▼]

The reason for the meeting is to discuss the new credit control procedures.

Regards

AAT Student

448

Picklist:

Chat / Meeting / Meeting notification
James Bright / James Brite / Simon West
1pm / 2pm / 3pm / 4pm / 5pm
Boardroom / Green room / Grey room

Solutions

1 **(a)** The correct answer is:

MONDAY To Do List	Order of task completion
Mail distribution	First task
Fixed (non-current) asset analysis	Second task
Bank statement reconciliation	Third task
Wages analysis	Fourth task
Departmental meeting	Fifth task

(b) The correct answer is:

	✓
Your manager would not be able to attend the meeting.	
Your manager would not have the necessary information to support his discussions with the bank manager.	✓
The organisation may face financial difficulty if it does not secure the finance required.	✓
Your colleagues would be unable to complete their work on time.	

2   **(a)**

Silver

14 High Street, Wallington, WA11 4GX

SALES INVOICE 336

Date: **11 July 20XX**

To: Beard and Son   Customer account code: BEA003

Redcar Road

Wallington, WA15 0MX   Purchase order no: **B392**

Quantity of units	Product code	Price each £	Total amount after trade discount £	VAT £	Total £
85	BC765	3.55	277.61	55.52	333.13

Tutorial note.

Workings:

85 × £3.55 × 92% = £277.61

£277.61 × 0.2 = £55.52

(b)

Day book:	Sales day book

Customer	Customer code	Invoice number	Total £	VAT £	Net £
Beard and Son	BEA003	336	333.13	55.52	277.61

(c)   The words you should have selected are in bold and underlined.

> **Deer** Mr Beard
>
> Please find enclosed an invoice in respect of the **Professional** IT Manual delivered last month.

> Our records show that this amount is still outstanding. Our **terms** of payment are strictly 30 days and therefore this invoice is overdue for payment.
>
> If **their** is any reason why the amount outstanding has not been paid you should contact the Accounts Department immediately. Alternatively you should ensure your payment in full settlement reaches us within 7 days of this letter.
>
> We look forward to hearing from you.
>
> Yours **faithfully** [Tutorial note: should be **sincerely**]

3 **(a)** **Sales ledger**

Account name	Amount £	Debit ✓	Credit ✓
Web Designers	564		✓

(b) **General ledger**

Account name	Amount £	Debit ✓	Credit ✓
Sales returns	470	✓	
VAT	94	✓	
Sales ledger control	564		✓

(c)

From:	AATstudent@silver.co.uk
To:	swest@silver.co.uk
Subject:	Meeting notification

Hello Simon

There is a meeting planned with James Bright at 3 pm on Friday in the Green room

The reason for the meeting is to discuss the new credit control procedures.

Regards

AAT Student

Glossary of terms

It is useful to be familiar with interchangeable terminology including IFRS and UK GAAP (generally accepted accounting principles).

Below is a short list of the most important terms you are likely to use or come across, together with their international and UK equivalents.

UK term	International term
Profit and loss account	**Statement of profit or loss (or statement of profit or loss and other comprehensive income)**
Turnover or Sales	Revenue or Sales Revenue
Operating profit	Profit from operations
Reducing balance depreciation	Diminishing balance depreciation
Depreciation/depreciation expense(s)	Depreciation charge(s)
Balance sheet	**Statement of financial position**
Fixed assets	Non-current assets
Net book value	Carrying amount
Tangible assets	Property, plant and equipment
Stocks	Inventories
Trade debtors or Debtors	Trade receivables
Prepayments	Other receivables
Debtors and prepayments	Trade and other receivables
Cash at bank and in hand	Cash and cash equivalents
Long-term liabilities	Non-current liabilities
Trade creditors or creditors	Trade payables
Accruals	Other payables
Creditors and accruals	Trade and other payables
Capital and reserves	Equity (limited companies)
Profit and loss balance	Retained earnings
Cash flow statement	**Statement of cash flows**

Accountants often have a tendency to use several phrases to describe the same thing! Some of these are listed below:

Different terms for the same thing
Nominal ledger, main ledger or general ledger
Subsidiary ledgers, memorandum ledgers
Subsidiary (sales) ledger, sales ledger
Subsidiary (purchases) ledger, purchases ledger

Index

Supplier code, 21, 27

T

Tabular format for double entry, 157
Tendering, 107, 130
Till receipt, 27
Timing difference, 130
Trade creditors or Creditors, 83
Trade debtors or Debtors, 83
Trade discount, 64, 74
Trade payables, 83
Trade receivables, 83
Trial balance, 335
Two-column cash book, 38, 201, 230

U

UK terminology, 83

V

Value Added Tax (VAT), 61, 74
VAT, 12
VAT and discounts, 66
VAT and double entry, 243
VAT and prompt payment discounts, 66
VAT calculation, 61
VAT control account, 244
VAT credit note, 66, 74
VAT rates, 61
VAT return, 61, 74

Notes

Notes

Notes

Notes

REVIEW FORM

How have you used this Course Book?
(Tick one box only)

☐ Self study

☐ On a course_____

☐ Other _____

Why did you decide to purchase this Course Book? *(Tick one box only)*

☐ Have used BPP materials in the past

☐ Recommendation by friend/colleague

☐ Recommendation by a college lecturer

☐ Saw advertising

☐ Other _____

During the past six months do you recall seeing/receiving either of the following?
(Tick as many boxes as are relevant)

☐ Our advertisement in Accounting Technician

☐ Our Publishing Catalogue

Which (if any) aspects of our advertising do you think are useful?
(Tick as many boxes as are relevant)

☐ Prices and publication dates of new editions

☐ Information on Course Book content

☐ Details of our free online offering

☐ None of the above

Your ratings, comments and suggestions would be appreciated on the following areas of this Course Book.

	Very useful	Useful	Not useful
Chapter overviews	☐	☐	☐
Introductory section	☐	☐	☐
Quality of explanations	☐	☐	☐
Illustrations	☐	☐	☐
Chapter activities	☐	☐	☐
Test your learning	☐	☐	☐
Keywords	☐	☐	☐

	Excellent	Good	Adequate	Poor
Overall opinion of this Course Book	☐	☐	☐	☐

Do you intend to continue using BPP Products? ☐ Yes ☐ No

Please note any further comments and suggestions/errors on the reverse of this page. The BPP author of this edition can be emailed at: lmfeedback@bpp.com

Alternatively, the Head of Programme of this edition can be emailed at: nisarahmed@bpp.com.

REVIEW FORM (continued)

TELL US WHAT YOU THINK

Please note any further comments and suggestions/errors below